SMART VACATIONS

▶▶

SMART VACATIONS

The Traveler's Guide to Learning Adventures Abroad

EDITED BY

PRISCILLA TOVEY

Council on International Educational Exchange

St. Martin's Press

New York

SMART VACATIONS. Copyright © 1993 by the Council on International Educational Exchange. All rights reserved. Printed in the United States of America. No part of this book may be used or reproduced in any manner whatsoever without written permission except in the case of brief quotations embodied in critical articles or reviews. For information, address St. Martin's Press, 175 Fifth Avenue, New York, N.Y. 10010.

Library of Congress Cataloging-in-Publication Data
Smart vacations : the traveler's guide to learning adventures abroad /
    Council on International Educational Exchange.
        p.   cm.
    Includes index.
    ISBN 0-312-08823-X (pbk.)
    1. Travel.   2. Vacations.   I. Council on International Educational Exchange.
G151.S63   1993
910'.2'02—dc20   92-43173
                                                                           CIP

Design by Susan Hood
FIRST EDITION: March 1993
10 9 8 7 6 5 4 3 2 1

CONTENTS

ACKNOWLEDGMENTS

Producing a new book is always a formidable task involving a great deal of time, effort, and thought. *Smart Vacations: The Traveler's Guide to Learning Opportunities Abroad* was no exception. Conceptualizing, researching, compiling, organizing, writing, and rewriting were only some of the tasks that yielded the finished product now in your hands. At each stage of the process a number of people were involved in different capacities, and I want to take this opportunity to thank these people on behalf of the Council on International Educational Exchange.

First and foremost, gratitude must be expressed to the publications staff at the Council on International Educational Exchange, especially Priscilla Tovey, who served as the book's editor. Her long hours of work are largely responsible for the existence of this book. In addition, credit needs to be given to Lazaro Hernandez, who played an important role in the conceptualization, compilation, and final editing of the book. Thanks also to the other members of CIEE's publications staff, Richard Christiano, Jon Howard, Max Terry, and Nicole Ellison, who assisted in many phases of the development of *Smart Vacations.*

In addition, thanks must be expressed to Pat Koch Thaler, Associate Dean at New York University's School of Continuing Education, for her help in reviewing the manuscript and providing many positive suggestions. Finally, thanks to CIEE Deputy and Assistant Executive Directors Joe Hickey and Margaret Shiba for their support and suggestions throughout this project.

Del Franz
Director, Information and Student Services
Council on International Educational Exchange

ABOUT CIEE

The Council on International Educational Exchange (CIEE) is a non-profit, educational organization with offices in the United States, Europe, and Asia. In nearly 50 years of service to the educational community, CIEE and its travel subsidiaries, Council Travel and Council Charter, have emerged among the foremost organizations promoting international education and student travel.

CIEE was founded in 1947 to help reestablish student exchanges after World War II. In its early years, CIEE chartered ocean liners for transatlantic student sailings, arranged group air travel, and organized orientation programs to prepare students and teachers for educational experiences abroad. Over the years, CIEE's mandate has broadened dramatically as the interests of its member institutions and organizations have spread beyond Europe to Africa, Asia, and Latin America. Today CIEE's responsibilities include developing and administering study, work, and voluntary service programs throughout the world; publishing books, academic papers, and informational materials on international educational exchange; and facilitating inexpensive international travel for students, teachers, and other budget travelers.

STUDY ABROAD

Among CIEE's most widely recognized educational services are the academic programs that it administers in Argentina, Australia, Brazil, Chile, China, Costa Rica, Czechoslovakia, the Dominican Republic, France, Germany, the Netherlands, Hungary, Indonesia, Japan, Poland, Russia, Spain, Thailand, and Vietnam. These programs are administered by CIEE's University Programs Department on behalf of sponsoring colleges and universities that participate in policy and curriculum formation, assure academic credibility and quality, and serve the particular academic field for which the program has been developed. Programs are available on the undergraduate and graduate levels and are open to all qualified students. Financial assistance is available for participation in some of these programs.

WORK ABROAD

CIEE operates a series of reciprocal work exchange programs that enable college and university students to work in one another's countries, primarily during summer vacation periods. Through these programs, students are able to obtain temporary employment in Australia, Britain, Canada, Costa Rica, France, Germany, Ireland, Jamaica, New Zealand, Spain, and the United States. The Work Abroad programs allow students to cut through the red tape and bureaucratic difficulties that usually accompany the process of getting permission to work in another country. Along with the necessary employment authorization, Work Abroad participants receive general information on the country, tips on employment, and helpful hints on housing and travel. In each country the program is offered in cooperation with a national student organization or CIEE office that provides an orientation on the country's culture and society, advises on seeking jobs and accommodations, and serves as a sponsor during the participant's stay.

INTERNATIONAL VOLUNTARY SERVICE

CIEE's Voluntary Service Department operates an international work-camp program for young people interested in short-term voluntary service worldwide, including the United States. Volunteers are placed with organizations conducting projects in Algeria, Belgium, Canada, Czechoslovakia, Denmark, France, Germany, Ghana, Hungary, Lithuania, Morocco, the Netherlands, Poland, Slovenia, Spain, Russia, Tunisia, Turkey, Ukraine, and the United Kingdom. Projects include restoring historical sites; working with children or the elderly; constructing low-income housing; and taking part in nature conservation projects. Workcamps bring young people from many different countries together to work in a local community.

SECONDARY SCHOOL PROGRAMS

CIEE's Secondary Education Programs Department administers School Partners Abroad, a school-to-school partnership program that matches junior and senior high schools in the United States with counterpart schools in Costa Rica, France, Germany, Japan, Russia, and Spain. The program provides resources for the enhancement of foreign language and social studies curricula, as well as short-term reciprocal exchange opportunities for groups of students and teachers. Each exchange provides participants with the opportunity to live with local families and attend regular classes in the partner school.

ADULT/PROFESSIONAL PROGRAMS

The Professional and Continuing Education Programs Department designs and administers a wide variety of short-term seminars, study tours, and in-service training programs for groups of international professionals, including secondary school teachers and administrators, university faculty, business managers, and other "adult learners." Among these programs is the International Faculty Development Seminar series, for faculty and administrators at two- and four-year institutions of higher education. These overseas seminars and professional interchange opportunities are designed to assist institutions with internationalizing home-campus curricula. At the K-12 level, CIEE arranges short-term "teaching visit" opportunities in overseas schools for U.S. teachers, with reciprocal opportunities in the United States for educators from abroad.

STUDENT SERVICES

Through its Information and Student Services Department, CIEE administers the International Student Identity Card, the International Youth Card, and the International Teacher Identity Card in the United States.

Nearly 200,000 International Student Identity Cards are issued each year by CIEE's New York headquarters, its 38 Council Travel offices, and more than 450 issuing offices at colleges and universities across the country. Cardholders receive travel-related discounts, basic accident/medical insurance coverage while traveling abroad, and access to a 24-hour toll-free emergency hot line. The International Youth Card, for those under 26, and the International Teacher Identity

Card, for full-time faculty, both provide benefits similar to the student card.

PUBLICATIONS

In addition to *Smart Vacations,* CIEE's Information and Student Services Department produces the following books for travelers:

- *Work, Study, Travel Abroad: The Whole World Handbook,* published biennially by St. Martin's Press, includes all the essentials of working, studying, and traveling abroad. Divided into country-by-country sections covering six continents, this book includes information on work and study opportunities worldwide. It also shows the traveler how to experience another country as an insider.
- *Volunteer! The Comprehensive Guide To Voluntary Service in the U.S. and Abroad.* Published biennially in cooperation with the Council of Religious Volunteer Agencies, this book includes more than 200 organizations that sponsor service opportunities worldwide, including a section on the "basics" of volunteering and essays written by past volunteers.
- *Going Places: The High-School Student's Guide To Study, Travel, and Adventure Abroad,* published by St. Martin's Press, is an award-winning compendium of short- and long-term overseas opportunities for youths 12 to 18 years of age.
- *Where to Stay USA* is a state-by-state listing of more than 1,700 places to spend the night for less than $35, with special city sections and general travel advice for anyone touring the United States. This book is updated every other year by CIEE and published by Prentice Hall.

In addition to those books, CIEE also publishes a range of informational materials that are available free of charge. Among these are:

- *Student Travels,* a new 48-page travel magazine for college students, has replaced the *Student Travel Catalog.* The magazine includes "insider" stories, travel tips, where to go, what to do, and how to manage from the student's perspective. A special section contains information on the International Student Identity Card, the Work Abroad program, international volunteer workcamps, study abroad programs, and updates on Council Travel's student airfares and services.

- *Basic Facts on Study Abroad,* a booklet compiled in cooperation with the Institute of International Education and NAFSA: Association of International Educators, provides general information for students interested in an educational experience abroad.
- *A Guide to Educational Programs in the Third World* provides brief descriptions of more than 200 programs offered by CIEE member institutions in developing countries. Included are study, work, and volunteer programs.
- *Update,* CIEE's monthly newsletter, provides information on CIEE's programs and services, up-to-date coverage of issues in the field of international educational exchange, as well as developments in the travel industry.

SCHOLARSHIPS AND FELLOWSHIPS

CIEE provides financial assistance for U.S. students and professionals to participate in educational programs abroad. The following funds are available:

- *ISIC Fund.* The International Student Identity Card Fund provides travel grants to enable full-time high school or undergraduate students attending CIEE member institutions, or participating in a program sponsored by a CIEE member institution, to participate in study, work, volunteer, internship, or homestay programs in the developing nations of the world.
- *Education Abroad Scholarship Fund for Minority Students.* This recently established fund supports members of minority groups who want to participate in any of CIEE's educational programs, including study, work, voluntary service, internship, and professional opportunities. Funds are available for secondary, undergraduate, and graduate students, as well as professionals, who are U.S. citizens or permanent residents.

TRAVEL SERVICES

Council Travel, a subsidiary of CIEE, operates a network of 38 retail travel offices across the country that provide travel assistance to students, teachers, and other budget travelers planning individual or group trips to any part of the world. Council Travel's services and products include the following:

- low-cost flights between the United States and Europe, Asia, the South Pacific, Africa, the Middle East, Latin America, and the Caribbean on scheduled and charter carriers (some special fares are available only to students or young people and teachers/professors)
- rail passes, including Eurail, BritRail, and French Rail passes
- the International Student, Teacher, and Youth Identity Cards
- car-rental plans in Europe
- language courses in 17 European cities and Japan
- travel insurance, guidebooks, and travel gear
- the New York Student Center, a low-cost accommodations and travel advisory service for visitors to New York City

For Council Travel office locations in the United States and abroad, see the list following this section.

Charter Flights

Council Charter, another travel subsidiary of CIEE, has been a reliable consolidator for 43 years. It offers budget flights on scheduled and charter carriers between the United States and major European cities, including Paris, London, Amsterdam, Brussels, Rome, Madrid, and Milan. Council Charter fares, which are open to students and non-students alike, have no hidden charges and require no minimum or maximum stay or Saturday overnight stay. Council Charter's flexible service provides travelers with a unique low-cost cancellation waiver allowing cancellation for any reason up to three hours prior to departure; the option of flying into one city and returning from another; continued assistance through its European offices; and frequent departures.

CIEE MEMBERSHIP

At present, over 250 educational institutions and organizations in the United States and abroad are members of CIEE. As members, they can take advantage of CIEE's information and publications services; become involved in CIEE's advocacy, evaluation, and consultation activities; and participate in conferences and services organized by CIEE. Membership allows educational institutions and organizations to play a central role in the development and operation of exchanges at a national and international level. Members of the Council on International Educational Exchange are listed in the Appendix.

COUNCIL TRAVEL OFFICES

U.S.A.

Tempe
120 East University Drive
Suite E
Tempe, AZ 85281
(602) 966–3544

CALIFORNIA

Berkeley
2486 Channing Way
Berkeley, CA 94704
(510) 848–8604

La Jolla
UCSD Price Center
9500 Gilman Drive
La Jolla, CA 92093–0076
(619) 452–0630

Long Beach
1818 Palo Verde Avenue
Suite E
Long Beach, CA 90815
(310) 598–3338
(714) 527–7950

Los Angeles
1093 Broxton Avenue
Suite 200
Los Angeles, CA 90024
(310) 208–3551

Palo Alto
394 University Avenue
Suite 200
Palo Alto, CA 94301
(415) 325–3888

San Diego
953 Garnet Avenue
San Diego, CA 92109
(619) 270–6401

San Francisco
312 Sutter Street, Suite 407
San Francisco, CA 94108
(415) 421–3473

919 Irving Street, Suite 102
San Francisco, CA 94122
(415) 566–6222

Sherman Oaks
14515 Ventura Boulevard
Suite 250
Sherman Oaks, CA 91403
(818) 905–5777

COLORADO
Boulder
1138 13th Street
Boulder, CO 80302
(303) 447–8101

CONNECTICUT
New Haven
Yale Co-op East
77 Broadway
New Haven, CT 06520
(203) 562–5335

DISTRICT OF COLUMBIA
Washington
3300 M Street NW, 2nd floor
Washington, DC 20007
(202) 337–6464

FLORIDA
Miami
One Datran Center, Suite 320
9100 South Dadeland
    Boulevard
Miami, FL 33156
(305) 670–9261

GEORGIA
Atlanta
Emory Village
1561 North Decatur Road
Atlanta, GA 30307
(404) 377–9997

ILLINOIS
Chicago
1153 North Dearborn Street,
    2nd floor
Chicago, IL 60610
(312) 951–0585

Evanston
1634 Orrington Avenue
Evanston, IL 60201
(708) 475–5070

LOUISIANA
New Orleans
Joseph A. Danna Center
Loyola University
6363 St. Charles Avenue
New Orleans, LA 70118
(504) 866–1767

MASSACHUSETTS
Amherst
79 South Pleasant Street (2nd
    floor, rear)
Amherst, MA 01002
(413) 256–1261

Boston
729 Boylston Street, Suite 201
Boston, MA 02116
(617) 266–1926

Carl S. Ell Student Center
Northeastern University
360 Huntington Avenue
Boston, MA 02115
(617) 424–6665

Cambridge
1384 Massachusetts Avenue,
    Suite 201
Cambridge, MA 02138
(617) 497–1497

Stratton Student Center
MIT W20–024
84 Massachusetts Avenue
Cambridge, MA 02139
(617) 225–2555

MICHIGAN
Ann Arbor
1220 S. University Drive, #208
Ann Arbor, MI 48104
(313) 998–0200

MINNESOTA
Minneapolis
1501 University Avenue, SE,
  Room 300
Minneapolis, MN 55414
(612) 379–2323

NEW YORK
New York
205 East 42nd Street
New York, NY 10017
(212) 661–1450

New York Student Center
895 Amsterdam Avenue
New York, NY 10025
(212) 666–4177

148 West 4th Street
New York, NY 10012
(212) 254–2525

NORTH CAROLINA
Durham
703 Ninth Street, Suite B–2
Durham, NC 27705
(919) 286–4664

OHIO
Columbus
8 East 13th Avenue
Columbus, OH 43201
(614) 294–8696

OREGON
Portland
715 SW Morrison, Suite 600
Portland, OR 97205
(503) 228–1900

PENNSYLVANIA
Philadelphia
3606A Chestnut Street
Philadelphia, PA 19104
(215) 382–0343

RHODE ISLAND
Providence
171 Angell Street, Suite 212
Providence, RI 02906
(401) 331–5810

TEXAS
Austin
2000 Guadalupe Street
Austin, TX 78705
(512) 472–4931

Dallas
6923 Snider Plaza
Suite B
Dallas, TX 75205
(214) 363–9941

WASHINGTON
Seattle
1314 Northeast 43rd Street
Suite 210
Seattle, WA 98105
(206) 632–2448

219 Broadway Avenue East
The Alley Building, Suite 17
Seattle, WA 98102
(206) 329–4567

WISCONSIN

Milwaukee
2615 North Hackett Avenue
Milwaukee, WI 53211
(414) 332–4740

ABROAD

FRANCE
CTS
49, rue Pierre Charron
Paris 75008

CTS
31, rue St. Augustin
Paris 75002

CTS
16, rue de Vaugirard
Paris 75006

CTS
51, rue Dauphine
Paris 75006

CTS
12, rue Victor Leydet
Aix–en Provence 13100

CTS
37 bis, rue d'Angleterre
Nice 0600

CTS
36, quai Gailleton
Lyon 69002

CTS
20, rue de l'Université
Montpellier 34000

BRITAIN
CTS
28A Poland Street
London W1V 3DB
England

GERMANY
CTS
18, Graf Adolf Strasse
4000 Dusseldorf 1

JAPAN
CTC
Sanno Grand Building
Room 102
014–2 Nagata–cho 2–chome
Chiyoda–ku, Tokyo 100

Part One

▸━▸━▸━▸━▸━▸━▸

THE BASICS

Chapter 1

THE POSSIBILITIES

More than ever before, Americans are looking for vacations that don't involve merely lying on a beach or jumping on a bus tour that takes them to five cities in five days. In addition to basking in the sun or seeing the sights, they want to learn something new on their travels. Vacations with a special focus—whether it be studying Polish history in Warsaw, architecture in London, conservation ecology in Tanzania, or sea turtles on the coast of Mexico—provide that type of stimulation.

As the fastest-growing segment of the travel industry, learning vacations are increasing in both number and variety. Colleges and universities, museums, voluntary service and environmental organizations, and even traditional tour operators have developed overseas learning vacations with the adult traveler in mind. Whether you want to learn or brush up on a foreign language, do development work in Nicaragua, take French cooking lessons while residing in a château in Burgundy, or go on a Kenyan safari, you can find a program to suit your needs.

Have you ever dreamed of cycling through Italy, trekking in Nepal, or doing scientific research in the Amazon rain forest? What about doing voluntary service work like excavating an archaeological site in Israel? Perhaps you're interested in socially conscious travel and would like to participate in an overseas delegation promoting global friendship through meetings with local people. This book includes more than 240 institutions and organizations that sponsor a wide variety of learning vacations abroad:

- study tours with academic, environmental, and cultural themes
- outdoor adventures such as trekking, hiking, and mountain climbing

- archaeological digs that depend on volunteers to delve into the past
- the arts, including painting workshops and lectures on art history, cooking schools, dance theater, and opera tours
- language study, including programs in 16 languages

What distinguishes many of these programs from ordinary vacations is the caliber of the professionals who accompany the group. Tour and project leaders are generally experts in their fields; many have advanced degrees or extensive in-country experience. Another difference is that in most cases you needn't get bogged down in planning your itinerary and making reservations for places to stay. All of this is usually arranged, which frees you to concentrate on what interests you—to learn, to explore, to discuss, and to grow.

There are programs designed for virtually every interested traveler, from the amateur historian, gastronomist, or artist to the ecologically conscious and the adventurous. There are also programs for seniors, professionals, singles, and other special groups. The organizations and institutions listed in this book specialize in programs lasting one to six weeks.

The program listings are arranged alaphabetically according to the sponsoring organization or institution. They include a brief description of each sponsor and a summary of the programs offered, their duration, and their focus. In some cases, the listings include more detailed descriptions of specific programs. Most sponsors offer the same types of programs each year, although the exact focus or location might change. If you're looking for a certain kind of program, be sure to contact those sponsors that have offered similar opportunities in the past.

In addition to the institutions listed in this book, check with other colleges and museums to examine the educational travel programs they offer. Many colleges and universities offer programs that are open to the public. Contact the alumni associations at local institutions or at your alma mater to find out what programs they sponsor.

Learning vacations are not only opportunities for pleasurable ways to learn—they can also be useful for career enhancement. These vacations can yield practical benefits whether you are participating in a program specifically designed for your profession or a program to learn, or enhance your knowledge of, a foreign language to use at work. If you are a member of a professional organization, you should also check there for possible program offerings specifically tailored to your occupation. (For a breakdown of program types and sponsoring organizations, see pages 48–60.)

A learning vacation allows you to expand your understanding of the world and the ways of other people and cultures. You can learn something new or delve more deeply into something more familiar by meeting and traveling with others who share your interests. As you read through the listings, opportunities that you never thought about before may spark your interest. We hope this book starts you on a journey of discovery.

FURTHER READING

For more program ideas, you may want to consult the following:

- *Volunteer! The Comprehensive Guide To Voluntary Service in the U.S. and Abroad,* by the Council on International Educational Exchange, Publications Department, 205 East 42nd Street, New York, NY 10017 (fourth edition, $8.95 plus $1.50 postage). Strictly dedicated to voluntary service, this book includes short, medium, and long-term opportunities available worldwide.
- *Academic Year Abroad,* published annually by the Institute of International Education, 809 United Nations Plaza, New York, NY 10017 (1992–1993 edition, $39.95 plus $3 postage). Written primarily for U.S. undergraduate students, this book also includes study-abroad programs open to adults.
- *Vacation Study Abroad,* published annually by the Institute of International Education (see address above; 1992 edition, $36.95 plus $3 postage). This publication, designed for U.S. students looking for summer study-abroad opportunities, also includes many short-term programs open to adults that focus on topics of broad interest. Not limited strictly to summer programs, the book also lists short courses offered during the fall, winter, and spring.
- *The Educational Travel Planner: The Canadian Guide To Learning Vacations Around the World* provides more than 250 pages of alternative travel ideas. This guidebook includes study tours, language schools, volunteer opportunities, retreat centers, and cooking schools worldwide. The 1993 edition is available for $12.95 plus $2.25 postage (Canadian dollars) from Athabasca University, Marketing and Communications, Box 10,000, Athabasca, Alberta TOG 2RO, Canada.
- *The Educated Traveler,* an informative newsletter dedicated to learning vacations, includes information on a variety of inter-

esting programs that take place worldwide. Each issue includes a current list of program sponsors and an outline of their offerings. Articles written by people who have participated in these programs as well as those involved in the educational travel industry are also featured. Published ten times a year, the newsletter is available from The Educated Traveler, Inc., P.O. Box 220822, Chantilly, VA 22022; (703) 471–1063. An annual subscription is $75. (Single copies and back issues are available for $7.50 each.)

- *Transitions Abroad* magazine is an independent resource guide to living, learning, employment, and educational travel abroad. Published six times a year, it offers practical, usable information in articles and firsthand reports. A special supplement, the "Educational Travel Directory" is compiled annually and includes the best and most current information sources on work, study, travel, and living abroad. Subscription rates for U.S. residents are $18 for six issues, $34 for 12 issues; for Canadian residents, $24 (U.S. dollars only) for six issues. The "Educational Travel Directory" is available separately for $6.95. Order from Transitions Abroad, Department TRA, Box 3000, Denville, NJ 07834.

If you find *Smart Vacations* useful, you may also be interested in two similar books CIEE compiles on educational experiences abroad. These two books—one geared to college students and the other to high school and junior high school students—comprise with this book a complete series on learning abroad for all age groups. (All are published by St. Martin's Press.)

- *Work, Study, Travel Abroad: The Whole World Handbook,* available in bookstores or from the Council on International Educational Exchange, Publications Department, 205 East 42nd Street, New York, NY 10017 (1992–1993 edition, $12.95 plus $1.50 postage). Updated biennially, this handbook includes invaluable information and suggestions to help college students plan a work, study, or travel experience abroad. Included are descriptions of hundreds of specific study and work programs around the world, along with tips on the least expensive ways to travel.
- *Going Places: The High-School Student's Guide to Study, Travel, and Adventure Abroad.* This guide provides travelers between the ages of 12 and 18 with all the information they need for a successful trip abroad. Included are sections to help teens

find out if they're ready for travel abroad, make the necessary preparations, and get the most from their experience. The book describes more than 200 programs, including study tours, language programs, workcamps, summer camps, and homestays. Also included are interviews with teenagers who have participated in some of the programs listed. The 1993–1994 edition is available in bookstores and also can be ordered from CIEE (see address above; $13.95 plus $1.50 postage).

Chapter 2

CHOOSING THE RIGHT PROGRAM

Choosing the program that's best for you involves careful thought and research. You'll want to seize the opportunity that most interests you, but remember that traveling abroad requires flexibility, an open mind, and thorough preparation. To have the most rewarding experience possible, it is necessary to consider all your options. Ask questions and read the fine print. If information isn't provided in the program advertisement or descriptive brochure, call and inquire.

When you're embarking on an educational vacation, the learning begins with the decision to go. Nothing can take the place of doing some legwork to make the most of your time abroad. We hope the following guidelines will help you with your search.

PROGRAM FOCUS

Learning vacations have a special educational focus—and since there are so many to choose from, it's worthwhile to look at as many alternatives as possible. You may be the type of person who has many travel interests, and would be just as content studying history in Warsaw as architecture in Tokyo. Or perhaps you know quite specifically that you would like to take painting classes in the Bordeaux region of France. In either case, it's important to spend some time exploring specific programs to determine whether they meet your needs.

A realistic view of yourself and the program you're considering is essential. What are your expectations for this program? If you're interested in an intensive study of Turkish mosques, for example, you may be disappointed if you wind up in a program of short tours that take you on a casual saunter through several mosques. If you're interested in learning how to prepare entrées, you don't want to end up in a French culinary school that focuses on pastries and other desserts. To spare yourself disappointment later on, it's a good idea to discuss the program curriculum or itinerary with the director in advance. If you're not able to speak with the director, consult one of the staff at the sponsoring organization.

When looking into a specific program, ask the program director for the names and phone numbers of some past participants; then call them to discuss the program. If you're interested in a study tour, you may want to ask how effective the instructors were; how rigorous the study component was, or how much time, if any, was spent in the classroom. Do past participants recommend the program? Find out why or why not. Conversations with past participants will give you an insider's view of the program.

The length of time the program has been operating can affect the quality of your vacation. If it has been running for a number of years, chances are that the staff has worked out most of the "bugs." If it is a recently established program, it may not run quite as smoothly. You may not mind hopping on the pioneer's wagon, but it's a good idea to prepare yourself for rough spots along the way. Find out how much experience the tour leader has had in the program region. Taking the time to ask about these points can only add to the quality of your trip by helping you make an educated decision.

Every program involves some planned activity, whether it be going to the theater, visiting museums and restaurants, attending lectures, or biking to a certain town. While some programs require participants to attend all planned activities, others are more flexible. Think about what type of schedule would be most suitable for you. If you are constantly on the go and enjoy group activity, then a program that includes little independent time will be fine. If you'd rather have a balance of planned activities and time to yourself, you need a program with some flexibility. Find out how adaptable the itinerary is; some programs will give you the option to bow out of scheduled events. Whatever the case, you don't want to be frustrated or utterly exhausted on your trip abroad because you were constantly urged to hop from one place to the next.

It is also a good idea to find out whether the program includes an orientation. Some organizations run their orientations in the United States before the tour departs, while others provide an orientation overseas. These briefings usually include a basic introduction to the country and culture, information on the program itinerary, practical travel tips, and an opportunity to meet the tour leader and other members of the group. Participants may also be given a reading list of works relating to the focus of the program. If you have questions about the program, the orientation is a good place to bring them up. Chances are others in the group will have similar concerns. If you are unable to attend the orientation, ask whether there is any written introductory material the sponsor can mail or put aside for you.

DESTINATION

Most people already have some idea of where they would like to go. But even so, be sure to consider all your options before making a final decision. What opportunities are available around the world? While Europe tends to be the most popular destination for Americans, there are numerous programs that go to African, Asian, and Latin American countries. Why not think about going to a Third World country? The cultures and economies of these nations pose a vivid contrast to those of the United States and challenge travelers to reexamine their own values, assumptions, and beliefs. Talk to family members, friends, or teachers who have visited the country you're considering; find out where they went and what they did.

In deciding where you want to travel, remember that the program destination can have a substantial impact on the overall cost. Chances are that a two-week study tour in Japan, for example, will be significantly more expensive than a similar program in Mexico. Airfare alone will cost considerably more, and in-country expenses will be higher as well. Look into current airfares and use a recent travel guidebook to determine prices and exchange rates in the countries you're considering. Of course, the longer the program, the larger your budget needs to be.

THE PARTICIPANTS

Another important consideration in choosing a learning vacation is the other people in the group you'll be traveling with. Maybe you're looking for a marine biology program and would like to work with a serious group of researchers, gathering data on the habits of killer whales. Conversely, maybe you're interested in a more general study of sea life with a group of laypeople. Perhaps you would like to join a program that attracts participants from different parts of the world, instead of going abroad with a group of Americans. If you're in your 60s and most people participating in the program are in their mid-20s, you may feel more comfortable in a group closer to your age. Ask whether the program is designed for or tends to attract, a particular group of people such as seniors, singles, women, professionals, or college students.

A good way to get a general idea of the constituency of the group is to inquire about how the participants are recruited. Where and how does the sponsoring organization do its advertising? If you are interested in a study tour focused on European history and the program is primarily advertised on college campuses, chances are you'll be with a group of students. The volunteer program that interests you might recruit its participants from religious or political groups of one leaning or another. These things are worth knowing before you select your program, because your fellow travelers can have a strong effect on the quality of your experience.

TRAVEL

How much traveling would you like to do on your learning vacation? Some programs go from one city or country to the next, giving you the opportunity to explore a variety of places, while others involve bedding down in one spot and taking excursions to nearby historic sites, museums, theater performances, or wildlife sanctuaries. Staying in one place gives you the chance to become familiar with that area—an opportunity you won't have if you're only stopping off for a day or two. Consider the type of experience you would like to have, then look for a program that matches your preferences.

If you'd like a learning vacation that takes you to a number of different cities or countries, think about the mode of transportation that would be most suitable for you. Traveling by bus, train, or car gives you the opportunity to see the countryside as you journey from place to place. If you decide that you'd like to travel by air, you will be able to visit far-flung cities but won't always have the opportunity to see the areas in between.

An increasing number of luxury cruises have an educational theme. While this option offers many advantages in terms of comfort, remember that on most cruises you get only a brief and superficial view of the countries and ports at which the ship calls. You might think about combining different modes of travel: Some programs, for example, might include travel by ship along with rail or bus travel.

ACCOMMODATIONS

Depending upon the program you choose, accommodations may or may not be prearranged for you. They are included on most organized programs departing from the United States, but they might not be part of programs offered at language institutes overseas, or at other types of specialty schools.

Volunteer projects usually provide modest accommodations, often at no charge. However, although you may be interested in volunteering for an archaeological dig in Britain, the idea of sleeping in a tent on-site for two weeks may not appeal to you. On the other side of the coin, maybe you're considering a French program that includes accommodations in five-star hotels, but you would really rather stay with a French family; you want to experience the culture in a way that hotels simply prohibit. Ask the program staff whether you can seek alternative accommodations. Whatever your preference, it's important that you choose the type of accommodations where you will feel most comfortable.

If accommodations are included in the program itinerary, it's quite possible that the fees will be based on more than one person per room. Getting a single room may involve paying an additional fee; if you're interested, talk to the sponsoring organization to find out what can be arranged. If you'd like to attend a school that doesn't provide accommodations, be sure to ask about where to stay in the area, how much it will cost, and how long it will take you to get from there to the school each day.

Most programs include at least a few meals. While some provide breakfast and lunch daily, others only include meals from Monday to Friday. Some programs may include dinner daily, and others may not include dinner at all. Find out which meals you will be responsible for so you can work them into your budget. If you'd rather not eat on the program's meal plan, see if you can have this cost deducted from the overall fee.

FINANCES

Now it's time to examine the nuts and bolts of an educational vacation. There are many variables involved, so you need to take a realistic look at finances. How much are you willing to spend on this vacation? Do you have an overall budget? Factors that affect the cost of a program include destination, duration, accommodations, meals, excursions, and course fees (if any).

When considering these factors, it's important to scrutinize what is covered in the program fee. International airfare is usually included on study tours organized in the United States, but may not be included on voluntary service projects. Even if airfare comprises part of the program fee, find out which city the flight departs from. If you live in St. Louis and the flight leaves from New York, you'll have to get to New York and budget for that additional expense. If you want to make your own flight arrangements because you plan to go abroad before the program begins, or you have frequent-flier miles or another type of travel benefit, find out if you can meet up with the group outside the United States and have travel costs deducted. Read the fine print, and contact the organization with any questions you have about the potential expenses involved, so you can determine how much the trip will cost before selecting a program.

If classes are an integral part of the program, you may have to pay course fees. Find out whether these fees are included in the overall cost. Although some colleges and universities may not require participants to enroll for academic credit, it is likely that they charge a tuition fee. Depending upon the institution, these fees can vary considerably. It's also worth asking if you'll have to purchase books or other educational materials.

Whatever type of program you choose, you will need to know whether the fee includes excursions such as museum trips, tours of historical sites, and other types of outings. Often programs offer a combination of excursions; some are optional and some are not. Usually those that are part of the regular itinerary are included in the program fee, while the optional outings will involve additional expenses you'll have to pay while abroad.

You'll also need to find out if transportation is provided from the airport at which you land to the program site and back. Some programs have airport transfers prearranged for you; others require that you get to the program site on your own. Airport transfers can be expensive, so find out before you go if you'll have to arrange them on your own.

As you can see, there are many questions to address before deciding on an educational vacation that fits your budget and your interests. At a minimum, be sure to ask what is *not* covered in the overall fee, as well as which expenses may be subject to change. Most program fees do not include personal expenses, bank charges for currency exchange, airport taxes, medical-accident insurance, and other miscellaneous items. Plan for unanticipated expenses by setting some money aside. If you apply to a program and for some reason are unable to go, you'll want to know if the application fee is refundable.

In some countries you may be expected to tip in-country guides who take you on a tour. If guided tours are part of your program itinerary, ask the group leader whether tipping is appropriate and how much is recommended. These tips might be included in your program fee, but in most cases they are not.

PEOPLE WITH SPECIAL NEEDS

If you have special needs, whether they are related to a physical disability, dietary or other restrictions, you may need more information to select the right program. Don't hesitate to ask the program sponsor if the necessary accommodations can be made for you to participate. Have the sponsoring organization contact the airline, hotel, or other places you'll be staying to find out what can be arranged. When necessary, airlines will transport passengers via wheelchair or special vehicle from terminal to terminal in the United States and in major cities worldwide. They will also provide special meals if requested in advance, as will major hotels.

If you've traveled before and your needs have been accommodated in special ways, don't hesitate to tell the program director; it is safe to assume that he or she probably does not have experience with a situation like yours. Remember that with the passage in 1990 of the Americans with Disabilities Act, a civil rights law protecting people with disabilities from discrimination in employment, public accommodations, transportation, telecommunications, and the activities of state and local governments, U.S.-based organizations are required to take steps to make their programs accessible to persons with disabilities.

Chapter 3

PREPARING FOR YOUR LEARNING VACATION

No matter where you are traveling, there are certain official documents to be obtained and arrangements to be made before you leave. As soon as you decide to leave the United States, you should start getting the essentials out of the way.

PASSPORTS

U.S. citizens need a passport to enter just about every foreign country and to return to the United States. Exceptions include short-term travel between the United States and Mexico and Canada. For travel to many Caribbean countries, a birth certificate or voter registration card is acceptable proof of U.S. citzenship. However, even when it's not specifically required, a valid U.S. passport is the best travel documentation available.

Passports for U.S. citizens 18 years or over are valid for 10 years and cost $55 for first-time applicants plus a $10 execution fee (see below for details). For anyone under 18, they are valid for five years and cost $30, plus the $10 execution fee. Between March and August the demand is heaviest and the process will take longer than at other times of the year. Apply several months before departure, and if you're going to need visas, allow yourself even more time.

If it is your first passport application, you must apply in person at 1) a U.S. post office authorized to accept passport applications; 2) a federal or state court; or 3) one of the passport agencies located in Boston, Chicago, Honolulu, Houston, Los Angeles, Miami, New Orleans, New York, Philadelphia, San Francisco, Seattle, Stamford, or

Washington, DC. To apply, you'll need to bring proof of U.S. citizenship. This can be a certified copy of a birth certificate, naturalization certificate, or consular report of birth abroad. (Note: Your birth certificate must show that the birth record was filed shortly after birth and must be certified with the registrar's signature and raised, impressed, embossed, or multicolored seal.) You'll also need two identical photographs taken within six months of applying—photos must be two inches square with a white background (most vending machine photos are not acceptable)—and proof of identity, such as a valid driver's license (not a Social Security or credit card). Finally, you must complete the form DSP–11, "Passport Application."

You may apply by mail and avoid the $10 execution fee if 1) you have had a previous passport that was issued within 12 years of the new application; 2) you are able to submit your most recent passport with the application; and 3) you were 16 or older at the time of issuance. In addition to sending your previous passport and two new passport-size photographs, you must complete form DSP–82, "Application for Passport by Mail." It generally takes four to six weeks to process a passport, or even longer during the peak travel season.

Your passport should be kept with you at all times while traveling. American passports are coveted by those who wish to work or live in the United States but can't, due to visa restrictions. On the international black market, U.S. passports can sell for about $1,000. One good way to assure that your face remains in your passport is to carry it in a pouch tied at the neck or worn around the waist like a belt. This pouch can hold traveler's checks, too, and should always be kept inside your clothing. All Council Travel offices (see pages xv–xviii) carry passport holders and pouches.

Loss, theft, or destruction of a valid passport is a serious matter and should be reported immediately to local police and to the nearest U.S. embassy or consulate. If the loss occurs in the United States, notify Passport Services, 1425 K Street NW, Department of State, Washington, DC 20520. If you lose your passport in another country, you will need to get a replacement at a U.S. embassy or consulate. This process will be much easier if you have two extra passport photos with you and a photocopy of your original showing the number and date and place of issuance. In case your passport is stolen or lost, you also should have with you—but in a separate place from your passport—both proof of citzenship (an expired passport or copy of your birth certificate) and proof of identity (a driver's license or other photo ID).

You should also be aware that a number of countries will not place visas in passports that have a remaining validity of less than six months, and will not permit such visitors to enter. If you return to the United

States with an expired passport, you are subject to a passport waiver fee of $80.

Non-U.S. citizens—whether traveling with a travel permit or a valid passport from another country—will have to consult the embassy or consulate of the country they want to visit to obtain the appropriate visa requirements. Non-U.S. citizens without a valid passport from another country who have permanent residency in the United States can apply for a U.S. travel permit. This permit functions much like a passport and can be obtained from the Immigration and Naturalization Service in the state where the applicant resides. Note, however, that the requirements for obtaining visas in this case are usually different from those that apply to U.S. citizens.

VISAS

Depending on the country you visit and the length and purpose of your stay, you may also need a visa. A visa is an endorsement or stamp that is usually placed in your passport by a foreign government, permitting you to visit that country for a specified purpose and a limited time—for example, a three-month tourist visa. To study in a particular country, you may need a special student visa. In most cases, you'll have to obtain visas before you leave the United States. Apply directly to the embassies or nearest consulates of the countries you plan to visit, or check with a travel agent. The Passport Services office of the Department of State cannot help you get a visa.

Another source of information is the booklet *Foreign Entry Requirements,* which lists the entry requirements for U.S. citizens traveling to most foreign countries and tells where and how to apply for visas. Single copies are available for 50¢ from the Consumer Information Center, Department 454Y, Pueblo, CO 81009. Although this publication is updated annually, changes can occur without notice at any time. For the latest information, check with the embassy or the nearest consulate of the countries you plan to visit.

Since the visa is usually stamped directly onto one of the blank pages in your passport, you'll need to fill in a form and give your passport to an official of each foreign embassy or consulate. You may need one or more photos. (Have extras made when you're having passport pictures taken.) You'll have to pay for most visas. The whole process can take several weeks, so if you have more than one to get, start well in advance of your trip. Also, bear in mind that some countries require evidence that you have enough money for your trip and/or ongoing or return transportation tickets.

Some countries (Mexico, for example) allow U.S. citizens to enter and stay without a passport or visa but require a tourist card. If a country you plan to visit requires a tourist card, you can get one at the airport just before you depart the United States or at the border crossing when you enter the country. Some tourist cards require a fee.

CUSTOMS

When you come back to the United States, you'll have to go through customs. The U.S. government prohibits Americans from bringing back certain articles and imposes import fees or duties on other items. Everything that you'll need to know about customs regulations for your return to the United States can be found in *Know Before You Go,* a pamphlet available free from U.S. Customs Services, Box 7407, Washington, DC 20044. To order by phone, call (202) 566–8195.

HEALTH

Rather than go into specifics here about something as important as your health, we'll refer you to experts and a few good books on the subject. But before we do, we want to emphasize that the two greatest threats to travelers' health today are diseases against which you cannot be inoculated: diarrhea and malaria. Most types of malaria can be prevented, but you must begin taking antimalarial drugs before you arrive in the infected area and must continue taking them after you leave.

Some countries require international certificates of vaccination against yellow fever and cholera. Because smallpox has been virtually eradicated, vaccinations for that disease are rarely required. Check your health care records to ensure measles, mumps, rubella, polio, diphtheria, tetanus, and pertussis immunizations are up-to-date. The Centers for Disease Control has a hot line that tells travelers whether any special vaccinations are needed to visit a country, or if there are any dangerous outbreaks of disease in that country. The hot line number is (404) 332–4559.

One organization that has worked energetically to alert travelers about the risks of malaria and other health problems worldwide is the International Association of Medical Assistance to Travellers (IAMAT). IAMAT is a nonprofit organization with centers in 450 cities in 120 countries. Its members receive a pocket-size directory listing IAMAT centers abroad, a world immunization chart (which we particularly recommend), and various publications and maps that alert travelers to existing health problems throughout the world. Contact IAMAT at 417 Center Street, Lewiston, NY 14092; (716) 754–4883. Membership in this organization is free, but donations are appreciated.

When traveling, you should also be aware of the risk of contracting AIDS (Acquired Immunodeficiency Syndrome). Don't let exaggerated or distorted information alter your travel plans, but do inform yourself of the risks and make the necessary preparations. Be aware that some countries may require HIV (human immunodeficiency virus) antibody tests before they'll grant a visa for an extended period of time; tourists staying for 30 days or less are usually exempt. You might want to be tested before you depart; do so only at a center that offers pre- and post-test counseling, and allow two weeks for the testing process. While traveling, remember that the best way to deal with AIDS is through knowledge, foresight, and action, not ignorance and fear.

The Centers for Disease Control has issued the following advisory: "AIDS has been reported from more than 130 nations, but adequate surveillance systems are lacking in many countries. Because HIV and AIDS are globally distributed, the risk to international travelers is determined less by their geographic destination than by their individual behavior. HIV infection is preventable. There is no documented evidence of HIV transmission through casual contacts; air, food, or water routes; contact with inanimate objects; or through mosquitos or other arthropod (insect) vectors. HIV is transmitted through sexual intercourse, blood or blood components, and perinatally (at birth) from an infected mother. Travelers are at increased risk if they have sexual intercourse (homosexual or heterosexual) with an infected person; use or allow the use of contaminated, unsterilized syringes or needles for any injections, e.g., illicit drugs, tattooing, acupuncture, or medical/dental procedures; or use infected blood, blood components, or clotting factor concentrates."

The following books are recommended reading for overall health issues. You won't need to consult all of them, but do try to look through at least one. Getting sick while you travel is miserable.

- *The Pocket Doctor* is a pocket-sized publication written especially for travelers. You can order it for $3.95 (includes postage if prepaid) from The Mountaineers Books, 1011 SW Klickitat Way, Suite 107, Seattle, WA 98134; (206) 223–6303.
- *Health Information for International Travel,* published annually by the Centers for Disease Control and available for $5 from

the Superintendent of Documents, U.S. Government Printing Office, Washington, DC 20402–7325; (202) 783–3238.
* *Staying Healthy in Asia, Africa, and Latin America,* by Dirk Schroeder, is basic enough for the short-term traveler yet complete enough for someone living or traveling off the beaten path. Order it from Volunteers in Asia, Box 4543, Stanford, CA 94309 for $7.95 plus $1.50 postage.
* *The International Travel Health Guide* ($16.95), by Stuart R. Rose, M.D., is updated annually and includes country-by-country immunization, health, and safety listings. It also has chapters on AIDS, travel and pregnancy, and traveling with disabilities. Look for it in good bookstores or contact the publisher, Travel Medicine, Inc., 351 Pleasant Street, Suite 312, Northampton, MA 01060; (800) TRAV–MED.

Some general advice: Make sure you're in good general health before setting out. Go to the dentist before you leave on your trip, have an extra pair of eyeglasses or contact lenses made up (or at least have your doctor write out your prescription), and if you take along any prescription drugs, pack them in clearly marked bottles and have the prescription with you in case a customs officer asks for it.

SAFETY

Traveling outside the United States is not dangerous in and of itself; in fact, travelers will encounter few countries where the crime rate—especially the frequency of violent crime—equals that of the United States. But remember one thing: While traveling, you will be recognized as a foreigner. To some, this means you will be a novelty; to others, a rube. This means that you must be aware and thoughtful at all times. You can no longer rely on your instinctive knowledge of what may be considered unsafe, insulting, or provocative. This doesn't mean that you should not explore or stray off the tourist-beaten path. Depending upon the program, you may have a chance to do this, and if not, you might want to do some traveling on your own after the program ends. In any case, you should be aware of your passport and money at all times and take along a good guidebook that gives you a rough idea of the situations you will be getting yourself into. Try to determine which areas to avoid alone or at night, and try not to arrive in strange cities late at night unless you have a confirmed place to stay and a secure means of getting there. At home or abroad, you can't control everything that happens to you, but you can sway the odds.

If you're planning a trip to a spot where a political problem has existed for a while or just flared up, a reliable source of information is the Citizens Emergency Center (CEC), operated by the State Department in Washington, DC. This center will inform you of any State Department travel advisories that warn travelers of danger and recommend taking special precautions, or in more extreme cases, postponing travel to certain countries or regions. Recorded travel advisories can be obtained anytime from a push-button phone by calling (202) 647–5225. If you're using a dial phone, call between 8 A.M. and 10 P.M., Monday through Friday, or between 9 A.M. and 3 P.M. on Saturday.

INSURANCE

Check to see whether your medical and accident insurance policies are valid when you are traveling outside the United States. Never underestimate the importance of being insured when traveling abroad. Investigate the various plans for baggage and flight insurance. Baggage or personal insurance covers damage to or loss of your personal belongings while traveling. Flight insurance covers the cost of your fare if you are unable to take a flight you have already paid for.

One insurance package, Trip-Safe, provides a variety of options that can be purchased in any combination for any period from one month to one year. Included are basic sickness and accident, baggage, trip cancellation/interruption, and traveler's assistance coverage. Trip-Safe can be obtained at any Council Travel office (see list of offices on pages xv–xviii).

The international teacher, youth, and student cards (see below) include medical and accident insurance while traveling outside the United States, as well as a traveler's assistance service for help in a medical, financial, or legal emergency.

INTERNATIONAL IDENTITY CARDS

CIEE offers a variety of special internationally recognized identity cards for special groups, specifically teachers, persons under 26 years of age, and students. Because of their international recognition, these cards provide cardholders with special benefits while traveling abroad. All of these cards entitle the holders to special discounts on airfares, provide accident and hospitalization insurance while traveling outside the United States, and connect cardholders anywhere in the world via a toll-free telephone call to an emergency assistance service.

The International Teacher Identity Card

If you are a teacher at the elementary, secondary, or college/university level, you will probably want to get the International Teacher Identity Card before you go. The card provides basic medical and accident insurance while traveling abroad, as well as a free traveler's assistance service for help in a medical, financial, or legal emergency. Discounts abroad are not widely available with the International Teacher Identity Card; however, cardholders get a 10 percent discount on the teacher refresher language courses offered by Eurocentres (see pages 144–145).

Another benefit of the International Teacher Identity Card is access to special educator fares that CIEE/Council Travel offers on the regular international flights of a number of airlines. Teacher fares can cost as much as 50 percent less than regular commercial fares from the United States to cities in Africa, Asia, Europe, Latin America, and the South Pacific; age restrictions apply on some airlines. More information on these educator fares is available from Council Travel offices (see pages xv–xviii).

The International Teacher Identity Card is available by mail order from CIEE or can be obtained in person at all Council Travel offices and many of the same campus offices that issue the International Student Identity Card (see below). The cost of the 1993 card—valid from September 1, 1992, to December 31, 1993—is $16. For more information about the card, call CIEE's Information and Student Services Department, (212) 661–1414, extension 1108.

The International Youth Card

The benefits of the International Youth Card include the same insurance coverage and traveler's assistance service available with the teacher card (see above). In addition, cardholders gain access to special CIEE/Council Travel youth airfares on international flights with a number of airlines. Contact any Council Travel office (see pages xv–xviii) to find out the youth airfare to your destination abroad. Everyone purchasing an International Youth Card also receives a free booklet that lists hundreds of discounts in 40 countries for cardholders. The International Youth Card, available to anyone under age 26, is issued by CIEE, all Council Travel offices, and a limited number of travel agents. The 1993 card costs $15. For more information on the International Youth Card, call CIEE, (212) 661–1414, extension 1108.

International Student Identity Card

If you are a student in a degree program, you are eligible for the International Student Identity Card, a standard document of international student travel for more than 25 years. This card provides international recognition of student status so that you can take advantage of any student discounts available in the country you are traveling in. The International Student Identity Card provides the same insurance coverage and traveler's assistance emergency services that come with the International Teacher Identity Card (see above). Perhaps most important, cardholders also gain access to special student airfares that CIEE/Council Travel offers on regular international flights with a number of airlines. (Age restrictions apply on some airlines.) More information on student/youth fares is available from Council Travel offices (see pages xv–xviii).

The 1993 card—valid from September 1, 1992, to December 31, 1993—is available for $15. It can be obtained from CIEE, any Council Travel office, or from any of the 450 authorized issuing offices on college and university campuses across the country. For more information on the student card and issuing office locations, call 1–800–GET–AN–ID.

MAIL

If your educational vacation extends beyond a couple of weeks, you may want to give your relatives or friends an address where you can be reached. Most programs will have a mailing address. If your program does not, you can still receive mail by having it sent to you in care of poste restante (general delivery) at the central post office in the cities you'll be visiting. Simply go to the post office and pick up any mail that has arrived for you.

MONEY

Without a doubt, the best way to carry your money abroad is in traveler's checks, which can be replaced if lost or stolen. Most traveler's checks cost one percent of the total dollar amount you're buying (for example, $5 for $500 in traveler's checks). Traveler's checks in U.S. dollars are widely accepted around the world. However, it is also possible to purchase traveler's checks in other major currencies such as British pounds or German marks. If the dollar is falling in value relative to other major currencies, your money will go further if it is denominated in marks, pounds, or yen.

The most common traveler's checks are American Express, Citicorp, Thomas Cook, and Visa. In deciding what kind of traveler's checks you should buy, try to determine how widely the check is recognized and the number of offices the issuing agency has abroad (in case your checks are lost or stolen). Remember that you won't have to go to an overseas office of the issuing agency if you just want to convert your checks to local currency. Most banks will cash them readily; although some banks charge a fee to do this, in most European countries you'll get a better exchange rate with traveler's checks than with cash. Try to avoid changing your money in hotels and restaurants, where the rate of exchange is usually less favorable.

In many countries, especially those of the Third World, currency is often available in exchange shops (*bureaux de change* or *cambios*), where the rate of exchange is much better than that in a bank. Be sure to investigate all options for the best rate of exchange, especially if you're going to be changing large amounts of money. But be wary of currency exchange with money changers on the street: In most countries this type of transaction is illegal.

Conversion tables listing rates of exchange for dollars in different currencies are found in most guidebooks. Daily currency rates are quoted in many newspapers, including *The New York Times* and the *Wall Street Journal*. You'll be able to buy foreign currency in an air, ship, or train terminal when you arrive, but rates are often better once you're in town. It's a good idea, however, to have some local currency with you when you first arrive in a country, especially if it's late at night.

If you run short of money, traveler's checks or cash can be cabled to you from the United States in care of a bank or an agency, such as American Express or Thomas Cook. If your bank has a foreign branch, you can have money transferred to you there. It is best to do this in major cities and to make arrangements as far in advance of imminent destitution as possible. Don't be surprised if the bank requires you to open a special account with a high minimum balance in order to make the transfer. You can get more information on wiring money abroad from the agencies that issue your traveler's checks or from a Western Union office.

Your own credit card or ATM (automatic teller machine) card may allow you access to ATMs overseas. Check with the financial institution that issues the card to find out if it participates in an ATM network with overseas members. Also find out if you will need to change your personal identification number in order to use the card abroad. The PIN should be four numbers instead of six.

BECOMING INFORMED

To get the most out of your experience abroad, you'll need to do some reading on the countries you'll be visiting. Guidebooks, novels, movies, histories, and social, economic, and political studies are all helpful. Investigate your library, ask friends what they recommend, and check to see what your local bookstore has in stock. Though some programs will provide you with a suggested reading list before departure, it's also a good idea to do some preparation on your own. We especially recommend that you look at some books and movies from the country you will be visiting. Below are some reading suggestions appropriate for persons going anywhere from Canada to Madagascar.

No matter where you go, you'll be asked questions about U.S. foreign policy, especially matters that directly affect the countries you visit. The best thing to do is prepare yourself in advance by reading newspapers like *The New York Times,* the *Washington Post,* and the *Christian Science Monitor.* Although these papers are not always without bias, all are known for their coverage of international affairs. Especially valuable are the publications of the Foreign Policy Association, a nonprofit, nonpartisan organization dedicated to informing Americans of the complexities of foreign policy issues. *Great Decisions,* which describes the pros and cons of alternative courses of action on eight different foreign policy issues each year, is one of the best ways to quickly inform yourself about these topics. This book is available for $11 plus $2 postage and handling. Another good resource is the *Headline Series,* a set of booklets (usually 64 pages each) that cover major world areas and topics of current interest. These booklets are published four times a year, and single copies are available for $4. A subscription is $15 annually. These and other publications on foreign policy topics are available from the Foreign Policy Association, 729 Seventh Avenue, New York, NY 10019. To order, call toll-free (800) 477–5836; in New York, call (212) 764–4050.

For a quick and easy introduction to the culture of the country you're going to, we recommend *Culturgrams,* four-page profiles of the customs, manners, and life-styles you'll encounter in 105 countries. The briefings also discuss typical greetings and attitudes, religion, politics, and more. Published by Brigham Young University's David

M. Kennedy Center of International Studies, the guides are available for $1 each (50¢ each if you buy more than five) or $45 for the entire set of 105. Order them from the Center's Publication Services, 280 HRCB, Brigham Young University, Provo, UT 84602; (801) 378–6528.

Also useful in getting to know the country you're going to is the *Transcultural Study Guide,* prepared by Volunteers in Asia, an organization that emphasizes increased understanding between cultures. Believing that the questions asked to a large extent determine the answers and conclusions that follow, the guide suggests questions for looking at another culture from a humanitarian perspective. To order, write to Volunteers in Asia, Box 4543, Stanford, CA 94309 ($4.95 plus $1.50 postage).

DRUGS

More than 2,860 American citizens were arrested abroad in 1990. More than 1,180 of those arrested were held on charges of using or possessing drugs. The notion that drug laws (and their enforcement) in other countries are more lenient than the United States is simply not true. While a few countries might seem to have a more liberal attitude toward drugs, in most countries prosecution of offenders for both the possession and sale of drugs and narcotics can be more severe than in the United States. Many travelers assume that as American citizens they are immune from prosecution under foreign laws. The truth is that Americans suspected of drug violations can face severe penalties, even the death penalty, in some foreign countries. It is not uncommon to spend months or even years in pretrial detention, only to be sentenced to a lengthy stay without parole. Many countries do not permit bail in drug-trafficking cases.

Once an American leaves U.S. soil, U.S. laws and constitutional rights no longer apply. U.S. consular officers can visit jailed Americans to see that they are being fairly and humanely treated, but cannot get them out of jail nor intervene in a foreign country's legal system on their behalf. Should you get into some legal difficulty, the U.S. consulate can provide you with a list of local attorneys and contact your family at home for you—but it can't get you out of trouble or even furnish money for your legal fees.

Be particularly wary of persons who ask you to carry a package or drive a car across the border. Also, be sure that if you are required, for medical reasons, to take any drug that may be subject to abuse statutes, you have your prescription bottle and a copy of your prescription along with you. Remember, too, that the U.S. Bureau of Customs will inspect your baggage upon your return to the United States, and that is tightening its enforcement procedures.

For more information, consult the brochure entitled *Travel Warning on Drugs Abroad* (available free from the Bureau of Consular Affairs, Public Affairs Staff, Room 5801, Department of State, Washington, DC 20520).

FOR PERSONS WITH DISABILITIES

In the last decade, persons with disabilities have increased their participation in the world of international travel and exchange. This is partly the result of laws passed by the federal government that reflect a national commitment to end discrimination on the basis of handicaps and to bring persons with disabilities into the mainstream of American life. But it is primarily the result of a growing number of people with disabilities insisting upon their right to face the challenges and enjoy the benefits of international travel. Many of the programs listed in this book include information specifically for persons with disabilities. In addition, listed below are helpful organizations, videotapes, and publications developed and written for travelers with disabilities.

One organization active in the advocacy of travelers with disabilities is Mobility International. The organization, with its main office in London, was founded in 1973; the U.S. branch opened in 1981. Working with persons with disabilities as well as with the organizers and administrators of international educational exchange programs, Mobility International USA (MIUSA) has helped persons with disabilities participate more fully in the world community.

Besides publishing a quarterly newsletter called *Over the Rainbow,* MIUSA has put together two books, written and edited by Cindy Lewis and Susan Sygall, which are highly recommended. The first is entitled *A World of Options for the 90's: A Guide to International Educational Exchange, Community Service and Travel for Persons with Disabilities* ($14 for members, $16 for nonmembers). The book contains more than 300 pages of programs for volunteer, study, and host-family living especially for persons with disabilities. Participants provide first-hand accounts of what can be learned from international exchange. The second book, entitled *A New Manual for Integrating Persons with Disabilities into International Educational Exchange Programs,* is targeted mainly to the staff and volunteers of service and exchange organizations. It costs $16 for MIUSA members, $18 for nonmembers.

MIUSA has also produced four videocassettes about its work: *Mi*

Casa Es Su Casa describes a Costa Rica exchange; *Looking Back, Looking Forward* focuses on trips to England and Costa Rica described by student travelers with disabilities; *Home Is in the Heart* describes the accommodation of disabled persons into the homestay experience; and *Emerging Leaders* focuses on developing leadership skills as a disabled person. All of these are available in English and Spanish with captions for the hearing-impaired.

Books and tapes can be ordered from Mobility International-USA, P.O. Box 3551, Eugene, OR 97403; (503) 343–1284 (voice or TDD). In addition, MIUSA sponsors international exchanges for persons with and without disabilities.

Itinerary: The Magazine for Travelers with Physical Disabilities ($10 for six issues) is another publication of interest to those who want to travel in the United States or abroad. To subscribe, contact Whole Person Tours, P.O. Box 2012, Bayonne, NJ 07002–2012.

FOR FURTHER READING

The U.S. Department of State has several pamphlets that can help you make the necessary preparations. A good source of basic information, including such subjects as how to judge a travel program, information on charter flights, and where to get help when you are in trouble abroad, is *Your Trip Abroad.* Another Department of State pamphlet, *A Safe Trip Abroad,* reminds travelers of some common-sense precautions and also gives tips on protecting against the possibility of terrorism. These can be ordered for $1 each from the U.S. Government Printing Office, Washington, DC 20402; (202) 783–3238.

Chapter 4

MAKING YOUR OWN TRAVEL ARRANGEMENTS

Depending on the type of learning vacation you choose, you may have to make your own travel arrangements. Generally, study tours organized in the United States will incorporate most travel arrangements into the program itinerary, including flights, accommodations, and any program-related ground transportation. If, however, you're interested in attending a language school, culinary institute, or offering your services in a volunteer program, it is likely that you will have to make some or all of your own arrangements. This could involve purchasing airline tickets, arranging transportation from the airport to the program site and back, and finding a place to stay.

Making travel arrangements takes time and planning, so be sure to start at least three months in advance. It's always a good idea to begin by looking at a few good guidebooks—preferably those that give you a flavor of the country and culture, as well as practical travel tips and information (see Resources, pages 40–41). You may also want to request a free information packet from the tourist board of the country to which you're traveling. After getting some background information, you can make arrangements yourself or go to a travel agent and discuss the options that are best for you.

Unless the travel agency you deal with specializes in low-cost travel, it will generally provide you with the going rates on standard flights and accommodations. However, there are many other options. This chapter spells out some of the alternatives for travelers who are on a budget or looking for something other than conventional tourist offerings. It describes some low-cost alternatives for transportation and accommodations, as well as other tips on getting the most for your money.

TRAVEL AGENCIES FOR THE BUDGET TRAVELER

Few travel agencies specialize in budget travel. Most are simply not set up to arrange the cheapest flight or arrange any type of accommodation abroad other than standard hotels. If you are interested in budget travel or want to explore somewhat unusual alternatives, do some basic investigation on your own and then go to a travel agency geared specifically to the budget or alternative traveler. Such agencies frequently advertise in the travel sections of major newspapers such as *The New York Times,* the *Chicago Tribune,* and *The Los Angeles Times.*

Specializing in low-cost travel for all ages, Council Travel, CIEE's travel office network, has 38 branches located throughout the United States with a wide selection of information and services on travel, work, and study abroad. (Additional offices are located in Europe and Asia; see pages xv–xviii for a complete list.) Council Travel provides details on low-cost flights, accommodations, and car rentals worldwide, as well as rail passes and special student, youth, and teacher airfares to all parts of the world. In addition, travel guidebooks, youth hostel memberships, international student, youth, and teacher identity cards, travel insurance, and even travel gear are available from all offices nationwide. Council Travel also sells charter airline tickets on behalf of Council Charter, CIEE's charter division. Flights are available to most major European cities.

AIRFARES

Although there is no shortage of bargain airfares, they usually go hand in hand with a number of restrictions. Use caution when investigating your options, and be sure to read the fine print. As a general rule of thumb, the more limitations attached to a fare, the less expensive it will be. When looking for the most economical fares, take some time to gather and compare flight information. To get started, contact Council Travel (see list of locations on pages xv–xviii) for an "Airfare Update," a seasonal list of its lowest fares to destinations throughout the world. Also be sure to check the Sunday travel sections of large metropolitan newspapers like *The New York Times, The Los Angeles Times,* and the *Chicago Tribune.*

When you're considering your options, it's important to keep a few fundamental things in mind. The time of year you decide to travel can affect the cost. June through September is the peak travel season in the Northern Hemisphere and is more expensive than other seasons, while November through February is the peak season in the

Southern Hemisphere. Traveling during the off-peak seasons can save you a substantial amount of money. Other factors that can have an impact on the cost of your flight include the length of time you spend abroad; the day of the week you travel (fares to overseas destinations are more expensive on weekends than they are on weekdays); your airline choice; and whether you fly on a charter or regularly scheduled flight.

Charter flights and consolidators generally offer the best deals. A charter flight is one in which a tour operator charters a plane to fly a specific route on a specific date. Consolidators buy unsold seats from airlines at a substantial discount and then sell them to travel agents, other consolidators, or directly to the public through newspaper ads. In both cases, these seats usually are nonrefundable and cannot be changed. This isn't true of all charters and consolidators, however: CIEE's Council Charter, which runs charters to most major European cities, will give you a partial refund as long as you cancel before your scheduled departure from the United States. For a $75 fee you can also change your return ticket in Europe. Tickets are available from all Council Travel offices (see pages xv–xviii for a list of offices).

Special fares on many international flights are available to senior citizens, young people, students, and teachers. Seniors can often get discounts directly from the airline (see Discounts for the 50 + Traveler, pages 37–40). If you're under 26, a student in a degree program at an accredited institution, or a full-time teacher, you should look into the special youth, student, and teacher fares CIEE has negotiated with a number of international airlines. These fares, not available directly from the airline, can cost as much as 50 percent less than the regular fare. Contact any Council Travel office for fare information. Eligibility for the youth fare is limited to persons under 26, and student fares on most airlines require the traveler to be under 31 years of age; purchase of the International Youth Card, International Student Identity Card, or International Teacher Identity Card is required for these special fares (see pages 22–23).

If you are not eligible for special youth, student, or teacher fares, you should also ask your travel agent about Advance Purchase Excursion Fares (APEX). These fares generally cost 30 to 40 percent less than regular economy-class tickets, but usually carry restrictions such as cancellation and change penalties, minimum- and maximum-stay requirements, and stopovers. You are also required to purchase your tickets within seven to 30 days prior to departure.

You may also want to keep your eyes open for special advertised bargain or promotional fares. Usually available during slow periods, promotional fares come up sporadically. In most cases, however, you have to purchase them right away and be ready to travel soon after you buy your ticket.

GETTING AROUND ONCE YOU'VE ARRIVED
Rail Travel

Traveling by rail can be one of the most convenient and economical ways to get around, especially if you plan on taking long trips. Most trains have meal cars to satisfy your hunger pangs, as well as sleeping quarters in case you want to travel overnight. If you like the idea of meeting people and seeing the countryside, trains are good way to do both. You'll find well-developed rail networks throughout Europe, as well as in Japan, Canada, Argentina, China, India, and Thailand.

Special rail passes are usually available in those countries that have extensive rail lines; for a reduced price, most of these passes allow unlimited travel within a designated region for a certain period of time. Some passes must be purchased in the United States, while others are only available abroad. Among the most widely known passes are Eurailpasses, for travel throughout Europe.

Traveling by rail in Europe is one of the most popular ways for tourists and natives alike to see the continent. The rail network is reasonably priced, convenient, and fast. It stretches throughout the continent, covering more than 15 countries. Eurailpasses allow unlimited travel in most European countries and are available in various forms: the Youthpass, Youth Flexipass, Eurailpass, Saverpass, and Flexipass. All of these passes must be purchased in the United States and vary according to your age, duration of travel, and whether you're traveling first or second class. Eurail passes are ideal if you plan on going to a number of different countries.

For more information on the Eurail and other rail passes, check with Rail Europe (800) 345–1990, the nearest Council Travel office, or a local travel agency. You may also want to pick up a copy of *Eurail Guide: How to Travel Europe and All the World by Train,* which includes information on train travel in 141 countries worldwide (see Resources, pages 40–41, for ordering information).

Bus Travel

Bus systems vary from country to country. Some are efficient and luxurious, while others are slow, antiquated, and downright uncomfortable. In some of the less-developed nations of the world, they are the only means of public transportation. However, there are a couple of things you can count on with buses: They are one of the most inexpensive ways to get around, and they usually go to even the smallest and most out-of-the-way destinations. In some countries you may even be able to purchase passes that provide you with unlimited travel for a designated time period. Check with your travel agent or consult a good guidebook for up-to-date information on the bus lines in the country you're traveling to (see Resources, pages 40–41).

Car Rental

Most travelers rely on public transportation to get around, but renting a car is always an option, especially if you like your independence and are interested in traveling to places off the beaten path. Some rental companies may tell you that all you need is a valid U.S. driver's license to rent a car anywhere in the world, which may be true; however, to drive legally in most countries, you need an International Driver's Permit. The permit is available from any local office of the American Automobile Association (AAA), or from the main office at 1000 AAA Drive, Heathrow, FL 32746; (800) 556–1166. Though the permit is an official translation of your license, you are required to carry both with you when driving.

It's a good idea to arrange a rental in the United States before you go abroad. You can do it through any Council Travel office, as well as through multinational agencies such as Hertz, Budget, or Avis. Rental agreements vary substantially from country to country and from company to company. If you plan to travel long distances, check out the weekly unlimited mileage rates and be prepared to pay very high prices for gasoline, especially in Europe.

If you are going to Europe and want to combine travel by train with travel by rental car in your trip, several new rail pass options allow this kind of flexibility within one package price. Check with Council Travel for information on combined rail/car rail pass options.

PLACES TO STAY

Accommodations vary in quality and price, depending upon where you're traveling. In general you can find hotels, hostels, rooms in private homes, or university dormitories in most countries throughout the world. Especially popular in Europe are guesthouses and pensions. In Britain and Australia, bed and breakfasts are quite widespread and economical.

When deciding on the most suitable establishment in which to hang your hat, do not overlook its location. You may find a place that sounds as if it's just what you're looking for; when inquiring further, however, you find that it's beyond walking distance from the program site and not readily accessible by public transportation. Another detail to consider is how safe the location is, especially if you're considering budget accommodations. A good guidebook will be of enormous help (see Resources, pages 40–41).

Following are brief descriptions of the types of accommodations you may want to consider staying in while you're abroad.

Hotels

A wide range of hotels is available in nearly all destinations around the world. Travel guidebooks are one of the best sources of information on hotels. Even if you don't use the recommendations of a guidebook, you will at least gain an idea in advance of how much you will have to spend.

Reservations at the more expensive hotels overseas can be booked by travel agents in the United States; most international hotel chains even have 800 numbers in the United States that you can call to make a reservation at any of their locations worldwide. If you're looking for a budget hotel, however, it will be more difficult to make arrangements in advance. At most destinations in Europe, Latin America, Africa, and Asia, rooms in budget hotels can generally be found without advance reservations if you arrive before noon. At resort areas in peak season, finding an inexpensive hotel may be more difficult.

Your best bet when looking for budget accommodations is to consult a good guidebook that lists these places (see Resources, pages 40–41). If you're traveling in a major city, check the rail station for a tourist information center when you arrive. Many times these establishments have lists of inexpensive local accommodations and will call ahead and reserve a room for you. To book a room in advance, consult with a budget travel agency. These agencies usually advertise in the travel sections of major newspapers such as *The New York Times*, the *Chicago Tribune*, and *The Los Angeles Times*.

Hostels

Hostels, as a rule, are the least expensive type of accommodation you'll come across. To stay in most of the 5,300 hostels affiliated with Hostelling International worldwide, you must purchase the American Youth Hostels membership card before leaving the United States. Available for $25 for those over 18 and under 55, and $15 for those

55 and over, the card can be obtained at any Council Travel office (see list on pages xv–xviii), as well as at any American Youth Hostels office; for the office nearest you, contact AYH, National Office, P.O. Box 37613, Washington, DC; (202) 783–6161.

Hostels generally have dormitory-style rooms ranging from about $8 to $10 per night including bed mattresses and blankets (though it's not a bad idea to bring your own sleeping bag, especially if you're traveling during a peak season). Fellow hostelers are required to bunk together—at least six people in a room is not uncommon. Quarters can get a bit cramped during peak travel seasons, especially in popular tourist areas. This is something to think about if your learning vacation requires some studying. The chances of being able to hit the books in a hostel packed with travelers are slim. Also, some hostels permit a maximum stay of only three nights and have a curfew, usually sometime around 10 P.M.

YMCAs

Often equipped with swimming pools, recreational facilities, restaurants, and libraries, YMCAs are typically more expensive than hostels. YMCA residences are located in 27 countries in North America, Europe, and Asia, and accommodate both men and women. In most countries a private room with a shared bath is provided. Advance reservations can be made for establishments in England, Hong Hong, Thailand, Israel, and New Zealand through the YMCA's central reservation office, the Y's Way, at (212) 308–2899. Room rates generally run from about $30 to $50 per night.

Pensions, B&Bs, and Guesthouses

In most countries around the world you will find family-run establishments such as pensions, guesthouses, Japanese *minshuku*, and British bed and breakfasts (also common in Australia and Canada). Usually smaller than hotels, these accommodations also tend to be less expensive. For some names and addresses of places like these, consult a good guidebook (see Resources, pages 40–41), or contact a local tourist office.

Private Rooms

Renting rooms in private homes, particularly in Europe, can be even less expensive than pensions, guesthouses, or B&Bs. Local tourist offices usually have lists of rooms available that can be rented when you arrive at your destination. Some will even call ahead and make reservations for you. Unlike homestays, which usually have to be arranged through a homestay organization, travelers do not share in the daily life of the host family.

College Dormitories

Another economical alternative that has grown more popular in recent years is renting a dormitory room on a university campus. Generally dorms are a bit more expensive than hostels, but single rooms are usually available. Many also serve inexpensive meals on campus. *The U.S. and Worldwide Travel Accommodations Guide* lists dorm rooms available for $12 to $24 a night in more than 30 countries outside the United States; most are in Europe. (See Resources, pages 40–41, for ordering information). Tourist offices in university towns may also have lists of dorms open to travelers.

Homestays

If you're interested in real cultural enrichment, consider a homestay, the opportunity to live with a family abroad. It's a wonderful way to get an insider's view of a country and, if you're studying a language, a great place to practice it. A number of programs listed in this book include homestays. If the learning vacation you choose does not include such arrangements, you may be able to set up a short-term homestay on your own with the help of one of these organizations:

- U.S. SERVAS, 11 John Street, Room 407, New York, NY 10038; (212) 267–0252. As a member of SERVAS, you are entitled to contact host families on its membership list for stays of no longer than two days (unless the family agrees to let you stay longer). To become a member, you must apply and be interviewed by a SERVAS staff member. If your membership is approved, you are given host lists and an introductory letter to contact the families you'd like to stay with. SERVAS has hosts in 120 countries. The annual membership fee is $55.
- Federation EIL, P.O. Box 595, Putney, VT 05346; (802) 387–4210. Although this organization does not sponsor homestays, it serves as a clearinghouse for information on longer-term (one- to four-week) homestays in 17 countries worldwide. Federation EIL will provide you with information on homestay organizations in a particular country that have homes open to travelers.

Home Exchanges

Home exchanges are one of the most economical ways to find accommodations if you're willing to host visitors from abroad. In most cases you pay a fee to join a home exchange organization, which publishes directories of its members' homes that are available for short-term stays. As a member, you are entitled to contact other members and arrange a homestay; in return you are expected to host members who contact you. Two of these organizations are described below:

- Intervac U.S., P.O. Box 590504, San Francisco, CA 94159; (800) 756–HOME. The largest home exchange organization in the world, Intervac U.S. publishes three directories per year that include descriptions of more than 8,000 houses and apartments for exchange in about 25 countries. Home exchanges are generally available for one to four weeks.
- The Hospitality Exchange, 4908 East Culver #2, Phoenix, AZ 85008; (602) 267–8000. Exchange opportunities outside the United States are available in about 25 to 30 countries, with a high concentration in France and Germany. Three host directories, which describe the types of accommodations available, are published annually.

DISCOUNTS FOR THE 50+ TRAVELER

If you are at least 50 years old, you are a member of the distinguished segment of society that spends the most money on leisure travel. As a result, you are one of the travel industry's most cherished clients. Tour companies and educational and cultural institutions are continually designing programs with you in mind. Growing numbers of companies, including airlines, hotels, and car rental agencies, offer you special discounts on their services.

This section will give you some basic information about some advantages available to travelers, including the 50 plus special discounts, as well as age-related organizations and their benefits. Since travelers in this age group also take more cruises than any other, a short section on educational cruise lines is included.

Airlines

If you're 62 or over, watch the airline advertisements for special airfare deals. Many airlines sell senior coupons that provide attractive discounts. Issued in books of four or eight, these coupons allow you to fly for a good deal less than the lowest sale airfares. Coupon flights also accumulate frequent-flier mileage on most airlines. When deciding which type of coupons to purchase, make sure to read the fine print and consider any restrictions that apply: limitations on when seat reservations can be made; the time period in which the coupons are valid; and the number of seats reserved for coupon holders. While you might prefer the carrier that offers the best selection of flights from your home city to your destination, the restrictions may make you reconsider.

Coupon programs are not the only special programs available. Most airlines, for example, offer a 10 percent senior discount. Generally these discounts cannot be applied to reduced or sale tickets, but if you aren't able to find a coupon deal that's worthwhile, don't forget to ask about them.

Accommodations

Many hotel chains provide special discounts to travelers who are at least 50 years of age, although they may not be available at every one of the chain's locations. While some may require that you be a member of a particular organization such as the American Association of Retired Persons (AARP) or Mature Outlook (see descriptions below), others ask only for proof of your age. Discounts usually range from 10 to 50 percent and generally apply to rooms only; some also pertain to meals and items purchased at the hotel gift shops. Some participating worldwide chains include the Days Inns, Quality Inns, Radisson Hotels, and Hyatt Hotels.

Cruises

A different type of vacation—and one of increasing popularity—is a vacation at sea, with excursions in selected ports. If the idea of combining a cruise with a learning vacation sounds appealing, you may want to look at the growing selection of theme cruises. A number of cruise lines have expanded their offerings to include educational and special-interest cruises in which experts conduct shipboard lectures, lead excursions in port, answer questions, and so on. Theme cruises are available in a variety of fields ranging from the ancient history of the Eastern Mediterranean to opera music, from culinary art to the ecology of the Amazon rain forest. The lectures, educational excursions, and readings are generally optional, but for interested travelers, opportunities for serious learning abound.

Ask your travel agent about current offerings for educational vacations aboard ships. Options range from luxury cruise ships sailing on the most popular routes to smaller ships with fewer amenities sailing to out-of-the-way places, including Antarctica, the Galapagos Islands, or the Nile River. The following cruise lines sponsor educational voyages:

- Royal Viking Line, 95 Merrick Way, Coral Gables, FL 33134; (800) 422–8000.
- Sun Line Cruises, 1 Rockefeller Plaza, Suite 315, New York, NY 10020; (800) 445–6400.
- Seabourn Cruise Line, 55 Francisco Street, San Francisco, CA 94133; (800) 351–9595.

Cruise lines generally do not offer age-related discounts, but prices tend to be lower during off-peak periods.

Organizations

A couple of the most well-known organizations for mature Americans are described below. As a member, you receive travel discounts and a variety of other benefits for a minimum membership fee.

- American Association of Retired Persons (AARP), 400 Pinnacle Way, Norcross, GA 30071; (202) 872–4700. AARP provides its members with information on a variety of life issues ranging from job opportunities to insurance, health care, and travel. For $5 annually you can become a member of AARP and receive special hotel and car rental discounts worldwide. The organization is open to those 50 years old and above.
- Mature Outlook, 6001 North Clark Street, Chicago, IL 60660; (800) 336–6330. This organization, run by the Sears Family of Companies, provides special discounts to its members on selected hotels and car rentals worldwide. Discounts are also available at Sears stores. The annual membership fee is $9.95 per couple.

Further Information for the Mature Traveler

- *The 50 + Traveler's Guidebook: Where to Go, Where to Stay, What to Do,* by Anita Williams and Merrimac Dillon ($12.95). Published by St. Martin's Press (175 Fifth Avenue,

New York, NY 10010), this book includes information on accommodations, cruises, airlines, and other travel services for those at least 50 years of age.

- *Elderhostel: The Students Choice,* by Mildred Hyman ($15.95). Published by John Muir Publications (P.O. Box 613, Santa Fe, NM 87504), this book describes over 200 Elderhostel programs available worldwide and includes candid critiques provided by past participants. Elderhostel programs are designed for those at least 60 years of age.

Resources

In an era of increasing international travel, guidebooks to other countries have become plentiful. There's a wide selection to choose from at most bookstores, and your decision will probably depend on the type of traveler you are. In this section we've listed some travel guidebook series that we often recommend. Most of these are geared to budget travelers and those who want to get off the beaten path and do some independent exploration.

- *Let's Go* series. Compiled by Harvard Student Agencies, this family of guidebooks is packed with information for the budget traveler. Updated annually, these books cover most European countries, as well as Mexico, Israel, Egypt, and Turkey. *Let's Go* books, published by St. Martin's Press, are available in most bookstores and at Council Travel offices nationwide (see list of locations on pages xv–xviii).
- Lonely Planet Series. Compiled by Lonely Planet Publications, these guidebooks cover countries that are off the beaten tourist path, including many in Asia, Africa, the Middle East, and Central and South America. Lonely Planet has two travel series: *Travel Survival Kits* includes information for a range of budgets and styles; the *On a Shoestring Series* is specifically written for budget travelers. For a publications list, write to Lonely Planet Publications, Embarcadero West, 155 Filbert Street, Suite 251, Oakland, CA 94607. Many of these books can be purchased at your local bookstores or at Council Travel offices nationwide (see list of locations on pages xv–xviii).
- *Real Guides.* Published by Prentice-Hall Travel, this family of guidebooks covers a collection of countries in Europe, Asia, Africa, and Central and South America. Although not primarily written for the budget traveler, these guides include historical

and cultural introductions to the countries covered and provide you with some insight into contemporary attitudes. The *Real Guides* are available at most travel bookstores.

- Moon *Handbooks*. These guides, written for the budget traveler and covering destinations that are off the beaten path, include countries in Asia, the South Pacific, the Middle East, and Central America. For descriptions of the individual guidebooks, contact the publisher for a catalog: Moon Publications, 722 Wall Street, Chico, CA 95928; (800) 345–5473.
- *The U.S. and Worldwide Accommodations Guide.* This annual guide lists college and university dormitories around the world that rent rooms to travelers when school isn't in session. Information on nearby points of interest is also included. Compiled by Campus Travel Service, P.O. Box 8355, Newport Beach, CA 92660, this guide is available for $13 plus $1.50 postage.
- *Eurail Guide: How to Travel Europe and All the World by Train.* This book is available for $17 from Eurail Guide Annual, 27540 Pacific Coast Highway, Malibu, CA 90265; (310) 457–7286.

Chapter 5

LEADING A GROUP ABROAD

If you've had extensive overseas travel experience, you may be qualified to lead a group abroad. There are organizations that employ people to do just that. Usually the sponsoring organization plans the program itinerary, then hires leaders to accompany the group and oversee activities. Opportunities range from leading a cycling or hiking group on a short sojourn to taking a group of high school or college students abroad on a formal study program. For most group leader positions, you must be proficient in the language of the host country and have experience traveling or living abroad. Some programs require that you complete a leadership training program. Though you shouldn't expect to get paid much, usually part or all of your travel expenses will be covered.

The following organizations have positions available for group leaders:

- American Youth Hostels (AYH), Programs and Education Department, P.O. Box 37613, Washington, DC 20013. AYH seeks people interested in leading small groups on hiking, cycling, and public transportation or van transportation trips. Leaders must be at least 21 years old and have completed an AYH training course. Opportunities are available in Europe.
- World Learning Inc., Kipling Road, P.O. Box 676, Brattleboro, VT 05302; (802) 257–7751 (VT residents) or (800) 345–2929 (outside VT). World Learning sends small groups of high school and college students abroad for the summer. Leaders should be at least 24 years of age, be fluent in the language of the host country, and have previous cross-cultural

and leadership experience. Leaders must complete a training course. All expenses are paid, and leaders receive a $200 stipend upon completion of the program.

If you're under the age of 30, you may want to think about leading a group in a different sort of way—by becoming a camp counselor. The YMCA's International Camp Counselor Program seeks volunteers for their camps throughout the world. Some programs require fluency in a foreign language. Room and board are provided. Applicants must have completed at least one year of college and have experience in teaching or counseling in a group setting. For more information, contact YMCA, ICCP Abroad, 356 West 34th Street, New York, NY 10001; (212) 563–3441.

If you're an educator or business person interested in developing a program abroad on behalf of your employer, CIEE can provide you with consulting, development, and support services. These custom-designed programs are structured by the requesting institutions or corporations in consultation with CIEE staff. For more information, contact CIEE's Department of Professional and Continuing Education Programs, at 205 East 42nd Street, New York, NY 10017; (212) 661–1414.

Perhaps you're a French, Spanish, or German teacher in a high school or junior high school and would like to take your students abroad to live the language and experience the culture firsthand. CIEE administers School Partners Abroad, a program that enables teachers and their students to live with families while studying at schools abroad. This school-to-school exchange program matches U.S. junior and senior high schools with counterpart schools in Europe, Asia, and Latin America. During the three- to four-week exchange, visiting students and teachers participate fully in the life of the host school, attending regular classes, joining in extracurricular activities, and living with host families. Group leaders are required to attend a daylong orientation. Contact the Department of Secondary Education Programs for information on how this can be arranged (address same as above).

Part Two

▶▶⇒▶▶⇒▶▶⇒▶▶⇒▶▶

THE
PROGRAMS

USING THE LISTINGS

This section is designed to help you find the right program. In addition to the breakdown of information in the index, we have provided a few other ways to tackle the bulk of programs listed in this book. The first part of this section, **How to Find the Program You Are Interested In**, contains lists of the programs according to their subject or theme, specific design for special groups, and location. In **How to Read the Listings**, we explain the format we have used to describe the programs.

HOW TO FIND THE PROGRAM YOU ARE INTERESTED IN

The wide range of program possibilities makes it difficult to divide the organizations into neat categories. Instead, the program descriptions in this book appear alphabetically according to the name of the organization sponsoring the program. If you're specifically interested in a certain subject or activity, however, this section includes a breakdown of the organizations according to the major subject focus of their programs. A brief explanation of these categories is also included to give you an idea of what kinds of programs we have classified under each heading. Since some organizations offer more than one type of program, we have listed them under each category that may be applicable. This cross-referencing system is also used in the second breakdown, by the particular interest group for which the program is designed. The third grouping is by program destination, which in many cases is based on the previous or current locations of programs, as well as future ones when provided by the organization.

Subject or Theme of the Program

Following is a breakdown of the organizations and institutions listed in this book according to the type of programs each one offers. We have tried to group the listings by major subject areas, not by specific focus. For example, a sponsor offering a program dealing with interior design would appear under the *Design* category, along with a sponsor running a program on fashion design. For a more specific breakdown, please consult the index.

ARCHAEOLOGY

Listed here are organizations that offer programs with an archaeological focus, including volunteer excavations at biblical sites in Israel, field research projects in Cyprus, study tours of Ancient Rome, and programs for those who want to attend lectures while participating in an excavation.

Andante Travels
Antichita
Archaeological Tours
The Art Institute of Chicago
University of California Los
    Angeles Extension
California State University–Sac-
    ramento
Chichester Interest Holidays
The Council for British Archae-
    ology
Council on International Educa-
    tional Exchange
Earthwatch
Field Studies Council
Foundation for Field Research
Fudan Museum Foundation
Israel Antiquities Authority
Kent State University
Mexi-Mayan Academic Travel
National Trust for Places of

Natural Beauty and Historic
    Interest
Oceanic Society Expeditions
Oideas Gael
OPA Tours Greece
Purdue University
Ramapo College of New Jersey
San Francisco State University–
    Extended Education
Saskatchewan Archaeological
    Society
The Texas Camel Corps at the
    Witte Museum
The University Museum of Ar-
    chaeology and Anthropology
University Research Expeditions
    Program (UREP)
Volunteers for Peace, Inc.
Western Washington Univer-
    sity–Office of Foreign Study
Wildland Adventures/Earth
    Preservation Fund

ARCHITECTURE AND URBAN PLANNING

The following organizations offer study tours as well as courses with an emphasis on architecture and urban planning. This list includes tours of museums and architectural monuments, cruises with architectural historians, courses in architecture, and study programs in urban planning and city development.

Angkor Wat Adventures
The Art Institute of Chicago
University of California Berkeley Extension
University of California Los Angeles Extension
California State University—Sacramento
Coopersmith
Cornell's Adult University (CAU)
Solomon R. Guggenheim Museum

Journeys East
Michigan State University
The Minneapolis Institute of Arts
National Trust for Historic Preservation
Recursos de Santa Fe
Santa Barbara Museum of Art
University of Utah—International Center
Western Michigan University
Wilson & Lake International
The 92nd Street YM—YWHA

THE ARTS

These organizations offer a variety of arts programs ranging from the general liberal arts to art history, drama, music, and culinary instruction. Among the listings are a calligraphy program in China, watercolor painting in Mexico, and photography in New Zealand. You can take folk dance lessons, learn how to make wine in the French countryside, or take in opera and theater festivals. There are programs for the literary buff and for those interested in film and media studies. There are organizations that run programs for the practitioner as well as the observer.

Amazonia Expeditions
American Heritage Association
Archaeological Tours
The Art Institute of Chicago
Backroads Bicycle Touring
Big Five Tours and Expeditions, Ltd.
Bike Across Italy
University of California Berkeley Extension
University of California Los Angeles Extension
California State University—Fresno

California State University—Sacramento
Central American Institute for International Affairs (ICAI)
Centro Mexicano Internacional (CMI)
CET
Chateau de Saussignac Cooking School
Chopsticks Cooking Centre
Cincinnati Art Museum Travel Program
Close-Up Expeditions
Community College Tours
Cookery at the Grange

Coopersmith
Le Cordon Bleu
Cornell's Adult University (CAU)
The Cousteau Society
Craft World Tours/Camera World Tours
Cross-Culture
Cultural Folk Tours International
Deutsch in Graz
Dillington House
Dora Stratou Dance Theatre
The Earnley Concourse
Earthwatch
Eastern Michigan University
Elderhostel
English Literature Summer Schools
Farm Tours, Etc.
Federation of Ontario Naturalists
Field Studies Council
Galápagos Travel
German Wine Academy
Solomon R. Guggenheim Museum
Heritage Touring
Indiana University at Indianapolis
Institute for British and Irish Studies
Institute for Readers Theater
International Council for Cultural Exchange
Kay Pastorius' School of International Cuisine
Kosciuszko Foundation
The Lisle Fellowship
University of La Verne
University of Louisville
Michigan State University
Minneapolis Institute of Arts

Mozart's Europe Tours
National Trust for Historic Preservation
Natural Gourmet Cookery School
University of New Orleans
New York University
Northern Illinois University
Ohio University
Oideas Gael
University of Oklahoma
The Old Corner House, Woebley
OPA Tours Greece
Opera Education International/ OEI & OEI Tours
Paris en Cuisine
The Partnership for Service-Learning
Photo Adventure Tours
Plantagenet Tours
Podere Le Rose-Centro Pontevecchio
Purdue University
Rockland Community College
La Romita School of Art
San Francisco State University–Extended Education
Santa Barbara Museum of Art
Skidmore College
Smithsonian Odyssey Tours/ Saga Holidays
Storyfest Journeys
Studio Art Centers International
Syracuse University
Trinity College
Tulane University
University of Utah–Center for Adult Development
University of Utah–International Center
University Vacations
Voyagers International

Westchester Community College
Western Michigan University
Western Washington University—Department of Communications
Western Washington University—Office of Foreign Study
Wilson & Lake International

University of Wisconsin—Madison, Department of Continuing Education in the Arts
University of Wisconsin—Madison, Division of University Outreach
World Learning Inc.
The 92nd Street YM—YWHA

DESIGN

This grouping includes organizations that offer programs or short courses in interior design, textiles, fashion, sewing, and antique restoration. You can study interior design in Italy or delve into the history of costume, lace, Victoriana, and vintage collectibles in England. There are programs that focus on fiber arts in India, as well as classes in wool weaving and textile design in Ireland.

University of California Los Angeles Extension
Dillington House
Dyfed County Council
The Earnley Concourse

Professor Polly Guerin
Michigan State University
Oideas Gael
Textile Museum

LANGUAGE AND CULTURE

In this grouping are organizations that offer foreign language programs, as well as programs with a cultural emphasis. Most programs, regardless of their primary focus, place some emphasis on culture. Most programs include language instruction on all levels, whether you're a beginner, intermediate, or advanced learner. Many also include excursions to local places of cultural and historical interest. In many instances you can combine a homestay with language study to gain firsthand experience of the country's culture. Some programs combine culture with history, the natural sciences, or an outdoor activity.

Above the Clouds Trekking
AFS Intercultural Programs
Alternative Tour Thailand
American Heritage Association
American-International Homestays
American Jewish Congress
American Museum of Natural History

Andante Travels
Angkor Wat Adventures
The Athens Centre
Bike Across Italy
University of California Berkeley Extension
University of California Los Angeles Extension

California State University–Sacramento
California State University–Fresno
Casa Xelaju de Español
C/E/I–Club des 4 Vents
Central American Institute for International Affairs (ICAI)
Centre International D'Etudes
Centro de Idiomas, S.A.
Centro di Cultura Italiana
Centro di Cultura Italiana in Casentino
Centro Internazionale Dante Alighieri
Centro Linguistico Sperimentale
Centro Mexicano Internacional (CMI)
Centro Pontevecchio
CET
China Advocates
Cincinnati Art Museum Travel Program
Citizen Exchange Council
Craft World Tours/Camera World Tours
Cross-Culture
Cuauhnahuac
Cultural Folk Tours International
Deutsch in Graz
Did Deutsch-Institut
Dillington House
Dyfed County Council
Earnley Concourse
Eastern Michigan University
English Literature Summer Schools
Eurocentres
Federation of Ontario Naturalists
Folkways Institute

Foreign Language/Study Abroad Programs
Forum International
French-American Exchange
French & American Study Center
Fudan Museum Foundation
Goethe-Institut
Home and Host International
Home Language International
Independent Travel in Asia
Insight Travel
Institute for Shipboard Education
Institute of China Studies
Institute of Noetic Sciences
Institut Français des Alpes
Institut Mediterraneen d'Initiation à la Culture Française, (IMICF)
Instituto Universal Idiomas
Interhostel
International Bicycle Fund
International Council for Cultural Exchange
International Expeditions
International House
International House Language School
ISOK (Voor een vreemde tall naar het vreemde land)
International Peace Walk
Journeys East
Kent State University
Kosciuszko Foundation
Language Studies Abroad
University of La Verne
University of Louisville
LEX America
The Lisle Fellowship
Merkure Institut
Mexico Study Groups
Mexi-Mayan Academic Travel

Minneapolis Institute of Arts
Mir Initiative
Mountain Travel-Sobek: The Adventure Co.
Mozart's Europe Tours
National Registration Center for Study Abroad (NRCSA)
National Trust for Historic Preservation
Nature Expeditions International
University of New Orleans
Northern Illinois University
The Ohio State University
University of Oklahoma
Oideas Gael
OPA Tours Greece
Opera Education International/ OEI & OEI Tours
Partnership for Service Learning
Plantagenet Tours
Podere Le Rose-Centro Pontevecchio
Project RAFT
Purdue University
Ramapo College of New Jersey
Rockland Community College
St. Olaf College
San Diego State University
San Francisco State University– Extended Education
San Francisco State University– Wildlands Studies
Santa Barbara Museum of Art

Scandinavian Seminar
School Year Abroad
Seniors Abroad International Homestays
Skidmore College
Studio Art Centers International
Taleninstituut Regina Coeli B.V.
Tamu Safaris
The Texas Camel Corps at the Witte Museum
Torre Di Babele
Travelearn
Tulane University
University of Minnesota
University of Utah–Center for Adult Development
University of Utah–International Center
University Vacations
Voyagers International
Westchester Community College
Western Michigan University
Wilderness Southeast
Wildland Adventures/Earth Preservation Fund
Wilson & Lake International
University of Wisconsin–Madison, Division of University Outreach/Liberal Studies
World Affairs Council of Philadelphia
World Learning Inc.

NATURE AND SCIENCE

Organizations that sponsor programs in natural history, ecology, zoology, wildlife, biology, geography, and oceanography, among other sciences, are listed below. Most are concerned with environmental protection and responsible tourism. A sample of these programs includes trekking in Thailand, combined with rafting and elephant riding; expeditions in the Amazon rainforest; field research projects on dolphins and whale watching and the protection of endangered sea turtles in Costa Rica. Wildlife management and conservation in Ireland, study tours in the tropical forests of Latin America, and wilderness tours in Japan are also included.

Adventure Associates
Alternative Tour Thailand
Amazonia Expeditions
American Museum of Natural History
Big Five Tours and Expeditions, Ltd.
Borrobol Birding
Brazilian Views, Inc.
University of California Los Angeles Extension
California State University—Sacramento
Caribbean Conservation Corporation
Central American Institute for International Affairs (ICAI)
Chichester Interest Holidays
Community College Tours
Cornell's Adult University (CAU)
Corrib Conservation Centre
Council on International Educational Exchange
The Cousteau Society
Earth Island Institute
Earthwatch
Ecotour Expeditions
Federation of Ontario Naturalists
Field Studies Council
Folkways Institute
Forum International
Foundation for Field Research
Galápagos Travel
Institute for British and Irish Studies
Institute for Food and Development Policy

International Bicycle Tours
International Expeditions
International Oceanographic Foundation
International Zoological Expeditions
Journeys East
Learning Alliance: Options for Education and Action
The Lisle Fellowship
Marine Sciences Under Sails
Mexi-Mayan Academic Travel
Michigan State University
Mir Initiative
Mountain Travel-Sobek: The Adventure Co.
National Trust for Places of Natural Beauty and Historic Interest
Natural History Museum of Los Angeles County
Nature Expeditions International
New York Botanical Garden
Northern Illinois University
Oceanic Society Expeditions
Ohio University
Portland State University
Purdue University
Questers Tours and Travel
Ramapo College of New Jersey
Recursos de Santa Fe
San Diego Natural History Museum
San Francisco State University—Extended Education
San Francisco State University—Wildlands Studies

Sea Quest Expeditions/Zoetic
   Research
Sierra Club Outings
Smithsonian Odyssey Tours/
   Saga Holidays
Tamu Safaris
The Texas Camel Corps at the
   Witte Museum
Travelearn
University of Utah, Interna-
   tional Center

University Research Expeditions
   Program (UREP)
Volunteers for Peace
Voyagers International
Wilderness Southeast
Wildland Adventures/Earth
   Preservation Fund
Woodswomen
Zoological Society of Philadel-
   phia

OUTDOOR ADVENTURE

These organizations sponsor adventure travel programs that involve
outdoor activities such as hiking, rafting, or camping. Sample programs
include walking tours in Madagascar, hiking in the Swiss Alps, cycling
in Austria, and backpacking in Argentina. There are wildlife safaris
in Kenya and camping-photo tours in India. There are programs for
bird watchers in Scotland, mountain climbers in East Africa, and skiers
in the French Alps. Water lovers can sail in the British Virgin Islands,
white-water raft in Russia, and snorkel or fish in Mexico.

Above the Clouds Trekking
Adventure Associates
American Jewish Congress
Angkor Wat Adventures
Backroads Bicycle Touring
Big Five Tours and Expeditions,
   Ltd.
Bike Across Italy
Borrobol Birding
The Cousteau Society
The Earnley Concourse
Footloose & Fancy Free
Hostelling International/Ameri-
   can Youth Hostels
Institut Français des Alpes
International Bicycle Fund
International Bicycle Tours
International Oceanographic
   Foundation
International Peace Walk

Learning Alliance: Options for
   Education and Action
Marine Sciences Under Sails
Mobility International USA
   (MIUSA)
Mountain Travel Sobek: The
   Adventure Co.
National Outdoor Leadership
   Schools (NOLS)
Oceanic Society Expeditions
Offshore Sailing School
Oideas Gael
Photo Adventure Tours
Project RAFT
Red Coat Tours
Sea Quest Expeditions/Zoetic Re-
   search
Sierra Club Outings
The Texas Camel Corps at the
   Witte Museum
Travelearn

University of Utah–International Center
Western Michigan University

Wilderness Southeast
Woodswomen

RELIGION AND PHILOSOPHY

This roster includes organizations that sponsor programs or short courses focused on religion and philosophy, including Buddhist studies in Bhutan, India, and Nepal; noetic sciences and local religions in Brazil, Australia, and Turkey; and Christianity and liberation theology in Colombia.

Angkor Wat Adventures
Brigham Young University Travel Study
Dillington House
GATE–Global Awareness Through Experience
Insight Travel
Institute of Noetic Studies

Journeys East
Program of Conscientization for North Americans
Ramapo College of New Jersey
University of Wisconsin–Madison, Division of University Outreach/Liberal Studies

SOCIAL AND POLITICAL ISSUES

Organizations that offer programs focused on social and political issues can be found below. There are study tours that include lectures on political science, sociology, or economics, as well as programs that arrange meetings between participants and the people of the country to explore these issues. You can discuss contemporary issues and international events affecting Nicaragua and Costa Rica with high-level government officials in these countries, or participate in a program that includes meeting with the poor in Guatemala, Czechoslovakia, or Zimbabwe. You can take courses in politics and sociology in Germany or combine the study of sociology with community service work in Jamaica, Ecuador, or France, just to name a few.

Amazonia Expeditions
American Heritage Association
American Jewish Congress
APSNICA (Architects and Planners in Support of Nicaragua)
University of California Berkeley Extension
California State University–Sacramento
Canadian Light Brigade

The Center for Global Education
Central American Institute for International Affairs
CET
Committee for Health Rights in Central America
Cornell's Adult University
Council on International Educational Exchange
Earthwatch

Empire State College
GATE–Global Awareness
    Through Experience
Global Volunteers
Institute for Food and Develop-
    ment Policy
Institute for Shipboard Education
International Bicycle Fund
International Executive Service
    Corps
International Movement ATD
    Fourth World
International Peace Walk
University of La Verne
Learning Alliance: Options for
    Education and Action
The Lisle Fellowship
University of Louisville
Los Niños
Our Developing World
The Partnership for Service
    Learning

Plowshares Institute
St. Olaf College
San Francisco State University
Sierra Club Outings
The Texas Camel Corps at the
    Witte Museum
Travelearn
The University Museum of Ar-
    chaeology and Anthropology
University Research Expeditions
    Program
University of Utah
University of Wisconsin–Madi-
    son, Division of University
    Outreach/Liberal Studies
Venceremos Brigade
World Affairs Council of Phila-
    delphia
World Learning Inc.
World Neighbors

VOLUNTARY SERVICE

These are organizations that offer voluntary service programs ranging from development assistance work around the world to workcamps that might involve construction, historic preservation, farm, or recreation work. There are opportunities to live and work on kibbutzim in Israel, to volunteer on scientific research expeditions worldwide, and to work with the disabled in England. Some programs combine study with community service.

APSNICA (Architects and Plan-
    ners in Support of Nicaragua)
Canadian Light Brigade
Council on International Educa-
    tional Exchange
Foundation for Field Research
Global Volunteers
International Executive Service
    Corps
International Movement ATD
    Fourth World

International Peace Walk
Kibbutz Aliya Desk
Mir Initiative
Mobility International USA
    (MIUSA)
National Trust for Places of
    Natural Beauty and Historic
    Interest
The New York Botanical Gar-
    den
Los Niños

The Partnership for Service
  Learning
Queen Elizabeth's Foundation
  for the Disabled
La Sabranenque

Service Civil International/Inter-
  national Voluntary Service
  USA
Volunteers for Peace, Inc.

HISTORY

The organizations below sponsor programs that include a historical focus. There are programs held on university campuses that offer history courses and on-site lectures at places of historic interest, as well as study tours in which participants stay in hotels while traveling to various sites. Included among the listings are European history programs that take participants to gardens and manor homes in Europe, as well as Russian history study tours, and historical tours in Canada.

American Heritage Association
American Jewish Congress
Andante Travels
Archaeological Tours
University of California Berke-
  ley Extension
California State University–
  Fresno
Centro Mexicano Internacional
  (CMI)
Community College Tours
Coopersmith
Cornell's Adult University
Cross-Culture
Cultural Folk Tours Interna-
  tional
Eastern Michigan University
English Literature Summer
  Schools
Federation of Ontario Natural-
  ists
Field Studies Council
Fudan Museum Foundation
German Wine Academy
Professor Polly Guerin
Interhostel

International Peace Walk
Kent State University
The Kosciuszko Foundation
University of Louisville
National Trust for Historic
  Preservation
Northern Illinois University
University of Oklahoma
The Partnership for Service-
  Learning
Plantagenet Tours
Red Coat Tours
Rockland Community College
San Diego State University
Smithsonian Odyssey Tours/
  Saga Holidays
State University of New York
  at Oswego
Storyfest Journeys
Syracuse University
Travelearn
Tulane University
University of Utah–Center for
  Adult Development
University of Utah–Interna-
  tional Center

University Vacations
Western Michigan University
Wilson & Lake International

University of Wisconsin–Madison, Division of University Outreach/Liberal Studies
The 92nd Street YM–YWHA

Programs for Particular Groups

FOR MATURE TRAVELERS

Here you'll find organizations that sponsor programs especially designed for travelers who are at least 50 years of age. Among the listings is Elderhostel, which runs study tours in 44 countries focused on the liberal arts and sciences. Natural history and homestay programs are also available, as well as programs focused on the aging process across cultures.

American Jewish Congress
Backroads Bicycle Touring
Elderhostel
Folkways Institute
Hostelling International/American Youth Hostels
Interhostel

International Bicycle Tours
University of Oklahoma
Scandinavian Seminar
Seniors Abroad International Homestay
Trinity College

FOR EDUCATORS

Listed in this section are organizations offering programs for teachers, educational administrators, aspiring educators, or those with an interest in education. Some of the programs include spending a summer in Chile as a volunteer teacher, teaching in France or England while living with a European family, or spending three weeks in China visiting educational institutions and meeting with Chinese faculty and administrators. There are seminars designed for university-level faculty and administrators focused on current events and rapidly changing political and social conditions in Vietnam, Russia, and Poland. If you're a foreign language teacher, there are teacher refresher courses in France, Italy, Germany, Switzerland, and Spain. You can study elementary education in Britain, learn about elementary and secondary education in El Salvador, or spend three weeks looking at schooling in Costa Rica.

AFS Intercultural Programs
American Heritage Association
Central American Institute for International Affairs (ICAI)

Council on International Educational Exchange
Eastern Michigan University
Eurocentres

Foreign Language/Study Abroad Programs
Foundation for International Education
Hope College
Indiana University at Bloomington
Indiana University at Indianapolis
University of Louisville
Michigan State University
University of Minnesota
National Trust for Places of Natural Beauty and Historic Interest
Network of Educators on Central America
University of New Orleans
Los Niños
The Ohio State University
Rockland Community College
St. Olaf College
School Year Abroad
Travelearn
University of Utah, International Center
Westchester Community College
Western Washington University—College of Education
Zoological Society of Philadelphia

FOR OTHER PROFESSIONALS

Organizations that offer programs for a range of professionals, including social service workers, public administrators, business people, lawyers, and health care workers, are listed here. Among the listings are a program for social workers interested in short-term work in an agency abroad, a public administration and management program in Eastern Europe, as well as an international law program in France. For health professionals there is a work/study program in Latin America, and for retired business executives, a volunteer program to serve in the developing nations of the world.

Center for Cuban Studies
Central American Institute for International Affairs (ICAI)
Citizen Exchange Council
Committee for Health Rights in Central America
Deutsch in Graz
Empire State College
Foreign Language/Study Abroad Programs
Foundation for International Education
International Executive Service Corp
University of La Verne
University of Louisville
University of Minnesota Law School
Mobility International USA (MIUSA)
National Central America Health Rights Network
Northern Illinois University
Rockland Community College
St. Olaf College
San Francisco State University—Extended Education
University of New Orleans
University of Utah—International Center

Geographical Breakdown According to Destinations of the Programs

Organizations are arranged below according to geographical areas in which their programs take place. If you are looking for a specific country instead of a whole region, consult the index.

AFRICA

Above the Clouds Trekking
Adventure Associates
American Jewish Congress
American Museum of Natural History
Andante Travels
Archaeological Tours
Big Five Tours and Expeditions, Ltd.
Brigham Young University Travel Study
University of California Los Angeles Extension
California State University—Sacramento
Center for Global Education
Council on International Educational Exchange
Craft World Tours/Camera World Tours
Earthwatch
Elderhostel
Folkways Institute
GATE—Global Awareness Through Experience
Global Volunteers
Institute of Noetic Studies
International Bicycle Fund
International Executive Service Corps
International House
University of La Verne
University of Louisville
Mountain Travel-Sobek: The Adventure Co.

National Outdoor Leadership School (NOLS)
National Trust for Historic Preservation
Natural History Museum of Los Angeles County
Nature Expeditions International
Oceanic Society Expeditions
Ohio University
Our Developing World
Plowshares Institute
Purdue University
Questers Tours and Travel
San Francisco State University—Extended Education
Santa Barbara Museum of Art
Sierra Club Outings
Smithsonian Odyssey Tours/Saga Holidays
Tamu Safaris
The Texas Camel Corps at the Witte Museum
Travelearn
University Research Expeditions Program (UREP)
Volunteers for Peace
Voyagers International
Western Michigan University
University of Wisconsin—Madison, Division of University Outreach/Liberal Studies
World Affairs Council of Philadelphia
Zoological Society of Philadelphia

THE AMERICAS

Adventure Associates
AFS Intercultural Programs
Amazonia Expeditions
American Museum of Natural History
APSNICA (Architects and Planners in Support of Nicaragua)
Art Institute of Chicago
Backroads Bicycle Touring
Big Five Tours and Expeditions, Ltd.
Brazilian Views, Inc.
University of California Los Angeles Extension
California State University—Fresno
California State University—Sacramento
Canadian Light Brigade
Caribbean Conservation Corporation
Casa Xelaju de Espanol
Center for Cuban Studies
Center for Global Education
Central American Institute for International Affairs
Centro de Idiomas, S.A.
Centro Mexicano Internacional (CMI)
Cincinnati Art Museum Travel Program
Close-Up Expeditions
Committee for Health Rights in Central America
Cornell's Adult University (CAU)
Council on International Educational Exchange
Craft World Tours/Camera World Tours
Cuauhnahuac

Earth Island Institute
Earthwatch
Ecotour Expeditions
Elderhostel
Federation of Ontario Naturalists
Field Studies Council
Folkways Institute
Foreign Language/Study Abroad Programs
Forum International
Foundation for Field Research
Galápagos Travel
GATE—Global Awareness Through Experience
Global Volunteers
Solomon R. Guggenheim Museum
Home and Host International
Home Language International
Indiana University
Institute for Shipboard Education/University of Pittsburgh
Institute of Noetic Sciences
Instituto Universal Idiomas
Interhostel
International Executive Service Corps
International Expeditions
International House
International Oceanographic Foundation
International Peace Walk
International Zoological Expeditions
Kay Pastorius' School of International Cuisine
Language Studies Abroad
University of La Verne
Learning Alliance: Options for Education and Action

Lisle Fellowship
Marine Sciences Under Sail
Mexico Study Groups
Mexi-Mayan Academic Travel
Michigan State University
Mobility International USA
(MIUSA)
Mountain Travel-Sobek: The
Adventure Co.
National Central America
Health Rights Network
National Outdoor Leadership
School (NOLS)
National Registration Center for
Study Abroad
National Trust for Historic
Preservation
Natural History Museum of Los
Angeles County
Nature Expeditions International
Network of Educators on Central
America
New York Botanical Garden
Los Niños
Northern Illinois University
Oceanic Society Expeditions
Offshore Sailing School
Ohio University
Ohio State University
University of Oklahoma
Our Developing World
Partnership for Service Learning
Plowshares Institute
Portland State University
Program of Conscientization for
North Americans
Purdue University
Questers Tours and Travel

Ramapo College of New Jersey
Recursos de Santa Fe
Red Coat Tours
Rockland Community College
San Diego Natural History Museum
San Diego State University
San Francisco State University–
Extended Education
San Francisco State University–
Wildlands Studies
Saskatchewan Archaeological
Society
Sea Quest Expeditions/Zoetic
Research
Sierra Club Outings
Smithsonian Odyssey Tours/
Saga Holidays
The Texas Camel Corps at the
Witte Museum
Textile Museum
Travelearn
University Museum of Archaeology and Anthropology
University Research Expeditions
Program
University of Utah–International Center
Venceremos Brigade
Voyagers International
Wilderness Southeast
Wildland Adventures/Earth
Preservation Fund
Woodswomen
World Learning Inc.
World Neighbors
92nd Street YM–YWHA
Zoological Society of Philadelphia

ANTARCTICA

International Oceanographic Foundation
Mountain Travel-Sobek: The Adventure Co.
Natural History Museum of Los Angeles County
Oceanic Society Expeditions
World Affairs Council of Philadelphia

ASIA

Above the Clouds Trekking
AFS Intercultural Programs
Alternative Tour (Thailand)
American Heritage Association
American-International Home-
    stays
American Jewish Congress
Angkor Wat Adventures
Archaeological Tours
Art Institute of Chicago
Backroads Bicycle Touring
Big Five Tours and Expeditions,
    Ltd.
University of California Los
    Angeles Extension
California State University–Sac-
    ramento
Center for Global Education
CET
China Advocates
Chopsticks Cooking Centre
Cincinnati Art Museum Travel
    Program
Close-Up Expeditions
Community College Tours
Le Cordon Bleu
Council on International Educa-
    tional Exchange
Craft World Tours/Camera
    World Tours
Cross-Culture
Earthwatch
Elderhostel
Eurocentres

Field Studies Council
Folkways Institute
Foreign Language/Study Abroad
    Programs
Forum International
Fudan Museum Foundation
Global Volunteers
Solomon R. Guggenheim Mu-
    seum
Home and Host International
Home Language International
Independent Travel in Asia
Insight Travel
Institute for Food and Develop-
    ment Policy
Institute of China Studies
Interhostel
International Council for Cul-
    tural Exchange
International Executive Service
    Corps
International Oceanographic
    Foundation
International Peace Walk
Journeys East
LEX America
Lisle Fellowship
Mexi-Mayan Academic Travel
Michigan State University, Of-
    fice of Overseas Study
Minneapolis Institute of Arts
Mir Initiative
Mobility International USA
    (MIUSA)

Mountain Travel-Sobek: The Adventure Co.
National Outdoor Leadership School (NOLS)
National Registration Center for Study Abroad
National Trust for Historic Preservation
Natural Gourmet Cookery School
Natural History Museum of Los Angeles County
Nature Expeditions International
Northern Illinois University
Oceanic Society Expeditions
University of Oklahoma
Ohio University
Partnership for Service-Learning
Photo Adventure Tours
Plowshares Institute
Portland State University
Purdue University
Questers Tours and Travel
Rockland Community College
San Francisco State University—Extended Education

San Francisco State University—Wildlands Studies
Seniors Abroad International Homestay
Sierra Club Outings
Smithsonian Odyssey Tours/Saga Holidays
Textile Museum
Travelearn
University Museum of Archaeology and Anthropology
University of Utah—Center for Adult Development
University Research Expeditions Program (UREP)
Volunteers for Peace
Voyagers International
University of Wisconsin—Madison, Division of University Outreach/Liberal Studies
Woodswomen
World Affairs Council of Philadelphia
World Learning Inc.
92nd Street YM—YWHA

AUSTRALIA AND THE SOUTH PACIFIC

American Jewish Congress
Backroads Bicycle Touring
Big Five Tours and Expeditions, Ltd.
University of California Los Angeles Extension
Close-Up Expeditions
Community College Tours
Cornell's Adult University (CAU)
Cousteau Society
Earthwatch
Eastern Michigan University
Field Studies Council
Folkways Institute
Forum International

Foundation for International Education
Independent Travel in Asia
Institute of Noetic Sciences
Interhostel
International Executive Service Corps
Lisle Fellowship
University of Louisville
Michigan State University, Alumni Lifelong Education
Mountain Travel-Sobek: The Adventure Co.
National Trust for Historic Preservation

Natural History Museum of Los Angeles County
Nature Expeditions International
Oceanic Society Expeditions
Portland State University
Questers Tours and Travel
San Francisco State University

Seniors Abroad International Homestay
Sierra Club Outings
Smithsonian Odyssey Tours/ Saga Holidays
Travelearn
Woodswomen

EUROPE

Above the Clouds Trekking
American Heritage Association
American-International Homestay
American Jewish Congress
American Museum of Natural History
Andante Travels
Antichita
Archaeological Tours
Athens Centre
Backroads Bicycle Touring
Big Five Tours and Expeditions
Bike Across Italy
Borrobol Birding
University of California Berkeley Extension
University of California Los Angeles Extension
California State University– Fresno
California State University–Sacramento
C/E/I–Club des 4 Vents
Centre International d'Etudes
Centro di Cultura Italiana
Centro di Cultura Italiana in Casentino
Centro Internazionale Dante Alighieri
Centro Linguistico Sperimentale
Centro Pontevecchio

Château de Saussignac Cooking School
Chichester Interest Holidays
Cincinnati Art Museum Travel Program
Citizen Exchange Council
Close-Up Expeditions
Community College Tours
Cookery at the Grange
Coopersmith
Le Cordon Bleu
Cornell's Adult University (CAU)
Corrib Conservation Centre
Council for British Archaeology
Council on International Educational Exchange
Craft World Tours/Camera World Tours
Cross-Culture
Deutsch in Graz
Did Deutsch-Institut
Dillington House
Dora Stratou Dance Theatre
Dyfed County Council
The Earnley Concourse
Earthwatch
Eastern Michigan University
Elderhostel
Empire State College
English Literature Summer Schools
Eurocentres
Farm Tours, Etc.

Federation of Ontario Naturalists

Field Studies Council

Folkways Institute

Footloose & Fancy Free

Foreign Language/Study Abroad Programs

Forum International

Foundation for Field Research

Foundation for International Education

The French-American Exchange

The French & American Study Center

GATE–Global Awareness Through Experience

German Wine Academy

Global Volunteers

Goethe-Institut

Professor Polly Guerin

Solomon R. Guggenheim Museum

Heritage Touring

Home and Host International

Home Language International

Hope College

Hostelling International/American Youth Hostels

Indiana University at Indianapolis

Institute for British and Irish Studies

Institute of Noetic Sciences

Institute for Readers Theater

Institut Français des Alpes

Institut Mediterraneen d'initiation à la Culture Française

Interhostel

International Bicycle Tours

International Council for Cultural Exchange

International Executive Service Corps

International House

International House Language School

International Movement ATD Fourth World

International Oceanographic Foundation

ISOK (Voor een vreemde taal naar het vreemde land)

Kay Pastorius' School of International Cuisine

Kent State University

Kosciuszko Foundation

Language Studies Abroad

University of La Verne

University of Louisville

Merkure Institut

Michigan State University, Alumni Lifelong Education

Michigan State University, Office of Overseas Study

Minneapolis Institute of Arts

University of Minnesota

University of Minnesota Law School

Mir Initiative

Mobility International USA (MIUSA)

Mountain Travel-Sobek: The Adventure Co.

Mozart's Europe Tours

National Registration Center for Study Abroad

National Trust for Historic Preservation

National Trust for Places of Natural Beauty and Historic Interest

Natural History Museum of Los Angeles County

University of New Orleans

New York University

Northern Illinois University

Oceanic Society Expeditions
Ohio University
Oideas Gael
University of Oklahoma
Old Corner House, Woebley
OPA Tours Greece
Opera Education International/
OEI & OEI Tours
Paris en Cuisine
Partnership for Service-
Learning
Photo Adventure Tours
Plantagenet Tours
Plowshares Institute
Podere Le Rose-Centro Ponte-
vecchio
Project RAFT
Purdue University
Queen Elizabeth's Foundation
for the Disabled
Questers Tours and Travel
Ramapo College of New
Jersey
Rockland Community College
La Romita School of Art
La Sabranenque
St. Olaf College
San Diego State University
San Francisco State University–
Extended Education
Santa Barbara Museum of
Art
Scandinavian Seminar
School Year Abroad
Seniors Abroad International
Homestay
Service Civil International/Inter-
national Voluntary Service
USA
Sierra Club Outings
Skidmore College
Smithsonian Odyssey Tours/
Saga Holidays

State University of New York
at Oswego
Storyfest Journeys
Studio Art Center International
Syracuse University
Taleninstituut Regina Coeli
B.V.
The Texas Camel Corps at the
Witte Museum
Textile Museum
Torre Di Babele
Travelearn
Trinity College
Tulane University
University Research Expeditions
Program (UREP)
University Vacations
University of Utah–Interna-
tional Center
Volunteers for Peace
Westchester Community Col-
lege
Western Michigan University–
Office of International Affairs
Western Washington Univer-
sity–College of Education
Western Washington Univer-
sity–Department of Commu-
nication
Western Washington Univer-
sity—Office of Foreign Study
Wilson & Lake International
University of Wisconsin–Madi-
son, Department of Continu-
ing Education in the Arts
University of Wisconsin–Madi-
son, Division of University
Outreach/Liberal Studies
Woodswomen
World Affairs Council of Phila-
delphia
World Learning Inc.
92nd Street YM–YWHA

THE MIDDLE EAST

American Jewish Congress
Archaeological Tours
Art Institute of Chicago
Brigham Young University
  Travel Study
California State University—Sac-
  ramento
The Center for Global Educa-
  tion
Close-Up Expeditions
Cornell's Adult University
  (CAU)
Craft World Tours/Camera
  World Tours
Cultural Folk Tours Interna-
  tional
Elderhostel
Folkways Institute
Forum International
Institute of Noetic Sciences
International Executive Service
  Corps
International House
Israel Antiquities Authority

Kibbutz Aliya Desk
University of Louisville
Minneapolis Institute of Arts
National Trust for Historic
  Preservation
Ohio University
Ramapo College of New Jersey
Rockland Community College
San Francisco State University—
  Extended Education
Santa Barbara Museum of Art
Service Civil International/Inter-
  national Voluntary Service
  USA
Textile Museum
Travelearn
University Museum of Archae-
  ology and Anthropology
Volunteers for Peace
Western Michigan University,
  Office of International Affairs
University of Wisconsin—Madi-
  son, Division of University
  Outreach/Liberal Studies

HOW TO READ THE LISTINGS

The fact that a program is listed here does not mean that it is without fault or that it has the endorsement of the Council on International Educational Exchange (CIEE). We have simply compiled information on the programs available; now it's up to you to get more specific information to choose the program that's right for you. Under **Institution/Organization** we've identified educational organizations and institutions that are members of the Council on International Educational Exchange (CIEE). CIEE member programs are all operated on a nonprofit basis; they include some of the largest and best-established international exchange programs available. As part of the membership review process, they have undergone the scrutiny of the CIEE Membership Committee, which has examined their programs and services as well as their organizational structure. As members of CIEE, they have demonstrated an interest in maintaining high standards and a willingness to contribute to the development of the field of international exchange.

Format for the Listings

We've tried to present all the information we've received in a format that will give the reader a feel for what the program is really about. Here's how the information in the listings is arranged:

INSTITUTION/ORGANIZATION: This describes, in broad terms, what the sponsoring group is all about; in most cases it will specify whether the organization is nonprofit or commercial.

PROGRAMS: This describes the program(s) that the organization sponsors, its subject or focus, and other pertinent details.

ELIGIBILITY: Described here are any skills or other requirements necessary to participate in the program.

LOCATION: Here you will find the country or countries, and sometimes the city, in which the program is held.

TIME OF YEAR: In most cases the seasons the program is offered in are listed here. If the program runs in all seasons, it states that the program runs throughout the year. In some cases specific months are listed.

DURATION: The length of time the program runs is described here.

ACCOMMODATIONS: The type of lodgings provided, such as hotels, college dormitories, tents, or private homes, is described here.

COST: In addition to the program fee, the specific expenses covered— room, board, airfare, and so on—are usually listed.

AGE OF PARTICIPANTS: Here you will find the average age or the range of ages of participants.

PERSONS WITH DISABILITIES: This category lists the policy of the organization regarding participation by persons with disabilities.

COMMENTS: Here we have included any other information that would be of interest to the reader and does not fit under the other categories.

Not every listing has every category; for some programs one or two of the items do not apply, and in other cases the information was not provided by the sponsoring organization. Finally, remember that we've only summarized the programs. Finding out all the information you need is up to you.

PROGRAM LISTINGS

Above the Clouds Trekking
P.O. Box 398
Worcester, MA 01602
Phone: (508) 799-4499
Fax: (508) 797-4779

INSTITUTION/ORGANIZATION: Founded in 1982, Above the Clouds Trekking is a commercial tour operator specializing in small-group, cross-cultural expeditions.

PROGRAMS: Above the Clouds organizes adventure travel programs that include walking tours in Europe and trekking (rigorous hiking) and camping expeditions in Nepal and Madagascar. The staff places strong emphasis on assisting the participants in adapting to the new culture. Programs are led by guides with outdoor leadership, language, and cultural skills; many guides are nationals of the countries visited. Participants are encouraged to interact with the local people. Groups are limited to 15 participants.

ELIGIBILITY: Interested persons should be in good health and physical condition.

LOCATION: Walking tours take place in Ireland, Scotland, England, France, Switzerland, and Italy; trekking and camping expeditions take place in Nepal and Madagascar.

TIME OF YEAR: Options are available throughout the year.

DURATION: Two to three weeks on average.

ACCOMMODATIONS: Inns on the walking tours; tents on the trekking and camping expeditions.

COST: Cost averages $100 a day, which covers virtually all in-country expenditures. Airfare is additional.

PERSONS WITH DISABILITIES: Participation by persons with disabilities is generally impossible, due to the rigors of walking and trekking.

Adventure Associates

P.O. Box 16304
Seattle, WA 98116
Phone: (206) 932-8352

INSTITUTION/ORGANIZATION: Adventure Associates is a commercial tour operator that offers adventure travel programs with an "educational focus on native cultures and nature awareness."

PROGRAMS: Programs include a Kenya wildlife and sailing safari, tropical jungle exploration in Costa Rica, a Tanzanian Maasailand safari, and a tour of Morocco. Guides are natives of the regions and have had formal study and training in one of the following areas: ecology, environmental science, cross-cultural studies, anthropology, or park management.
ELIGIBILITY: Applications accepted from all interested persons.
LOCATION: Costa Rica, Kenya, Morocco, Tanzania.
TIME OF YEAR: Winter and summer.
DURATION: Two to three weeks.
ACCOMMODATIONS: Homestays and camping in tents.
COST: Costs range from $2,000 to $6,000, including airfare and 95 percent of all in-country expenses.
AGE OF PARTICIPANTS: The average age of participants is usually between 35 and 55.
COMMENTS: Each program is limited to 10 participants.

AFS Intercultural Programs

313 East 43rd Street
New York, NY 10017
Phone: (800) AFS-INFO
Fax: (212) 949-9379

INSTITUTION/ORGANIZATION: Founded in 1947, AFS is one of the world's oldest and largest nonprofit international student and teacher exchange organizations. AFS is a member of the Council on International Educational Exchange.

PROGRAMS:
- "AFS-USA's Volunteer Educator Program." Offered in Thailand and Chile during the summer for three to 10 weeks, this program enables teachers to observe and teach in local schools. Participants provide conversational English skills and serve as general educational resources. While living with host families, teachers are encouraged to become involved in community activities. An orientation seminar is provided, and various enrichment activities are organized throughout the duration of the program. Persons interested in the Chile program should be proficient in Spanish and have two years of teaching experience; there are no prerequisites for Thailand. The approximate cost for the program in Thailand is $2,750; Chile is $2,500. Both fees include international airfare from gateway city, room, board, predeparture and in-country orientation, excursions, international support and counseling. Some funding is available to participants. Contact AFS for more information.
- "China Language and Culture Study." Offered for three to 10 weeks during the summer, this program takes place in Kunming, Hangzhou, China. Participants study Mandarin language, Chinese culture, Asian studies, and international education. Instructors are native Chinese, with teaching certification and many years of classroom experience. Also included are courses in calligraphy and painting. Lectures are combined with excursions. Participants live in college dormitories. The cost is approximately $3,000, which includes international airfare, room, board, predeparture orientation, classes, some excursions, group leader, international support and counseling. Some funding might be available; contact AFS for more information. Applications accepted from all interested persons.

ELIGIBILITY: Varies according to program. See descriptions of programs above.

LOCATION: Thailand, Chile, and China.

TIME OF YEAR: Time of year varies; see descriptions of programs above.

DURATION: Programs vary from three to 10 weeks.

PERSONS WITH DISABILITIES: AFS tries to accommodate persons with disabilities; individuals are considered on a case-by-case basis.
COMMENTS: Interested participants can receive units of continuing education credit from the American Council on Education. Contact AFS for more information.

Alternative Tour Thailand

14/1 Soi Rajatapan
Rajaprarop Road, Payathai
Bangkok 10400
THAILAND
Phone: (66-2) 245-2963
Fax: (66-2) 246-7020

INSTITUTION/ORGANIZATION: Alternative Tour Thailand (ATT) is a commercial tour operator that organizes tours focused on developing awareness and sensitivity toward the environment and cultures of Thailand's mountain people. ATT is concerned with responsible tourism and development projects in rural and urban Thailand.

PROGRAM: "Trekking Tour Program for Environmental Awareness." This tour takes participants to different villages to observe the local culture; rafting and elephant riding are the main forms of transportation between villages.
ELIGIBILITY: Applications accepted from all interested persons.
LOCATION: Thailand.
TIME OF YEAR: Options are available throughout the year.
DURATION: Treks run for five days.
ACCOMMODATIONS: Participant live in villages.
COST: Price depends on the size of the group. For six to 10 people, the total cost per person is approximately $200 and includes accommodations, most meals, transportation from village to village, and guide. International airfare is additional.

▶➡▶➡▶

Amazonia Expeditions
1824 NW 102nd Way
Gainesville, FL 32606
Phone: (904) 332-4051

INSTITUTION/ORGANIZATION: Founded in 1981, Amazonia Expeditions is a commercial tour operator that offers a variety of expeditions in the Amazon rain forest.

PROGRAMS: Expeditions focus on anthropology, botany, ecology, nature photography, or zoology. Expeditions are led by Paul Beaver, who has a Ph.D. in zoology and is an expert on the Amazon rain forest. The maximum group size is 15.
ELIGIBILITY: Applications are accepted from all interested persons.
LOCATION: Iquitos, Peru.
TIME OF YEAR: Options are available throughout the year.
DURATION: Two to 12 weeks.
ACCOMMODATIONS: Tents and mosquito nets.
COST: Cost depends on length of trip. A two-week expedition costs $1,800 and includes round-trip airfare, meals, ground transportation, guides, accommodations, and boat trips.
AGE OF PARTICIPANTS: The average age of participants is usually about 40.
PERSONS WITH DISABILITIES: Handled on a case-by-case basis.

▶➡▶➡▶

American Heritage Association
P.O. Box 147
Marylhurst, OR 97036
Phone: (503) 635-3702
Fax: (503) 635-8751

INSTITUTION/ORGANIZATION: Founded in 1957, the American Heritage Association is a nonprofit organization that coordinates study-abroad programs for college, high school, and adult students. The American Heritage Association is a member of the Council on International Educational Exchange.

PROGRAMS: The American Heritage Association offers summer travel and study programs focused on topics including history, culture, area studies, language, art, literature, art history, education, politics, and current issues facing the country visited. The instructors are employed by the site's local university and have had prior teaching experience. Lectures, which are given in English, are combined with discussions and walking excursions.

ELIGIBILITY: None, although language facility may be recommended for some programs.

LOCATION: France, Austria, Czechoslovakia, Hungary, Poland, Italy, the United Kingdom, and China.

TIME OF YEAR: Summer.

DURATION: Programs run from three to five weeks.

ACCOMMODATIONS: Private homes, hotels, and college dormitories.

COST: In 1992 the approximate costs ranged from $1,898 for the United Kingdom to $2,800 for Vienna, Austria, and Eastern Europe. The fee included room, board, tuition, textbooks, some meals, excursions, local transportation if applicable, insurance, and an orientation; airfare was additional.

AGE OF PARTICIPANTS: For most programs, the average age of participants is between 30 and 40.

PERSONS WITH DISABILITIES: The American Heritage Association does not discriminate; individuals are handled on a case-by-case basis.

COMMENTS: Interested travelers can earn academic credit for participation. Contact the American Heritage Association for more information. Participants are usually United States residents.

➤➤➤

American-International Homestays

Route 1, Box 68
Iowa City, IA 52240
Phone: (800) 876-2048
        (319) 626-2125
Fax: (319) 626-2129

INSTITUTION/ORGANIZATION: Founded in 1988, American-International Homestays (AIH) is a commercial tour operator that sponsors homestay travel programs.

PROGRAMS: Homestay programs provide participants with the opportunity to gain firsthand experience of a country and culture by living with local families. A special language program is available to interested travelers to supplement the homestay experience. Private tutors can be provided. The homestay itinerary is set by the individual participant and the host.

ELIGIBILITY: Applications are accepted from all interested persons.

LOCATION: Homestays are available in Russia, Ukraine, Kazakhstan, Kirghizia, Estonia, Latvia, Lithuania, Germany, Poland, Czechoslovakia, Hungary, and Mongolia.

TIME OF YEAR: Options are available throughout the year.

DURATION: Two weeks. Interested persons can arrange longer stays.

ACCOMMODATIONS: Private homes.

COST: Varies. Programs generally range from about $2,100 to $3,000 and include round-trip airfare from New York, accommodations, all meals, English-speaking hosts, internal transportation, and entrance fees.

AGE OF PARTICIPANTS: Participants range in age from 18 to 80.

PERSONS WITH DISABILITIES: AIH places no limitations on participation, although accessibility may be limited by the destination.

COMMENTS: Usually about 95 percent of the participants are from the United States.

▶⇒▶⇒▶

American Jewish Congress

15 East 84th Street
New York, NY 10028
Phone: (800) 221-4694
Fax: (212) 249-3672

INSTITUTION/ORGANIZATION: Founded in 1918, the American Jewish Congress (AJC) is a nonprofit organization of American Jews that support the state of Israel, religious liberty, and civil rights.

PROGRAMS: According to the organization's literature, "The focus of the American Jewish Congress International Travel Program is to learn how Jews live today, or once lived, throughout the globe." Guided by scholars or others with strong background in their fields, tours include lectures and small groups discussions, with visits to places of historic and contemporary Jewish interest. Adventure tours and cruises have also been offered in past years. Some programs are designed for particular groups, including singles, singles under 40, travelers over the age of 50, families, and so on. The maximum number of participants on any one program is 32. AJC runs more than 30 programs annually.

ELIGIBILITY: Membership in the American Jewish Congress is required (open to Jews over the age of 18).

LOCATION: Destinations in past years have included Africa, Asia, Europe, Australia, and the Middle East.

TIME OF YEAR: Options are available throughout the year.

DURATION: Programs run from nine to 22 days.

ACCOMMODATIONS: Hotels and cruise ships.

COST: Varies depending on location, duration, and time of year. In 1992 costs for a two-week program in Israel ranged from $2,808 to $3,623 and included round-trip airfare, hotel accommodations, most meals, excursions, and taxes.

AGE OF PARTICIPANTS: The average age of participants is usually 55 to 60.

PERSONS WITH DISABILITIES: Open to persons with disabilities if accompanied by an able-bodied person.

▶▶⇒▶▶⇒▶▶

American Museum of Natural History

Discovery Tours
Central Park West at 79th Street
New York, NY 10024
Phone: (800) 462-8687
        (212) 769-5700
Fax: (212) 769-5755

INSTITUTION/ORGANIZATION: The American Museum of Natural History is a nonprofit institution. The museum houses the largest natural history collection in the world and has conducted international study trips open to the general public since 1953.

PROGRAMS: "Discovery Cruises and Tours." These educational travel programs combine cruises with tours and take participants to major wildlife and anthropological sites around the world. AMNH prides itself on conducting tours that protect the natural environment and respect the cultures of the regions visited. Focused on natural history, anthropology, and conservation science, programs are led by museum curators and other experts in the appropriate areas. Lectures and small group discussions are combined with site visits. Program offerings in 1992 included "Voyage of the Vikings: Norway, Faroe Islands & West Greenland"; "To the Land of the Eagles: Art and Wildlife from Vancouver to Glacier Bay"; "French Caves and Castles"; "The Great Apes and Great Lakes of East Africa"; "Rediscovering Russia and the Baltics"; "Exploring Ancient Britain"; and "Trans-Siberia: Across the Russian Republic by Luxury Private Train." Land-based programs range in size from 15 to 30 people; cruises range from 62 to 120.

ELIGIBILITY: Applications are accepted from all interested persons.

LOCATION: Destinations vary each year. Previous destinations have included Norway, Iceland, Greenland, Canada, France, Kenya, Tanzania, Zaire, Russia, Lithuania, Latvia, Estonia, Poland, and Britain.

TIME OF YEAR: Summer and winter.

DURATION: Programs generally run two to three weeks.

ACCOMMODATIONS: Hotels and cruise ships.

COST: Varies according to the program. Contact AMNH for specific information.

AGE OF PARTICIPANTS: Most participants are usually 50 and older.

PERSONS WITH DISABILITIES: The museum will accommodate disabled persons whenever possible. Some of the cruise ships, however, are not accessible.

Andante Travels

Grange Cottage
Winterbourne Dauntsey
Salisbury SP4 6ER
UNITED KINGDOM
Phone: (44) 980 610979

INSTITUTION/ORGANIZATION: Founded in 1985, Andante Travels is a commercial tour operator that leads study holidays.

PROGRAMS: Study holidays focused on archaeology and ancient cultures and civilizations are conducted by experts in the appropriate fields, who provide lectures and guided tours. The following tours are available: "Celts and Romans in Southern Germany"; "Romans and the Romanesque in the Rhineland"; "Paleolithic Cave Paintings of the

Dorgogne"; "Viking Denmark"; "Pompeii, Herculaneum and the Lands of the Samnites"; "The Culture of the Etruscans"; "Carthage and Classical Tunisia"; "Ancient Sicily-Sicilia Antiqua."

ELIGIBILITY: Applications accepted from all persons 18 and over with "reasonable physical fitness."

LOCATION: Denmark, France, Germany, Italy, and Tunisia.

TIME OF YEAR: Programs are offered once or twice per year in the spring, summer, or fall months.

DURATION: Programs vary from eight to 10 days.

ACCOMMODATIONS: Participants stay in hotels.

COST: Costs vary greatly, from about $920 for studying the classical sites in Tunisia to about $1,750 for studying archaeology at ancient sites in Sicily. Cost includes airfare from London to sites, as well as bed and breakfast in hotels, picnic lunches, private coach, and insurance. Air transportation to London is additional.

PERSONS WITH DISABILITIES: Because of the rough terrain of the archaeological sites, persons with difficulty in mobility cannot be accommodated.

▶⇒▶⇒▶

Angkor Wat Adventures

653 Pleasant Road
Toronto M4S 2N2
CANADA
Phone: (416) 482-1223
Fax: (416) 486-4001

INSTITUTION/ORGANIZATION: Founded in 1973, Angkor Wat Adventures is a commercial tour operator that sponsors adventure travel programs focused on culture, history, archaeology, and architecture.

PROGRAM: The "Angkor Wat Indochina Adventure" study tour focuses on the development of religion, culture, and architecture in Indochina. Tour leaders hold advanced degrees in Asian history, religion, art, or architecture and provide on-site lectures. Participants visit architectural monuments, shrines, wats (Buddhist temples or monastaries in Cambodia), and museums. Groups are limited to 16 people.

ELIGIBILITY: Applications are accepted from all interested persons.

LOCATION: Laos, Cambodia, and Vietnam.

TIME OF YEAR: The program is offered monthly throughout the year.

DURATION: Program runs for 19 days.

ACCOMMODATIONS: Hotels.

COST: The price is approximately $5,000 and includes round-trip airfare (departing from Seattle, WA), room, most meals, site entrance fees, and excursions. Travel to Seattle is additional.

AGE OF PARTICIPANTS: The average age of participants is usually about 52.

PERSONS WITH DISABILITIES: Contact Angkor Wat Adventures for information.

COMMENTS: About 65 percent of the participants are from the United States.

➤➡➤

Antichita

P.O. Box 156
St. Catharines
Ontario L2R 6S4
CANADA
Phone: (416) 682-8124
Fax: (416) 684-8875

INSTITUTION/ORGANIZATION: Founded in 1985, Antichita is a commercial tour operator that organizes cruises and tours as well as field schools in the eastern Mediterranean focused on archaeology.

PROGRAM: The "Antichita Archaeological Research Team Research Assistant Program" is designed for people with no previous archaeological experience or knowledge. This program takes place at various sites in Cyprus. Lectures are combined with hands-on fieldwork and conducted by an experienced field archaeologist. Expeditions range in size from five to 12 participants.

ELIGIBILITY: Applications accepted from all interested persons. Antichita looks for persons with enthusiasm, dedication, and motivation to work hard.

LOCATION: Various locations in Cyprus.

TIME OF YEAR: Summer.

DURATION: Three weeks.

ACCOMMODATIONS: Participants stay in college dormitories.

COSTS: The program is $1,495, which includes background reading materials, room, board (except weekend lunches and dinners), local transportation during working hours, equipment, and two excursions. Airfare is not included.

AGE OF PARTICIPANTS: The average age is usually about 22.

COMMENTS: Usually about 80 percent of the participants are from the United States.

⇥⇒⇥⇒⇥

APSNICA (Architects and Planners in Support of Nicaragua)

P.O. Box 1151
Topanga, CA 90290
Phone: (213) 455-1340
Fax: (213) 455-3312

INSTITUTION/ORGANIZATION: Founded in 1984, APSNICA is a nonprofit organization that sponsors volunteers and supports economic development projects in Nicaragua.

PROGRAM: The "Technical Assistance and Work Brigades" program places volunteers in Nicaragua to work with local organizations while living with host families. Placements are available in all fields, including engineering, architecture, carpentry, plumbing, education, information technology, and so on.

ELIGIBILITY: Applications are accepted from all interested persons.

LOCATION: Nicaragua.

TIME OF YEAR: Options are available throughout the year.

DURATION: Flexible.

ACCOMMODATIONS: Private homes.

COST: The program fee is $300. Participants are responsible for all expenses including airfare, accommodations, and meals.

AGE OF PARTICIPANTS: The average age of participants is usually about 25.

PERSONS WITH DISABILITIES: Open to those with disabilities, bearing in mind the physical hardship of life in Nicaragua.

▶▶⇒▶▶⇒▶▶

Archaeological Tours

30 East 42nd Street, Suite 1202
New York, NY 10017
Phone: (212) 986-3054
Fax: (212) 370-1561

INSTITUTION/ORGANIZATION: Founded in 1970, Archaeological
Tours is a commercial tour operator that runs study tours worldwide.

PROGRAMS: Study tours focused on archaeology, art, and history are
led by distinguished scholars. All instructors are either university pro-
fessors, museum curators, or archaeologists. Lectures are combined
with small group discussions. The maximum group size ranges from
24 to 30.
ELIGIBILITY: Applications are accepted from all interested persons.
LOCATION: Destinations vary each year. Previous destinations have
included China, India, Indonesia, Thailand, Japan, Greece, Tunisia,
Malta, Brittany, Turkey, Egypt, Israel, Yemen, Guatemala, Spain,
France, and Italy.
TIME OF YEAR: Options are available throughout the year.
DURATION: Programs vary from two to four weeks.
ACCOMMODATIONS: Hotels.
COST: Program costs range from approximately $2,500 to $4,000 and
include most meals, lecturer, accommodations, ground transportation,
and tips. Airfare is additional.
AGE OF PARTICIPANTS: The average age of participants is usually
between 50 and 60.
PERSONS WITH DISABILITIES: Individuals are handled on a case-by-
case basis.

▶▶⇒▶▶⇒▶▶

The Art Institute of Chicago

Michigan at Adams Street
Chicago, IL 60603
Phone: (312) 443-3917
Fax: (312) 443-0849

INSTITUTION/ORGANIZATION: Founded in 1879, The Art Institute
of Chicago is a nonprofit, world-class art museum.

PROGRAMS: The Art Institute sponsors a variety of programs focused on the study of art, architecture, and archaeology. Both land- and ship-based programs have been offered. The instructors are generally curators, staff lecturers, and other art historians; slide presentations are combined with on-site lectures.

ELIGIBILITY: Art Institute membership is encouraged but not required.

LOCATION: Program destinations have included Venezuela, Portugal, Turkey, Indonesia, Alaska, and the Far East.

TIME OF YEAR: Options are available throughout the year.

DURATION: Programs usually run for two weeks.

ACCOMMODATIONS: Hotels and cruise ships.

COST: Trips generally range from $3,500 to $6,000 and include airfare, hotel, sight-seeing and admission fees, along with some meals.

AGE OF PARTICIPANTS: The average age of participants is usually between 50 and 60 years old.

PERSONS WITH DISABILITIES: Persons with disabilities will be accommodated whenever possible.

COMMENTS: The maximum number of participants on the land-based programs is 20 to 30; for the ship-based programs, 80.

▶⇒▶⇒▶

The Athens Centre

48 Archimidous Street
Athens 116 36
GREECE
Phone: (30) 1 701 2268
Fax: (30) 1 701 8603

INSTITUTION/ORGANIZATION: Founded in 1969, The Athens Centre is a nonprofit educational organization that sponsors academic and cultural activities in Greece.

PROGRAM: The "Modern Greek Language Program" offers Greek language courses on all levels, taught by instructors with university degrees in literature and/or teaching Greek as a foreign language. Lectures are combined with small group discussions, and classes have no more than 15 students.

ELIGIBILITY: Applications are accepted from all interested persons.

LOCATION: Athens, Greece.

TIME OF YEAR: Options are available throughout the year.

DURATION: Courses run for three, four, seven and 10-week terms.

ACCOMMODATIONS: Participants live in hotels, hostels, private homes, or studio apartments, when available.

COST: As of September 1991, the cost was $260 (50,000 drachmas), which covered tuition and registration fees only, plus about $5 (1,000 drachmas) for a one-year membership in the Athens Centre.

AGE OF PARTICIPANTS: The average age of participants is usually about 30.

PERSONS WITH DISABILITIES: The Athens Centre does not discriminate against persons with disabilities unless the disability renders them unable to attend classes.

COMMENTS: Usually about 20 percent of the participants are from the United States.

➤➤➤

Backroads Bicycle Touring

1516 5th Street
Berkeley, CA 94710
Phone: (510) 527-1555
Fax: (510) 527-1444

INSTITUTION/ORGANIZATION: Established in 1979, Backroads Bicycle Touring is a commercial tour operator offering bicycle and walking tours worldwide.

PROGRAMS: The "Backroads Bicycle and Walking Tours" are available for beginner, intermediate, and advanced riders and walkers in Europe, Canada, Asia, the Pacific, and the Caribbean. Special-interest trips for singles, students, and seniors are also available, along with camping trips. Other special-interest tours focus on art, photography, health, and fitness. Groups are limited to 26 people.

ELIGIBILITY: Applications are accepted from all interested persons.

LOCATION: Destinations have included Ireland, France, England, Italy, Mexico, New Zealand, Australia, Bali, Thailand, and China.

TIME OF YEAR: Options available throughout the year.

DURATION: Trips range from two to 16 days.

ACCOMMODATIONS: Châteaux, villas, homestays, tents, lodges, and hotels.

COST: Varies depending on the destination. Generally, trips range from about $695 for a camping trip in Mexico to $2,950 for a bicycle tour in China. Prices include room and most meals. Airfare is additional.
AGE OF PARTICIPANTS: Participants generally range in age from 28 to 50.
PERSONS WITH DISABILITIES: Backroads will work with disabled persons and try to accommodate them as much as possible. Individuals are handled on a case-by-case basis.

▶▶⇒▶▶⇒▶▶

Big Five Tours and Expeditions, Ltd.

110 Route 110
South Huntington, NY 11746
Phone: (800) 445-7002
　　　　(516) 424-2036
Fax: (516) 424-2154

INSTITUTION/ORGANIZATION: This 19-year-old self-described "soft adventure/ecotourism company" offers tours throughout Africa, Asia, Australia, New Zealand, and North and South America. Big Five Tours and Expeditions is a commercial tour operator with headquarters in Nairobi, Kenya.

PROGRAMS: Big Five's tours emphasize conservation and ecology. Examples include nature and photography tours of the Amazon and African wildlife safaris. Professional naturalists accompany each tour. Groups are usually limited to 11 participants.
ELIGIBILITY: Participants should be ecology-minded, physically fit, and tolerant of cultural differences.
LOCATION: Destinations outside the United States include Kenya, Tanzania, Botswana, Zimbabwe, South Africa, Indonesia, India, Nepal, New Guinea, Australia, New Zealand, Costa Rica, Ecuador, Peru, Brazil, Canada, and the United Kingdom.
TIME OF YEAR: Seasons vary according to destinations.
DURATION: Programs last from eight to 28 days.
ACCOMMODATIONS: Accommodations vary from hotels to camping in tents.
COST: Prices vary according to the destination, but most tours cost between $1,300 for a 10-day tour in Costa Rica to $5,000 for a 17-day safari in Tanzania.

AGE OF PARTICIPANTS: The average age of participants is usually 45 and over.

PERSONS WITH DISABILITIES: Participation by persons with disabilities depends on the destination. Travelers are handled on a case-by-case basis.

Bike Across Italy

1925 Wallenberg Drive
Fort Collins, CO 80526
Phone: (303) 484-8489

INSTITUTION/ORGANIZATION: Founded in 1985, Bike Across Italy is a family-run commercial tour operator specializing in bicycle tours for adults.

PROGRAMS: Bike Across Italy sponsors a number of different tours, including "Classic Bike Across Italy," which takes participants cycling from Venice to Pisa; the "Culinary Cycling Circus," which combines cycling with cooking lessons and demonstrations in the heart of Italy's famous pasta region, Emilia Romagna; and "Sardinia," which takes serious cyclists biking on the island from Alghero to Cagliari. These cultural tours are led by Paola and Rick Price, the founders and owners of the company. Both Paola, a professor of Italian, and Rick, a geographer, hold Ph.D.s and are fluent in English and Italian.

ELIGIBILITY: Interested persons should be in reasonable physical condition and able to use a ten-speed bike.

LOCATION: Italy.

TIME OF YEAR: Summer.

DURATION: Tours run for two weeks.

ACCOMMODATIONS: Hotels.

COST: In 1991 the cost ranged from $1,495 to $1,595 and included room, 12 meals, wine, bicycle, and sag wagon (van that accompanies the group and carries luggage, spare bicycle parts, weary bikers, etc).

AGE OF PARTICIPANTS: Most participants range in age from 35 to 45.

PERSONS WITH DISABILITIES: As long as the participant is able to ride a bike, he or she will be accepted.

COMMENTS: If you call, ask for Richard or Paola Price; both are employees of Colorado State University. They will be happy to give you the names of past participants so you can contact them yourself.

➤⇒➤⇒➤

Borrobol Birding

Borrobol,
Kinbrace,
Sutherland,
Scotland KW11 6UB
United Kingdom
Phone: (44) 43 13 264

INSTITUTION/ORGANIZATION: Founded in 1986, Borrobol Birding is a commercial tour operator that organizes bird-watching trips in Scotland.

PROGRAM: In the heartland of the roaming red deer population of the Northern Highlands, participants in the Borrobol Birding program spend one week bird-watching. In spring, over 100 bird species may be counted here. Other sights include castles, archaeological and historical sites, and the world-famous Dornoch golf course. Guides have experience with accredited U.K. nature organizations. Each excursion is limited to six participants. Guests dine on local fish and game prepared by a professional chef.

ELIGIBILITY: Applications accepted from all interested persons.

LOCATION: Kinbrace, Scotland.

TIME OF YEAR: May through July.

DURATION: One week.

ACCOMMODATIONS: Participants are based at Borrobol Lodge, a wood-paneled Edwardian sporting lodge. The lodge has six bedrooms, two drawing rooms, and a large dining room.

COST: Approximately $1,640, including all tickets, full board, wine and spirits, and travel from Kinbrace rail station. Airfare and travel to Kinbrace are additional.

AGE OF PARTICIPANTS: The average age of participants is usually about 45.

▸⇒▸⇒▸

Brazilian Views, Inc.

201 East 66 Street, Suite 21G
New York, NY 10021-6480
Phone: (212) 472-9539

INSTITUTION/ORGANIZATION: Brazilian Views, a commercial tour operator specializing in Brazil, has offered guided nature tours to Mountain Cloud Forest, part of Brazil's Mata Alantica rain forest nature preserve, for more than 10 years.

PROGRAMS: The owners of Mountain Cloud Forest, Dr. Richard Warren and David Miller, conduct field-study projects for high school and university students. Professional scientists and amateur enthusiasts are also welcome. The owners are local ornithologists, biologists, botanists, and zoologists. All field studies provide the opportunity to pursue individual or group research.
ELIGIBILITY: Applications are accepted from all interested persons.
LOCATION: State of Rio de Janeiro, Brazil.
TIME OF YEAR: February through May and August through December.
DURATION: 10 or 20 days.
ACCOMMODATIONS: Participants share a bunkhouse.
COST:$1,000 for 10 days, $1,200 for 20; includes lodging, meals, land transportation, and access to on-site scientists. Airfare is additional.
AGE OF PARTICIPANTS: Participants range in age from the late 20s through the 70s.
PERSONS WITH DISABILITIES: Persons are welcome as long as they can travel. Individuals are considered on a case-by-case basis.

▸⇒▸⇒▸

Brigham Young University Travel Study

310 Harman Building
Provo, UT 84602
Phone: (801) 378-3946
Fax: (801) 378-3949

INSTITUTION/ORGANIZATION: Brigham Young University (BYU) is an accredited university affiliated with the Church of Jesus Christ of

Latter-Day Saints. BYU is a member of the Council on International Educational Exchange.

PROGRAM: The "Holy Land Adult Study Program," which focuses on the study of the Old and New Testaments, is led by full-time or emeritus professors from Brigham Young University. Groups are limited to 35 participants. The program has been running for nine years.
ELIGIBILITY: Applications are accepted from all interested persons.
LOCATION: Israel and Egypt.
TIME OF YEAR: Spring and summer.
DURATION: Programs run from three to seven weeks.
ACCOMMODATIONS: Hotels and college dormitories.
COST: The price ranges from $2,500 to $5,000, depending on the program length, and includes airfare, room, most meals, and all other expenses.
AGE OF PARTICIPANTS: The average age of participants is usually about 45.
PERSONS WITH DISABILITIES: Persons with disabilities are considered on a case-by-case basis.
COMMENTS: Interested travelers can earn academic credit for participation. Contact BYU for more information.

▶⇒▶⇒▶

University of California Berkeley Extension
Travel/Study Office
UC Extension
55 Laguna Street
San Francisco, CA 94102
Phone: (415) 861-7720
Fax: (415) 552-4237

INSTITUTION/ORGANIZATION: UC Berkeley Extension is the continuing education division of the University of California at Berkeley. The Travel/Study Office has been running programs for more than 25 years. UC Berkeley is a member of the Council on International Educational Exchange.

PROGRAMS: The following are available in 1993:
  • "Oxford/Berkeley Program." Jointly sponsored by UC Berkeley Extension and the Department for Continuing Education

at the University of Oxford, this summer study program focuses on art, history, literature, and the social sciences. Participants choose from 24 seminars taught by Oxford dons. In concurrence with the Oxford tradition, the tutorial method of teaching is applied. This program has been in operation for over 20 years and is designed for the adult traveler. Participants live in college dormitories. In 1992 the cost was $2,800 for a three-week session and $5,200 for a double (six-week) session, including room, board, tuition, and general lectures. Airfare and field trips were not included. The average age of participants is usually between 40 and 60. This program has been running for more than 23 years. Courses are limited to 12 students.

- "Ireland: Myth and Literature." Offered for three weeks during the summer, this program focuses on Irish literature, mythology, and history. Participants spend two weeks at Trinity College, Dublin, and one week traveling through Ireland. Excursions to Sligo, Galway, the Aran Isles, and Dublin's Bloomsday festivities are included. Classroom and on-site lectures are provided by university faculty. Participants stay in hotels and college dormitories. This program costs approximately $3,100 and includes tuition, single room at Trinity College, shared rooms in hotels during week of travel, breakfast, some dinners, admission, field trips, and transportation within Ireland. Airfare is not included. The average age of participants is usually between 30 and 60. The program is limited to 28 participants.
- "Inside the London Theater Scene." Focused on the dramatic arts, this program takes participants to London for three weeks during the summer. Seminars are conducted by English drama critics and feature talks by leading actors, directors, and playwrights. Attendance at 12 theater performances is included. Participants stay in college dormitories. The approximate cost is $2,900 and includes tuition, theater tickets, single room, and breakfast daily. Airfare is not included. The average age of participants is usually between 30 and 60. Group size is limited to 42 participants. The program has been running for six years.
- "The Paris Program." Sponsored in cooperation with the Council on International Educational Exchange, this summer program runs for three weeks. Participants take classes in one of the following liberal arts subjects: French literature, art, history, architecture, or language. Taught by French university faculty members, on-site and classroom lectures are provided. Classes are limited to 20 students each. Participants live in

college dormitories. The program is approximately $2,800 and includes tuition, single room, most meals, field trips, and transportation within Paris. Airfare is not included. The average age of participants is usually between 30 and 60. This program has been running for six years.

- "Rome: The Eternal City." This three-week summer study program is focused on history, art history, and architecture. Participants travel to various cities throughout Italy to study the many layers of Italian civilization from the time of the Etruscans to the modern period. Courses are taught by university faculty, and lectures are provided on-site and in the classroom. Group size is limited to 28 people. Participants stay in hotels. The program cost is approximately $3,400 and includes tuition, shared room in hotels, some meals, admissions, field trips, and transportation within Italy. The average age of participants is usually between 30 and 60.

ELIGIBILITY: Participants must be at least 20 years old.

LOCATION: England, Ireland, France, and Italy.

TIME OF YEAR: Summer.

DURATION: All programs run for three weeks. Participants in the Oxford program have the option to study for six weeks.

▶▶⇒▶▶⇒▶▶

University of California Los Angeles Extension
10995 Le Conte Avenue
Los Angeles, CA 90024
Phone: (310) 825-1901
Fax: (310) 206-5123

INSTITUTION/ORGANIZATION: Founded in 1917, UCLA Extension, a division of the University of California, provides continuing education opportunities to more than 100,000 adult students each year who enroll in some 4,500 courses, conferences, and special programs. UCLA is a member of the Council on International Educational Exchange.

PROGRAMS: UCLA Extension offers a range of travel study programs led by experts in the appropriate disciplines who have had experience in the program region. Offerings in 1992 included "Tropical Ecology: The Amazon"; "Greece and the Greek Islands," with a focus on studio and art history; "Easter Island: Adventure in Archaeology"; "Under China Skies: Astronomy, Myth, & Society in Ancient China, Mongolia, and Tibet"; "Art, Architecture, and Interior Design Study Tour to the Heart of France"; and "The Ancient World of Greece and Italy," with a focus on archaeology.

ELIGIBILITY: Applications are accepted from all interested persons.

LOCATION: Destinations vary each year. Previous destinations have included Peru, Tahiti, Easter Island, China, Mongolia, Tibet, France, and Greece.

TIME OF YEAR: Varies. Previous programs have been offered in the summer and fall.

DURATION: Programs vary from two to three weeks.

ACCOMMODATIONS: Varies with the program.

COST: Varies with the program; contact UCLA Extension for specific program itineraries.

AGE OF PARTICIPANTS: Participants generally range in age from about 35 to 60.

PERSONS WITH DISABILITIES: Individuals are handled on a case-by-case basis.

▶⇒▶⇒▶

California State University—Fresno

Division of Extended Education
2450 East San Ramon
Fresno, CA 93740
Phone: (209) 278-2524
Fax: (209) 278-7090

INSTITUTION/ORGANIZATION: Founded in 1911, California State University—Fresno (CSUF) is a nonprofit state institution that is a member of the Council on International Educational Exchange.

PROGRAMS: The following programs will be offered in 1993:
- "History of England: University of York." This study program focuses on English history and takes participants to explore ancient city walls, country homes, monumental ruins, and museums. Led by CSUF faculty, lectures are combined with small group discussions. The program runs for three weeks during the summer and costs approximately $2,700. This fee includes round-trip airfare, accommodations in college dormitories,

meals, guest speakers, tours, and admission tickets. The average age of participants is usually about 40. Groups are limited to 30 people. Open to all interested persons.

- "Summer Study in Guanajuato, Mexico." This Spanish-language program runs for four weeks during the summer and emphasizes speaking, reading, and cultural interaction. Taught by CSUF faculty, lectures are combined with small group discussions. Participants stay in private homes. The program fee is $1,200 and includes accommodations, meals, lectures, tuition, and field trips. Airfare is additional. The average age of participants is usually about 24. Open to all interested persons.

- "London Theater Program." This two-week program takes place during the summer and the winter. Participants attend theater performances and are given a broad introduction to the cultural aspects of London. Led by CSUF faculty, lectures are combined with field trips. The fee is $2,000 and includes round-trip airfare, theater tickets, hotel accommodations, guest speakers, and tuition. The average age of participants is usually about 45. The maximum group size is 50. Open to all interested persons.

- "Cultural and Performing Arts in London and Paris." This two-week program runs during the winter and takes participants to a wide variety of cultural programs selected from concerts, ballet, museums, and theater. The first week is spent in London and the second week in Paris. Led by CSUF faculty, lectures and small group discussions are provided. The program fee is $2,000 and includes round-trip airfare (San Francisco–London/ Paris–San Francisco), coach between airport and hotel, hotel accommodations, tickets to museums and performances, guest speakers, and tuition. Meals are additional. The average age of participants is usually about 45. The maximum group size is 30. Open to all interested persons.

ELIGIBILITY: Applications are accepted from all interested persons.

LOCATION: England, Mexico, and France.

TIME OF YEAR: Summer and winter.

DURATION: Programs vary from two to four weeks.

▶➡▶➡▶

California State University–Sacramento

Regional & Continuing Education
650 University Avenue
Suite 101A
Sacramento, CA 95825
Phone: (916) 923-0441
Fax: (916) 927-4836

INSTITUTION/ORGANIZATION: CSU–Sacramento is a member of the
Council on International Educational Exchange. Founded in 1960, the
Regional and Continuing Education division of CSU–Sacramento offers workshops, courses, and programs for personal and professional
development.

PROGRAMS: CSU offers a combination of study, field research, studio
art, and independent travel programs. All instructors are approved by
CSU–Sacramento. The Regional and Continuing Education Department runs the following programs:
- "Spanish Language and Culture." This program focuses on the
  study of language and culture in Spain, Mexico, and Peru for
  six weeks during the summer. Participants live in hotels and
  private homes. Open to those who have at least one year of
  college-level Spanish. The cost is approximately $3,500, which
  includes all expenses except some meals and personal items.
  The program is limited to 30 participants.
- "Archaeological Field School at Tel Dor, Israel." This study
  program, which has been running for more than 12 years,
  enables participants to study at the largest excavation site in
  Israel. Fieldwork (excavation) is combined with lectures, excursions, and lab work. Offered for six weeks during the summer, the program focuses on anthropology as well as
  archaeology. Participants live in hotels and dormitories. The
  cost is approximately $3,700. The program is limited to 30 to
  40 participants.
- "The Land and People of Northeast Thailand." This study program, offered for four weeks during the summer, looks at the
  physical and cultural geography of Thailand, including rural
  development, markets, environmental change, history, wom-
  en's issues, and the economy. Lectures are combined with small
  group discussions and field study. The cost is approximately

$2,500, which includes all expenses except some meals and personal items. The program is limited to 20 participants.

- "Study in Paris, Florence or Heidelberg." Study French language and civilization in Paris; study music and art in Florence; or study German language and civilization in Heidelberg. Each program is offered during the summer for four weeks. (The Paris program can be extended to six weeks.) Lectures are combined with field study, small group discussions, and cultural tours. Participants live in hotels, private homes, or college dormitories. The cost is approximately $3,300, which includes all expenses except some meals and personal items. Programs are limited to 40 participants each.

- "African Adventure." This program, offered for two weeks during the summer, takes participants to Kenya and Tanzania to study wildlife centers, African culture, and the influences of Islam and Christianity, as well as foods, customs, and art. Lectures and small group discussions are combined with field study. Excursions are taken to villages, wildlife parks, cities, and farms. Participants live in hotels. The cost is approximately $4,000, which includes all expenses except some meals and personal items. Programs are limited to 25 participants.

- "Art Workshops in Puerto Vallarta, Mexico." This art studio program concentrates on watercolor painting or architectural design. Participants are given daily instruction and practice in watercolor medium or architectural design of southwest home planning. This program runs four times a year for three to six days during the Thanksgiving, Christmas, and Easter holidays, as well as the summer. The cost is approximately $1,000, which includes all expenses except meals and personal items. Programs are limited to 15 participants.

- "Independent Travel Study." Students, professionals, or interested others may earn academic credit for planned travel experiences undertaken individually or with a group (applies worldwide). The instructor of record is a university faculty member; generally, credit awarded is interdisciplinary.

ELIGIBILITY: For the "Spanish Language and Culture" program, participants should have at least one year of college-level Spanish; the other programs accept applications from all interested persons.

LOCATIONS: Destinations vary each year; see program descriptions for 1992–1993 destinations.

DURATION: Programs vary from three days to six weeks.

TIME OF YEAR: Time of year varies; see program descriptions above.

PERSONS WITH DISABILITIES: California State University abides by the state requirements for disabled persons; some individuals must bring an attendant or assistant.

COMMENTS: These programs are all subject to change, so be sure to call or write to the Regional & Continuing Education division for current offerings.

➤➡➡

Canadian Light Brigade

137 Beaconsfield Avenue
Toronto, Ontario M6J 3J5
CANADA
Phone: (416) 535-4810

INSTITUTION/ORGANIZATION: Founded in 1988, the Canadian Light Brigade is a "Nicaraguan Solidarity Group" founded in 1988 to support the Sandinista Revolution. This nonprofit organization sponsors work/study tours in Nicaragua.

PROGRAM: "Work/Study Tour of Nicaragua." Focused on development and assistance training, this program takes participants on tour in Nicaragua, where they participate in a voluntary service program reconstructing public buildings. Led by a tour guide with extensive experience in development assistance, participants meet with representatives from various Nicaraguan social and political organizations.

ELIGIBILITY: Physical fitness is necessary. In addition, proximity to Toronto is highly desirable, as extensive preplanning includes attending courses on the history and politics of Nicaragua, as well as fundraising activities. Tours are limited to 16 participants.

LOCATION: Nicaragua (various cities including Managua, Mateare, and Xiloa).

TIME OF YEAR: Summer.

DURATION: Four weeks: two weeks on tour and two weeks of service work.

ACCOMMODATIONS: Hotels and homestays.

COST: $1,500 (Canadian dollars), which includes travel from Toronto, meals, hotels, homestay, tour guide, bus transportation, and spending money.

AGE OF PARTICIPANTS: The average age of participants is usually about 25.

PERSONS WITH DISABILITIES: Participation by travelers with disabilities is discouraged due to the lack of accessible facilities in Nicaragua.
COMMENTS: Most participants are Canadians.

▸⇒▸⇒▸

Caribbean Conservation Corporation

P.O. Box 2866
Gainesville, FL 32602-2866
Phone: (904) 373-6441
Fax: (904) 375-2449

INSTITUTION/ORGANIZATION: Founded in 1959, the Caribbean Conservation Corporation is a nonprofit environmental organization dedicated to the protection of endangered sea turtles and their habitats through research, conservation, and education.

PROGRAM: "The Turtles of Tortuguero." This program is focused on sea turtle ecology and biology; participants tag endangered green sea turtles on the remote black sand beaches of Tortuguero, Costa Rica. Leaders have training (usually graduate level) in a related field. Group size usually ranges from eight to 10 people.
ELIGIBILITY: Applications are accepted from all interested persons.
LOCATION: Tortuguero, Costa Rica.
TIME OF YEAR: Between July 3 and August 30.
DURATION: Ten- or 17-day programs are available.
ACCOMMODATIONS: Participants stay in dormitories at a rustic, rural research station.
COST: From $1,675 to $1,900, depending on the length of the program. This includes round-trip airfare from Miami to San José, transport to Tortuguero, room and board at the research station, and hotel and meals in San José (upon arrival and departure).
AGE OF PARTICIPANTS: Participants range in age from 14 to 70.
PERSONS WITH DISABILITIES: Persons with disabilities are not excluded, but participants are expected to walk an average of four hours per night on beaches, guided by natural light only.

#⇒#⇒#

Casa Xelaju de Español

1022 St. Paul Avenue
St. Paul, MN 55116
Phone: (612) 690-9471
Fax: (612) 690-9471

INSTITUTION/ORGANIZATION: Founded in 1987, the Casa Xelaju de Español is a language school in Guatemala offering courses in Spanish as a second language.

PROGRAM: This Spanish language program provides participants with one-on-one instruction for five hours per day. Daily cultural and social activities are also an integral part of the program. Instructors are university-trained native Guatemalans. Students can begin their studies on any Monday.

ELIGIBILITY: Applications are accepted from all interested persons.

LOCATION: Quezaltenango, Guatemala.

TIME OF YEAR: Options are available throughout the year.

DURATION: Participants can study as long as they wish, though 10 weeks is recommended.

ACCOMMODATIONS: Private homes.

COST: The program costs approximately $600 per month, which includes private bedroom, board, laundry service, private teacher, and daily cultural activities. Airfare is additional.

COMMENTS: For summer and January classes, Casa Xelaju de Español recommends making reservations at least two weeks ahead of time.

C/E/I—Club des 4 Vents

1, rue Gozlin
75006 Paris
FRANCE
Phone: (33) 143-29-60-20
Fax: (33) 143-29-06-21

INSTITUTION/ORGANIZATION: C/E/I—Club des 4 Vents has more than 40 years of experience offering a variety of programs for people of all ages interested in learning French.

PROGRAM: C/E/I—Club des 4 Vents offers French language classes, which vary from 25 to 40 hours per week, depending on intensity. Classes usually have from 12 to 15 students, consist of conversation and lectures, and use modern methods of teaching, including videos and audiocassettes. For those who would like to take part in the life of a French family, homestay and language programs are available. Participants live with host families, who make the effort to show their guests around the region.

ELIGIBILITY: Applications are accepted from all interested persons; however, for homestays, participants should have studied French for at least one year.

LOCATIONS: C/E/I—Club des 4 Vents offers language classes throughout France. Some of their locations are Paris, Dourdan, Aix-en-Provence, Arcachon, Dinan, La Ciotat, Montpellier, St. Cyr/Mer Les Lecques, and Sète.

TIME OF YEAR: Options are available throughout the year.

DURATION: Classes run from one week to one month.

ACCOMMODATIONS: Participants stay with French families or in one of the organization's international residence centers.

COST: Costs vary from $340 and up per person (including tuition, full room, and board) for the week to about $1,610 per person for a month-long stay (room only). Airfare and surface travel to and from the site are not included.

▶▶⇒▶▶⇒▶▶

Center for Cuban Studies

124 West 23rd Street
New York, NY 10011
Phone: (212) 242-0559

INSTITUTION/ORGANIZATION: The Center for Cuban Studies is a nonprofit organization that promotes professional educational and cultural exchanges with Cuba.

PROGRAMS: The Center for Cuban Studies, which focuses on providing Americans with the opportunity to communicate with Cubans, sets up research tours in a variety of fields based on requests from professional groups interested in traveling to Cuba. In 1992 tours included medical professionals who traveled to hospitals and other facilities to meet with Cuban health professionals, and musicians who

met with their Cuban counterparts and attended concerts and other musical performances. Tours are open to all interested professionals.
ELIGIBILITY: Participants must be professionals.
LOCATION: Havana, Santiago de Cuba, Matanzas.
TIME OF YEAR: Options are available throughout the year.
DURATION: Generally one to two weeks.
ACCOMMODATIONS: Hotels.
COST: Approximately $1,000, which includes airfare, ground transportation, room and board, and most incidentals.
PERSONS WITH DISABILITIES: Tours are open to disabled individuals.

The Center for Global Education
Augsburg College
731 21st Avenue South
Minneapolis, MN 55454
Phone: (612) 330-1159
Fax: (612) 330-1695

INSTITUTION/ORGANIZATION: Founded in 1982, The Center for Global Education is a nonprofit institution affiliated with Augsburg College. The Center is committed to education that helps citizens expand their world views and deepen their understanding of international issues.

PROGRAMS: The Center coordinates "Travel Seminars" to destinations worldwide. These seminars examine the problems of international development and the dynamics of social change. Participants meet with a wide range of representatives in government, business, church, and grass-roots communities. These meetings are followed by discussions. Seminars are limited to 18 participants.
ELIGIBILITY: Applications are accepted from all interested persons, including church and civic groups.
LOCATION: Destinations include Guatemala, El Salvador, Nicaragua, Honduras, Mexico, South Africa, and Namibia, as well as locations in the Middle East, the Philippines, the Caribbean, and South America.
TIME OF YEAR: Options available throughout the year.
DURATION: Programs range from 10 to 21 days.
ACCOMMODATIONS: Hotels and retreat centers.

COST: Ranges from $1,800 to $3,000, depending on the program. Program fee covers airfare, room and board, land transportation, and airport taxes.

AGE OF PARTICIPANTS: The average age of participants is usually about 35.

PERSONS WITH DISABILITIES: Persons with disabilities have successfully participated in the program.

COMMENTS: Limited scholarships are available; awards are based on need.

➤➤➤

Central American Institute for International Affairs (ICAI)

PO Box 10302-1000
San Jose
COSTA RICA
Phone: (506) 33 85 71
Fax: (506) 21 5238

INSTITUTION/ORGANIZATION: Founded in 1984, the Central American Institute for International Affairs is an institution dedicated to teaching conversational Spanish, as well as offering other educational programs.

PROGRAMS: ICAI sponsors a variety of educational programs, including:

- "Learn Spanish in Costa Rica." Participants receive four hours of Spanish instruction daily and are taught by instructors with university degrees in linguistics. The Institute sponsors a number of different program options that combine language learning with daily cultural and sight-seeing activities. The price depends on the program and duration. For example, the 1992 cost of a two-week Spanish language program was $560, which includes transfer from the airport to the host family, room, two meals per day, laundry service, school materials, Spanish instruction (Monday through Friday), tours and excursions to historic sites, two conferences, and cultural workshops. Programs are available throughout the year.
- "Photographing the Natural Treasures of Costa Rica." Offered five times a year, this eight-day photo adventure tour takes the

amateur or professional photographer inside the rain forest to La Selva Biological Reserve and the small fishing village of Puerto Viejo. The tour is led by one of Costa Rica's most well-known nature photographers, Mayra Bonilla. In 1992 the program cost approximately $890, and included lodging and meals.

- "Central American Issues and Perspectives." This two-week program provides participants with the opportunity to study the major national and international events that affect Central America. The complex social, political, cultural, and economic factors that influence the development of the region are discussed. The program includes meetings with high-level government officials and representatives of political and religious groups in both Nicaragua and Costa Rica. In 1992 the program cost approximately $1,200.
- "Education and Society in Costa Rica." This three-week program provides an analytical look at contemporary Costa Rican society, with emphasis on education and schooling. Focused on the educational process from preschool through university, the program covers current technical and vocational trends and teacher preparation. Conferences, lectures, and field trips are conducted with educators from Costa Rica. In 1992 the program cost was approximately $950, and included lodging, meals, and classes.
- "Spanish and International Business." This three-week program is designed to examine international business practices in Costa Rica by visiting major industrial sites and government agencies, including the Ministry of Commerce, Ministry of Exports, Dole Enterprises, major newspapers, and the National Institute for Coffee Growers. Spanish vocabulary building takes place through student participation in real business situations of the Spanish-speaking world. Lectures and conferences on economic issues are conducted. In 1992 the approximate cost was $1,100, and included lodging, meals, and classes.

ELIGIBILITY: Applications are accepted from all interested persons.

LOCATION: Costa Rica.

TIME OF YEAR: Time of year varies. "Learn Spanish in Costa Rica" is available throughout the year. For the other programs, contact the Central American Institute for International Affairs.

DURATION: Programs vary from two to four weeks.

PERSONS WITH DISABILITIES: Persons with disabilities should inform the school of their special needs prior to arriving in Costa Rica. Private attendants can be provided.

▸⇒▸⇒▸

Centre International D'Etudes

Françaises De Touraine
Château du Bois Minhy
41700 Chemery
FRANCE
Phone: (33) 5479 5101
Fax: (33) 5479 0626

INSTITUTION/ORGANIZATION: Founded in 1980, the Centre International D'Etudes Françaises De Touraine is a private French language school located in the Loire Valley. The Centre occupies the Château du Bois Minhy, a Renaissance-style castle built in the late nineteenth-century and situated in a seven-acre private park.

PROGRAMS: Intensive French language courses are offered on the beginner and intermediate levels. Instruction is given in French only, and conducted by experienced instructors. Classes have a maximum of 15 students each. Excursions to surrounding castles are included.

ELIGIBILITY: There are no prerequisites for beginners; some knowledge of French is required for those interested in the intermediate courses.

LOCATION: Blois, France (in the village of Chemery-Contres).

TIME OF YEAR: Courses are offered throughout the year except in December and January.

DURATION: Participants have the option to enroll for four, eight, 12 or 16 weeks.

ACCOMMODATIONS: Students live in the Château du Bois Minhy.

COST: The cost varies, depending on the course taken. The approximate charge for a four-week course is $1,440, which includes room, board, and 25 hours of lessons per week. Airfare is additional.

AGE OF PARTICIPANTS: The average age of participants is usually between 25 and 30.

PERSONS WITH DISABILITIES: The school is open to enrolling students with disabilities; however, the château is not accessible.

COMMENTS: About 10 percent of the participants are usually from the United States.

Centro de Idiomas, S.A.

Belisario Dominguez 1908
Mazatlán, Sinaloa
MEXICO
Phone: (52) 69 82-20-53
Fax: (52) 69 85-56-06

INSTITUTION/ORGANIZATION: Founded in 1973, Centro de Idiomas, S.A., is a language center that offers Spanish and English conversation courses for adults.

PROGRAMS: The center offers small group and individual instruction in conversational Spanish. Field trips supplement class work. Teachers hold university degrees.
ELIGIBILITY: Interested persons must be at least 16 years old.
LOCATION: Mazatlán, Mexico.
TIME OF YEAR: Options are available throughout the year.
DURATION: Participants have the option to enroll for one to 12 weeks.
ACCOMMODATIONS: Hotels and private homes.
COST: Depends on the length of stay and type of accommodations; contact the Centro for a breakdown of options. In 1992 a one-week course including homestay was priced at about $450.
AGE OF PARTICIPANTS: The average age of participants is usually about 40.
PERSONS WITH DISABILITIES: Private classes are provided for those with speech and hearing disabilities.
COMMENTS: Usually about 80 percent of the participants are from the United States.

Centro di Cultura Italiana

via Pier de' Crescenzi, 14/2
I-40131 Bologna
ITALY
Phone: (39) 51 523486
Fax: (39) 51 5222095

INSTITUTION/ORGANIZATION: Founded in 1986, the Centro di Cultura Italiana is a small, nonprofit language institute with centers in Bologna and Manciano. Specializing in research in the fields of Italian language, teaching, communication, and cultural exchanges, the Centro works in cooperation with the City Councils of Bologna and Manciano.

PROGRAMS: This Italian language and culture program offers courses on the beginner through the advanced levels. Particular attention is given to oral comprehension and expression. Classes are combined with cultural activities tailored to the students' interests. Instructors hold university degrees.

ELIGIBILITY: Applications are accepted from all interested persons.

LOCATION: Bologna or Manciano, Italy.

TIME OF YEAR: The center in Bologna operates throughout the year; Manciano offers courses during the spring, summer, and winter only.

DURATION: Two-, three-, and four-week courses are available.

ACCOMMODATIONS: Hotels and private homes.

COST: The Centro charges a registration fee of approximately $120 (150,000 lire) plus a weekly charge of about $85 (105,000 lire), which covers only the course fee of 20 hours of instruction per week. All other expenses are additional.

AGE OF PARTICIPANTS: The average age of participants is usually between 22 and 28.

COMMENTS: The Centro di Cultura Italiana offers a certain number of scholarships every year to people who have assisted them with publicizing these programs. Qualified persons can be recommended by Italian institutes, embassies, universities, or other cultural and social organizations. In addition, the Centro offers a two-day trial period to give participants an opportunity to decide whether the course and the program meet their needs. If the student is not satisfied after the trial period, all course fees will be completely refunded.

➤➡➤➡➤

Centro di Cultura Italiana in Casentino

One University Place, Apt. 17-R
New York, NY 10003
Phone: (212) 228-9273
Fax: (212) 228-9273

INSTITUTION/ORGANIZATION: Founded in 1982, the Centro di Cultura Italiana in Casentino is a nonprofit Italian language school with intensive courses on all levels for international visitors.

PROGRAM: This Italian language program includes courses in grammar, syntax, and conversation. Lessons are conducted entirely in Italian and include lectures, tutorials, and small group discussions. Instructors hold university degrees and have teaching experience. Thematic trips, excursions, and seminars supplement the course work.

ELIGIBILITY: Applications are accepted from all interested persons.

LOCATION: Poppi, Italy.

TIME OF YEAR: Spring, summer, and fall.

DURATION: Two- and four-week courses are available.

ACCOMMODATIONS: Private homes, apartments, and cottages.

COST: The two-week course costs approximately $1,070 and includes single room; tuition and fees for 20 hours of lessons per week; practice and seminars; excursions; and dinner four nights a week. (The cost for a double room and all other items mentioned above is $950.) Airfare is not included. The four-week course with a single room costs approximately $1,947.

AGE OF PARTICIPANTS: The average age of participants is usually between 28 and 32.

COMMENTS: Tuition-free scholarships are available; the student pays travel and living expenses. Contact the Centro di Cultura Italiana for more information. Usually about five percent of the participants are from the United States.

Centro Internazionale Dante Alighieri

La Lizza, 10
53100 Siena
ITALY
Phone: (39) 577 49533
Fax: (39) 577 270646

INSTITUTION/ORGANIZATION: Founded in 1979, the Centro Internazionale Dante Alighieri conducts courses in Italian language and culture for international visitors.

PROGRAM: This Italian language program includes the study of grammar, conversation, and culture or phonetics. Taught by instructors with university degrees, lectures and tutorials are combined with small group discussions. New courses begin every month. The maximum number of students per class is 12.

ELIGIBILITY: Applications are accepted from all interested persons.

LOCATION: Siena, Italy.

TIME OF YEAR: Options are available throughout the year.

DURATION: One month.

ACCOMMODATIONS: Hotels, apartments, and private homes.

COST: Varies depending on program duration and accommodations. Single room with half board in a private home is approximately $610 (760,000 lire) per month; tuition, airfare, and other expenses are additional. A double or single room in an apartment costs approximately $240 to $325 (300,000 to 400,000 lire) per person per month; meals, tuition, airfare, and other expenses are additional.

PERSONS WITH DISABILITIES: Since the classrooms are located in old buildings without elevators, travelers who are unable to climb stairs are discouraged from participating. Blind students have been accommodated in the past.

COMMENTS: Scholarships to cover tuition fees are available. Contact the Dante Alighieri Society or an Italian consulate for more information.

►⟹►⟹►

Centro Linguistico Sperimentale

Via del Corso, 1
50122 Florence
ITALY
Phone: (39) 55 210592
Fax: (39) 55 289817

INSTITUTION/ORGANIZATION: Founded in 1979, the Centro Linguistico Sperimentale offers courses in the Italian language.

PROGRAMS: "Italian Language Courses." Designed to fulfill the needs of both students and professionals, the institute offers general language courses (four hours per day); total immersion courses (six hours per day); and individual intensive courses (designed to meet the student's needs). Cultural and recreational activities are an integral part of the programs; although students are not required to participate in these activities, they are strongly urged to do so.

ELIGIBILITY: Interested persons must be at least 16 years old.

LOCATION: Florence, Italy.

TIME OF YEAR: Options are available throughout the year.

DURATION: The general and immersion courses are structured in sessions of two and four weeks, but participants can enroll for a maximum of five months. For individual courses, a minimum of one week is required.

ACCOMMODATIONS: Hotels, pensions, private homes, and apartments.

COST: Depends upon the course and the accommodations. Contact the institute for current prices. In 1992 a two-week course was priced at approximately $220 (280,000 lire). Accommodations are arranged according to the needs of the participant.

AGE OF PARTICIPANTS: The average age of participants is usually between 20 and 25.

COMMENTS: The school will arrange lodging for persons who want to take advantage of this service. However, if you're interested in staying with an Italian family or in an apartment, there is no guarantee that these places will be closer than 20 minutes from the school on public transportation.

►►⇒►►⇒►►

Centro Mexicano Internacional (CMI)

Fray Antonio de San Miguel No. 173
P.O. Box 56
Morelia, Michoacán
MEXICO
Phone: (800) 835 8863
Fax: (52) 451 3 98 98

INSTITUTION/ORGANIZATION: Founded in 1968, the Centro Mexicano Internacional is a nonprofit organization that offers intensive Spanish language courses for all ages.

PROGRAMS: Spanish classes on all levels are conducted in groups of five or less and combined with lessons in arts and crafts, cooking, history, and culture. Participants are grouped according to age and ability.

ELIGIBILITY: Applications are accepted from all interested persons.
LOCATION: Morelia, Michoacán, Mexico.
TIME OF YEAR: Options are available throughout the year.
DURATION: Programs vary from two weeks to six months.
ACCOMMODATIONS: Hotels and private homes.
COST: The cost ranges from $225 to $275 per week for room and
board, instruction, materials, social activities, and local excursions.
Airfare is additional.
AGE OF PARTICIPANTS: The average age of participants is usually
between 30 and 40.
PERSONS WITH DISABILITIES: The Centro Mexicano Internacional
will provide transportation assistance and ground-level classrooms,
and identify families willing to provide homestay opportunities.

Centro Pontevecchio

Piazza Mercato Nuovo 1
50123 Firenze
ITALY
Phone: (39) 55 29 45 11
Fax: (39) 55 23 96 887

INSTITUTION/ORGANIZATION: Founded in 1986, this language
school is a training center for translators and interpreters.

PROGRAM: Courses in Italian language and culture are taught by in-
structors with language degrees. Classes are small and intensive.
ELIGIBILITY: Applications are accepted from all interested persons.
LOCATION: Florence, Italy.
TIME OF YEAR: Options are available throughout the year.
DURATION: Participants can study from two weeks to six months.
ACCOMMODATIONS: Hotels and private homes.
COST: Varies depending on course length and accommodations. A
one-month course costs approximately $425 (530,000 lire); accom-
modations cost approximately $305 (380,000 lire) and include use of
kitchen.
PERSONS WITH DISABILITIES: Applicants are considered on a case-
by-case basis.
COMMENTS: The average age of participants is usually about 24.

▶▶⇒▶▶⇒▶▶

CET

Washington Street
Lower Mills
Boston, MA 02124
Phone: (617) 296-0270
Fax: (617) 296-6830

INSTITUTION/ORGANIZATION: Founded in 1979, CET is a commercial tour operator that develops educational programs in China for academic institutions, museums, and individuals.

PROGRAMS:
- "China in Perspective." This four-week study program provides a comprehensive introduction to Chinese civilization, including history, language, economics, art, politics, literature, and more. Instructors include faculty from various universities and institutes in Beijing. Lectures are combined with small group discussions. Participants live in college dormitories. In 1992 the cost was $2,900 and included round-trip airfare from Los Angeles, room, tuition, books and materials, activity fees, visas, and field trips. For participants who departed from New York, the cost was $3,100 and included all items listed above. The average age of participants is usually about 32.
- "Brush Strokes: The Painting and Calligraphy of China." This three-week studio art program takes place in Beijing. Studio classes, lectures, and demonstrations on art and art history, calligraphy, and printing of China are taught by faculty of the Central Academy of Fine Art. In 1992 the program cost $2,995 and included round-trip airfare from Los Angeles, room, board, tuition, activity fees, field trips, books, materials, and visa. The average age of participants is usually about 30.

ELIGIBILITY: Applications are accepted from all interested persons.
LOCATION: Beijing, China.
TIME OF YEAR: Summer.
DURATION: Programs vary from three to four weeks.
PERSONS WITH DISABILITIES: CET attempts to meet individual needs with special facilities and services within the bounds of China's limited ability to accommodate persons with disabilities.
COMMENTS: Interested participants can earn academic credit for the study program. Contact CET for more information.

➤═➤═➤

Château de Saussignac Cooking School

Saussignac, 24240 Sigoules
FRANCE
Phone: (33) 53 27 80 78
Fax: (33) 53 57 33 30

INSTITUTION/ORGANIZATION: Founded in 1984, The Château de Saussignac is a private culinary school owned and operated by Fred and Joan Montanye, who have taught for more than 35 years and studied at Le Cordon Bleu and La Varenne, Paris.

PROGRAM: The Château offers French cooking lessons taught in English. Classes include lectures, lab work, and mini-demonstrations. Excursions to famous vineyards and other historic and cultural sites are also included. Instructors have been teaching for over 35 years. The Château prides itself on giving individual attention to its students; the maximum number of participants in each session is 10.
ELIGIBILITY: Applications are accepted from all interested persons.
LOCATION: Sigoules, France.
TIME OF YEAR: Spring and fall.
DURATION: Participants can enroll for a minimum of one week.
ACCOMMODATIONS: Private château (where classes are held).
COST: Ranges from about $2,107 to $2,239 (11,800 to 12,540 French francs) and includes lodging, all food, wine, cooking lessons, excursions, and transportation while attending the school. Airfare is additional.
AGE OF PARTICIPANTS: The average age of participants is usually between 35 and 60.
PERSONS WITH DISABILITIES: Although no special provisions are made for persons with disabilities, anyone who can actively participate in the program is welcome.

➤═➤═➤

Chichester Interest Holidays

14 Bay View Terrace
Newquay, TR7 TLR
UNITED KINGDOM
Phone: (44) 637 874216

INSTITUTION/ORGANIZATION: Established in 1982, Chichester Interest Holidays is a commercial tour operator.

PROGRAMS: The Chichester Interest Holidays attempt to provide participants with an introduction to Cornwall by offering vacation courses focusing on such areas as flora and fauna, geology, minerals, great homes, gardens, and the coast. A variety of vacation courses are offered, including "Walking and Nature Stalking," "Cornish Gardens and Great Houses," "Archaeology," and "Stained Glass."

ELIGIBILITY: Applications are accepted from all interested persons who understand English.

LOCATION: County Cornwall, England.

TIME OF YEAR: February through October.

DURATION: Eight days.

ACCOMMODATIONS: Participants stay at the Chichester, a large house in Newquay.

COST: About $255 (145 British pounds), plus entrance fees where applicable. This includes transport, meals, lodging, and all other expenses incurred during the courses. Airfare is not included.

AGE OF PARTICIPANTS: The average age of participants is usually 55 to 60.

PERSONS WITH DISABILITIES: Persons applying must have sight and be able-bodied.

COMMENTS: Usually about three to five percent of the participants are from the United States.

▶➡▶➡▶

China Advocates

1635 Irving Street
San Francisco, CA 94122
Phone: (800) 333-6474
Fax: (415) 753-0412

INSTITUTION/ORGANIZATION: Founded in 1987, China Advocates is a cultural organization that operates commercial tours to promote educational opportunities in China.

PROGRAM: A Chinese (Mandarin) language study program is offered at Beijing Univerity. The maximum number of participants is 30.

ELIGIBILITY: Applications are accepted from all interested persons.

LOCATION: Beijing, China.
TIME OF YEAR: Summer.
DURATION: Six weeks.
ACCOMMODATIONS: College dormitories.
COST: Approximately $2,700, which includes airfare, tuition, books, accommodations, cultural activities, and excursions.
AGE OF PARTICIPANTS: The average age of participants is usually about 35.

➤⇒➤⇒➤

Chopsticks Cooking Centre

108 Boundary Street
Ground Floor
Kowloon
HONG KONG
Phone: (852) 336-8433
Fax: (852) 336-8287

INSTITUTION/ORGANIZATION: Founded in 1971, Chopsticks Cooking Centre is primarily a catering school for professionals, but it also offers a variety of courses in Chinese cuisine for tourists.

PROGRAMS: Professional courses are available on the basic, intermediate, and advanced levels. "Tourist Courses" run from half a day to a one-week intensive course. Lectures are combined with demonstrations and practical cooking sessions. The maximum number of persons in each course is 12.
ELIGIBILITY: Applications are accepted from all interested persons.
LOCATION: Kowloon, Hong Kong.
TIME OF YEAR: Options are available throughout the year.
DURATION: Varies depending on the course. An intensive four-week professional course is offered, as well as half-day, one-day, three-day, and one-week tourist courses.
ACCOMMODATIONS: Though accommodations can be arranged in private hostels, they are not included as part of the course.
COST: Varies depending on the course. The four-week intensive course for beginners costs approximately $2,000; the advanced course costs about $2,500. The tourist courses range from approximately $40 to $60 for a half day to $600 for the one-week intensive programs.

These costs include demonstration classes, instruction, ingredients required, and a taste of the cooked food.

AGE OF PARTICIPANTS: The average age of participants is usually between 35 and 40.

COMMENTS: About 20 percent of the participants are usually from the United States.

➤➤═➤➤═➤➤

Cincinnati Art Museum Travel Program

Travel Planners
Volunteer Office
Cincinnati Art Museum
Eden Park
Cincinnati, OH 45202
Phone: (513) 721-5204
Fax: (513) 721-0129

INSTITUTION/ORGANIZATION: The Cincinnati Art Museum is a non-profit organization dedicated to the arts.

PROGRAMS: The museum conducts a variety of art/cultural study tours. Programs in the past have included a day trip to Louisville, Kentucky, to visit Kentucky's oldest museum, built from designs by Thomas Jefferson; Locust Grove, a restored Georgian mansion built in 1790; and Churchill Downs, a museum containing artifacts and objects connected with the Kentucky Derby. In 1992 the museum led a two-week tour to Scandinavia to visit many of its art treasures, including its ancient churches, stately châteaux, and thatched-roof cottages; museums in Copenhagen, Oslo, and Stockholm; as well as Rosenberg Castle and Christiansborg Palace. Also in 1992, the museum conducted a two-and-a-half-week trip to southern India: Madras and its nearby temple towns, the garden city of Mysore, 12th-century Hoysala temples at Belur and Halebid, and the port city of Cochin, winding up in Bombay, the "gateway to India." A number of other tours were given in 1992. For a more complete listing or information about tours in 1993, call the museum.

ELIGIBILITY: Museum membership ($27.50 for basic membership) is required for all participants.

LOCATION: Locations for 1992 included Columbus, Ohio; Indian-Lonapolis, Indiana; Pittsburgh, Pennsylvania; Southern India; Italy,

England, Mexico, the Netherlands, and Belgium. Projected destinations for 1993 include Dayton, Ohio; Arizona, the Pacific Northwest, Spain, and the south of France.

TIME OF YEAR: Options are available throughout the year.

DURATION: Trips range in length from one day to three weeks.

ACCOMMODATIONS: Participants generally stay in better hotels and bed and breakfasts.

COST: The cost of the trips varies greatly. A one-day trip to Louisville costs roughly $60 per person. A 10-day trip to Italy costs roughly $3,000 per person, including airfare, hotels, some meals, gratuities, and ground transportation. For each trip a deposit of $25 to $300 per person is required in advance.

▶⇒▶⇒▶

Citizen Exchange Council

12 West 31st Street, 4th Floor
New York, NY 10001
Phone: (212) 643-1985
Fax: (212) 643-1996

INSTITUTION/ORGANIZATION: Founded in 1962, the Citizen Exchange Council (CEC) is a nonprofit cultural exchange organization promoting ties to Russia, Ukraine, Latvia, Lithuania, and Estonia.

PROGRAMS: The Citizen Exchange Council sponsors educational and professional programs that take participants to Russia, Ukraine, Latvia, Lithuania, and Estonia to meet with people from these countries who share similar interests and professions. Offered throughout the year, the programs run for two to three weeks. Leaders have studied or lived in these countries and are fluent in the Russian language. Participants stay in hotels and private homes. The approximate cost ranges from $1,995 to $3,050 and includes round-trip airfare from New York, accommodations and meals, excursions, visa fees, travel insurance, and departure taxes. Programs are limited to 21 participants.

ELIGIBILITY: Applications are accepted from all interested persons.

LOCATION: Destinations include Russia, Ukraine, Latvia, Lithuania, and Estonia.

TIME OF YEAR: Time of year varies according to program.

AGE OF PARTICIPANTS: The average age of participants is usually 26. Programs are open to people of all ages.

DURATION: Two to three weeks.

PERSONS WITH DISABILITIES: Though persons with disabilities may participate, CEC cannot guarantee wheelchair-accessible facilities in these countries.

▶️⟹▶️⟹▶️

Close-Up Expeditions

1031 Ardmore Avenue
Oakland, CA 94610
Phone: (510) 465-8955
Fax: (510) 465-1237

INSTITUTION/ORGANIZATION: Founded in 1979, Close-Up Expeditions is a commercial tour operator that runs photography programs.

PROGRAMS: Close-Up Expeditions operates 20 photographic adventures around the world with professional photographer guides, small groups, and emphasis on cultural and natural history as well as photography. Programs are designed for active seniors ages 55 and over, and include informal lectures and discussions in the field with local and escorting guides. All guides have teaching experience. The maximum size of any group is 15; most are smaller.

ELIGIBILITY: Participants should have an interest in photography and other cultures.

LOCATIONS: Argentina, Belize, Canada, Chile, Austria, Czechoslovakia, Hungary, England, India, Indonesia, New Zealand, Thailand, Burma, and Turkey.

TIME OF YEAR: Options are available throughout the year.

DURATION: Two to three weeks.

ACCOMMODATIONS: On most programs, participants stay in hotels/motels, lodges, or inns. The Indonesian program also includes stays on a houseboat and in a village longhouse.

COST: The average cost is $180 a day, which includes all meals, ground transportation, accommodations, instruction, planning services, and orientation materials. Airfare is additional.

AGE OF PARTICIPANTS: The average age of participants is usually 68.

PERSONS WITH DISABILITIES: Each participant must be able to look after him/herself or have a companion who will do so. Pace of travel is usually slow and not strenuous.

COMMENTS: Most participants are from the United States.

▶⇒▶⇒▶

Committee for Health Rights in Central America

347 Dolores Street, #210
San Francisco, CA 94110
Phone: (415) 431-7760

INSTITUTION/ORGANIZATION: Established in 1983, the Committee for Health Rights in Central America (CHRICA) is a nonprofit organization that provides material and medical aid in Nicaragua. This organization, which supports the Sandanista Revolution in Nicaragua, sponsors professional exchanges and educational programs.

PROGRAM: CHRICA sponsors the "U.S.-Nicaragua Colloquium on Health," a delegation of professionals who visit health centers, hospitals, and other facilities. With a focus on medicine, nursing, rehabilitation, and mental health, the delegation is led by experts in the health care fields. The program includes a medical conference with presentations given by Nicaraguan and U.S. counterparts.

ELIGIBILITY: Knowledge of Spanish language is helpful but not necessary.

LOCATION: Managua, Nicaragua.

TIME OF YEAR: Spring.

DURATION: Ten days.

ACCOMMODATIONS: Hotels and guesthouses.

COST: Approximately $800, which includes room, board, and transportation within Nicaragua. Airfare to and from Managua is not included.

AGE OF PARTICIPANTS: The average age of participants is usually between 30 and 40.

PERSONS WITH DISABILITIES: Participation by persons with disabilities is encouraged. The delegation works heavily with disabled advocacy groups in Nicaragua. Accessible accommodations are provided, as is assistance with finding attendant care.

COMMENTS: A minimal amount of funding is available to assist participants with program-related expenses; awards are based on need. Interested persons can obtain units of continuing education credit for participation. Contact CHRICA for more information.

▶⇒▶⇒▶

Community College Tours
P.O. Box 620620
Woodside, CA 94062
Phone: (415) 851-1988

INSTITUTION/ORGANIZATION: Founded in 1984, Community College Tours is a commercial tour operator that organizes college-credit tours for older adults.

PROGRAMS: "Tours Worldwide." Focused on history, art history, and geography, these bus tours are accompanied by college professors.
ELIGIBILITY: Applications are accepted from all interested persons.
LOCATION: Australia, China, Europe, New Zealand, the United States.
TIME OF YEAR: Summer.
DURATION: Tours run from 17 to 28 days.
ACCOMMODATIONS: Hotels.
COST: Tours range from $2,000 to $4,000 and include airfare, hotels, buses, special excursions, admissions, and most meals (except lunches).
AGE OF PARTICIPANTS: The average age of participants is usually about 55. The programs are designed for people between the ages of 30 and 75.
PERSONS WITH DISABILITIES: They are welcome if they are able to manage a bus tour.
COMMENTS: Children are welcome.

▶⇒▶⇒▶

Cookery at The Grange
Whatley Vineyard
Whatley, Frome, Somerset BA11 3LA
UNITED KINGDOM
Phone: (44) 373 836579

INSTITUTION/ORGANIZATION: Established in 1981 in a 17th-century coach house, The Grange is a commercial cooking school located 15 miles outside the city of Bath.

PROGRAMS: The Grange offers a variety of programs ranging from a weekend course to a one-month certificate course. While students attend some class demonstrations and tutorials with instructors, they spend most of their time learning by cooking. Courses are generally small, with a maximum of 16 students.

ELIGIBILITY: Participants should have a reasonable grasp of English and be at least 18 years old.

LOCATION: Whatley, Frome, Somerset, England.

TIME OF YEAR: Options are available throughout the year.

DURATION: Courses range from two days to one month.

ACCOMMODATIONS: Participants have the option to reside at The Grange, a 17th-century coach house. They can also choose to stay in other country houses.

COST: The approximate cost for a weekend course is about $320 (180 British pounds); the month-long course costs about $2,100 (1,200 British pounds). Fees include room, meals, and linens Monday through Friday only. These prices are for those who reside at the Grange, and do not include airfare.

AGE OF PARTICIPANTS: The average age of participants in the month-long course is usually between 18 to 25. Ages vary widely in the other courses.

PERSONS WITH DISABILITIES: Participants should be sufficiently ambulant to reach kitchen, which is upstairs.

Coopersmith

6441 Valley View Road
Oakland, CA 94611
Phone: (510) 339-2499
Fax: (510) 339-7135

INSTITUTION/ORGANIZATION: Founded in 1984, Coopersmith is a commercial tour operator that specializes in garden, manor home, fine art, and literature tours of Britain and Europe.

PROGRAMS: "Garden and Literature Tours of Europe." These tours take participants to gardens and/or manor homes, cathedrals, museums, and palaces. Led by a tour manager with in-depth knowledge of British and European history, the programs focus on architecture, art, history, and literature. Groups are limited to 20 people.

ELIGIBILITY: Applications accepted from all interested persons.

LOCATION: France, Belgium, the Netherlands, Italy, and the United Kingdom.

TIME OF YEAR: Spring, summer, and fall.

DURATION: Tours run from 13 to 15 days.

ACCOMMODATIONS: Country inns, manor homes, and hotels.

COST: Approximately $4,000, which includes rooms with bathrooms, most meals, in-country transportation, entrance fees, service charges and taxes, airport transfers, porterage, and round-trip airfare from the East Coast.

AGE OF PARTICIPANTS: The average age of participants is usually between 40 and 70.

PERSONS WITH DISABILITIES: Coopersmith will make any necessary arrangements if at all possible.

▸⇒▸⇒▸

Le Cordon Bleu

8, rue Leon Delhomme
75015 Paris
FRANCE
Phone: (33) 148 56 06 06
Fax: (33) 148 56 03 96

INSTITUTION/ORGANIZATION: Founded in 1895, Le Cordon Bleu is a commercial operation that offers courses in classic French cuisine.

PROGRAMS: One-day workshops at Le Cordon Bleu last from two hours to a full day and are geared to specific culinary topics such as classical cuisine, pastry making, and chocolate confections. Workshops consist of demonstration, tasting, and practical instruction, or demonstration followed by tasting only. The two- to five-day courses are designed for those who would like to learn more about French cuisine and those who wish to improve or upgrade their skills. Sessions consist of demonstration and practical instruction. All culinary terms, techniques, and demonstrations are translated into English. All chefs are experienced teachers from Michelin-starred restaurants.

ELIGIBILITY: Participants must be at least 18 years of age and have a bachelor's degree.

LOCATIONS: London, Paris, and Tokyo.

TIME OF YEAR: Options are available throughout the year.

DURATION: One-day workshops are available, but most classes last two to five days.

COST: For a one-day workshop, price ranges from $30 to $135. Longer classes range from about $325 to $810. Fees cover class instruction only.

AGE OF PARTICIPANTS: The average age of participants is usually about 20 to 35.

▶⇒▶⇒▶

Cornell's Adult University (CAU)

626 Thurston Avenue
Ithaca, NY 14850
Phone: (607) 255-6260
Fax: (607) 255-7533

INSTITUTION/ORGANIZATION: Founded in 1968, CAU is Cornell's vacation college for alumni and friends of the university. It sponsors some 70 programs annually for 2,000 participants of all ages on the Cornell campus, around the United States and abroad. Cornell is a member of the Council on International Educational Exchange.

PROGRAMS: CAU sponsors study tours to destinations worldwide. All tours combine escorted travel with a complete educational program developed and led by members of the Cornell University faculty. The tours focus on such areas as history, art, politics, architecture, marine biology, geology, and botany, among others. Lectures and small group discussions are combined with readings, site visits, and guest speakers. Group sizes usually vary from 25 to 70, depending upon the study tour.

ELIGIBILITY: Applications are accepted from all interested persons.

LOCATION: Destinations vary each year. Previous destinations have included New Zealand, Belize, Tortola Island, Turkey, Scandinavia, the Baltics, and Russia.

TIME OF YEAR: Options are available throughout the year.

DURATION: Tours run from 10 days to three weeks.

ACCOMMODATIONS: Participants stay in hotels; some programs take place on cruise ships.

COST: In 1992, the cost of tours ranged from $1,800 to $4,900 and included room, most or all meals, site visits, entry fees, taxes, gratuities, escort services, books, and the educational program. International airfare is not included.

AGE OF PARTICIPANTS: Participants usually range in age from 35 to 70.

PERSONS WITH DISABILITIES: CAU tries to accommodate all who want to participate. Provisions made on past tours have included shortening walking itineraries and providing alternate activities as needed.

▶⟹▶⟹▶

Corrib Conservation Centre

Aronasillagh,
Oughterard,
County Galway,
IRELAND
Phone and Fax: (353) 91 82519

INSTITUTION/ORGANIZATION: Founded in 1978, the Corrib Conservation Centre is a commercial tour operator that promotes wildlife conservation through environmental education and research programs.

PROGRAMS: "Irish Wildlife Studies." The Center offers a variety of study, field research, and tutorial programs covering geology, climate, land use, flora, fauna, wildlife management, and conservation. Instructors have advanced degrees and teaching experience.

ELIGIBILITY: Applications accepted from all interested persons who have facility in English and are reasonably physically fit.

LOCATION: Oughterard/Galway, Ireland.

TIME OF YEAR: Spring, summer, and fall.

DURATION: Courses run for four or eight weeks.

ACCOMMODATIONS: Private homes and registered guesthouses.

COST: The four-week course is about $1,120 (695 Irish pounds); the eight-week course is about $2,090 (1,295 Irish pounds). Both include room, full board, tuition, course materials, travel within Ireland related to the course, and use of the center's facilities.

AGE OF PARTICIPANTS: The average age of participants is usually within the early 20s.

PERSONS WITH DISABILITIES: Open to those who feel they can benefit. All special diets can be arranged. Wheelchair access is limited.

COMMENTS: Students may be able to arrange academic credit through their home universities. All participants have been from the United States.

➤⇒➤⇒➤

The Council for British Archaeology

112 Kennington Road
London SE11 6RE
UNITED KINGDOM
Phone: (44) 71 582 0494
Fax: (44) 71 587 5152

INSTITUTION/ORGANIZATION: Founded in 1944, The Council for British Archaeology (CBA) is a nonprofit federation of universities, museums, societies, and professional archaeological units. Though CBA does not sponsor excavations, the organization publishes "British Archaeological News," which lists digs that need volunteers.

PROGRAMS: "Hands-on" learning takes place as volunteers excavate archaeological sites throughout England, Scotland, and Wales. Under the tutelage of archaeologists, volunteers have the option to participate in a formalized training excavation, which includes lectures, or a regular excavation without training.
ELIGIBILITY: Applications are accepted from all interested persons.
LOCATION: Excavations take place throughout the United Kingdom.
TIME OF YEAR: The majority of digs occur during the summer months.
DURATION: Varies according to dig site.
ACCOMMODATIONS: Tents, hostels, or college dormitories.
COST: Varies according to the dig site and type of excavation.
COMMENTS: A small stipend or living allowance is provided for volunteers who participate in the regular excavations, but not for those on the training digs.

➤⇒➤⇒➤

Council on International Educational Exchange

International Workcamps Department
205 East 42nd Street
New York, NY 10017
Phone: (212) 661-1414
Fax: (212) 972-3231

INSTITUTION/ORGANIZATION: Founded in 1947, the Council on International Educational Exchange (CIEE) is an international nonprofit organization. CIEE develops and administers international study, work, travel, and voluntary service programs throughout the world. CIEE's two travel divisions, Council Travel and Council Charter, specialize in budget travel for all ages.

PROGRAM: "International Workcamps." These short-term community service projects bring volunteers from different countries together to work on environmental, historic preservation, archaeological, renovation, and social projects. The 10 to 20 volunteers on each workcamp live together, sharing such responsibilities of daily life as cooking and cleaning, and organizing their own free time with social activities and excursions. Workcamps provide participants with an opportunity to learn from one another and the local community. Participants are recruited from around the world through an international network of voluntary service organizations, which also takes responsibility for organizing workcamps in their own countries. Generally there are no more than two or three volunteers from any one country on a workcamp.

ELIGIBILITY: Participants must be at least 18 years of age, open-minded, and willing to work, learn, and have fun. In some countries, knowledge of a foreign language is required.

LOCATION: Destinations outside the United States include Algeria, Belgium, Canada, Czechoslovakia, Denmark, France, Germany, Ghana, Hungary, Japan, Lithuania, Morocco, the Netherlands, Poland, Russia, Slovenia, Spain, Tunisia, Turkey, Ukraine, and Wales.

TIME OF YEAR: Most workcamps take place during the summer.

DURATION: Workcamps run from two to three weeks.

ACCOMMODATIONS: Community centers, schools, hostels, tents. Participants should expect spartan accommodations.

COST: A $135 placement fee covers all program expenses including room and board. Travel expenses are additional, and participants are responsible for making their own arrangements.

AGE OF PARTICIPANTS: Most volunteers are between 18 and 35; the average age of participants is about 21.

PERSONS WITH DISABILITIES: People with disabilities are encouraged to apply, and placements are made on an individual basis.

▶⇒▶⇒▶

Council on International Educational Exchange

Professional and Continuing Education Programs
205 East 42nd Street
New York, NY 10017
Phone: (212) 661-1414
Fax: (212) 972-3231

INSTITUTION/ORGANIZATION: Founded in 1947, the Council on International Educational Exchange (CIEE) is an international, nonprofit organization. CIEE develops and administers international study, work, travel, and voluntary service programs throughout the world. CIEE's two travel divisions, Council Travel and Council Charter, specialize in budget travel for all ages.

PROGRAMS: CIEE sponsors various programs for educators on the elementary, secondary, and university levels.
- "Teaching Visits." Offered annually in France and the United Kingdom, these programs provide educators with the opportunity to live with families in France or the United Kingdom, while spending each day with a host teacher at an elementary or secondary school. Educators gain an insider's perspective on the country's educational system through observing and participating in the host teacher's classes. An orientation is provided, which includes an introduction to the country's educational system and social structure. The French program takes place during the spring; the United Kingdom program takes place in the winter (February). The visits run for two weeks, and participants live in private homes but spend the first and last nights in hotels in London or Paris. In 1992 the French visit cost $1,450; the United Kingdom visit cost $1,300. Both program fees included round-trip airfare from New York, accommodations, most meals, and all educational expenses. All participants must be fluent in the language of the host country and be employed in the field of education. Programs in other countries may be offered in the future.
- "U.S.-China Educator Exchange." Offered annually during the summer, this reciprocal exchange program provides educators on the elementary, secondary, and university levels with the opportunity to spend three weeks in China. Participants travel within the country visiting schools; meeting with teachers, faculty members, and administrators; and exploring the cultural

wonders of the country. Destinations include Shanghai, Xi'an, Beijing, Dalian, and Guangzhou, where site visits are combined with small group discussions. Participants stay in hotels. In 1992 the program cost $3,520, which included round-trip airfare from the West Coast ($200 additional for New York departure), domestic airfare in China, all accommodations, meals, educational expenses, and transfers within China. All participants must be educators.

- "International Faculty Development Seminars." Hosted by universities around the world, these short-term, intensive, multidisciplinary seminars are designed for full-time faculty and administrators at two- and four-year institutions of higher education. Focused on current events and rapidly changing political and social environments, the seminars combine lectures and discussions with site visits. Program speakers include professors at host country institutions, business professionals, government officials, and community leaders. Seminars run from one to two weeks, depending on the location. Participants stay in hotels or university conference facilities. The seminars scheduled for 1993 will take place in the Netherlands, Vietnam, the Dominican Republic, Zimbabwe, Germany, Russia, Brazil, Hong Kong, Chile, Northern Ireland, Poland, and the United States. Seminar costs range from $1,150 to $1,800 and include accommodations, breakfast and lunch daily, tuition and seminar materials, admissions, local site visits, and receptions. Airfare is additional.

ELIGIBILITY: Varies according to program. See descriptions of programs above.

LOCATION: Destinations include France, the United Kingdom, China, the Netherlands, Vietnam, the Dominican Republic, Zimbabwe, Germany, Russia, Brazil, Hong Kong, Chile, Northern Ireland, and Poland.

TIME OF YEAR: Time of year varies. See descriptions of programs above.

DURATION: Programs vary from one to three weeks.

AGE OF PARTICIPANTS: The average age ranges from 30 to 70.

PERSONS WITH DISABILITIES: All qualified applicants will be considered for acceptance. CIEE will try to accommodate persons with disabilities whenever possible.

▶⇒▶⇒▶

The Cousteau Society

930 West 21st Street
Norfolk, VA 23517
Phone: (804) 627-1144
Fax: (804) 627-7547

INSTITUTION/ORGANIZATION: Founded in 1973, The Cousteau Society is a nonprofit environmental educational organization dedicated to protection and improvement of the quality of life for present and future generations.

PROGRAM: "Project Ocean Search." These field study programs include daily dives that focus on natural history, exploration, research, photography, resource management, and the humanities. Project leaders include Cousteau's staff of scientists and divers, a photography expert, visiting academics, and local guides. Lectures and small group discussions are combined with field trips. Usually the maximum group size ranges from 30 to 40 people.

ELIGIBILITY: Persons should be enthusiastic and in good health; minimum age is sixteen.

LOCATION: Destinations vary from year to year. In 1991 the projects took place in Fiji.

TIME OF YEAR: Summer.

DURATION: Projects usually run for two weeks, with two back-to-back sessions per year.

ACCOMMODATIONS: Vary according to location, but range from tents to full-service hotels. In Fiji, participants stay in traditional Fijan huts.

COST: Depends on the project. In 1991 the cost for Fiji was $3,900, which included room and board, diving, and airfare from Los Angeles to Fiji.

AGE OF PARTICIPANTS: The age of participants ranges from 16 up, and varies widely.

PERSONS WITH DISABILITIES: Applicants are considered on a case-by-case basis.

COMMENTS: Diving certification is strongly recommended for some projects. Financial assistance is available; awards are based on need.

Craft World Tours/Camera World Tours

6776 Warboys Road
Byron, NY 14422
Phone: (716) 548-2667
Fax: (716) 548-2821

INSTITUTION/ORGANIZATION: Founded in 1985, Craft World Tours/Camera World Tours is a commercial tour operator that offers photographic tours, as well as tours that focus on the crafts and folk art of the countries visited.

PROGRAM: "Craft World Tours and Camera World Tours." With an emphasis on culture, tours are accompanied by an expert on each country or by the director, Tom Muir Wilson, who has 20 years experience teaching art and photography at the Rochester Institute of Technology. Though not formal study tours, trips are educationally oriented. Groups are limited to 20 people.
ELIGIBILITY: Applications accepted from all interested persons.
LOCATION: Argentina/Chile, Myanmar, China, Eastern Europe, Egypt, India, Indonesia, Korea, Morocco, Nepal, New Zealand, Thailand, Turkey, and the United Kingdom.
TIME OF YEAR: Options are available throughout the year.
DURATION: Two to four weeks, depending on the program.
ACCOMMODATIONS: Hotels.
COST: Ranges between $2,500 and $4,500, including round-trip airfare, luggage handling, accommodations, most meals, tips, a bilingual guide, and tour escort.
AGE OF PARTICIPANTS: The average age of participants is usually between 50 and 80.
COMMENTS: Most participants are usually from the United States.

Cross-Culture

52 High Point Drive
Amherst, MA 01002
Phone: (413) 256-6303
Fax: (413) 253-2303

INSTITUTION/ORGANIZATION: Cross-Culture is a commercial tour operator that offers learning vacations led by educators from each country visited.

PROGRAMS: These learning vacations are designed to be a "comfortable balance between a study tour and a vacation," according to the sponsor. Lecturers provide background information on the history, culture, and contemporary life of the local people. All lecturers hold university degrees, and many are educators. Every attempt is made to bring participants into contact with the people of each country. Offerings in 1993 include "Journey to Old Japan," "Spanish Discovery," "Paris Plus," "Quintessential England," "Danish Delights," "The Loire Valley and Paris, Too," "Lake District Walks," "Exploring England," "Hungarian Holiday," "Viennese Waltzes," "Mozart's Salzburg," "Autumn in the South of France," and "Grecian Spring." Groups are limited to 25 people.
ELIGIBILITY: Applications are accepted from all interested persons at least 21 years of age.
LOCATION: Austria, Denmark, England, France, Hungary, Italy, Japan, and Spain.
TIME OF YEAR: Year-round, but mostly in the spring and fall.
DURATION: One to two weeks.
ACCOMMODATIONS: Hotels, as well as castles, châteaux, and manor homes.
COST: Ranges from $3,000 to $5,000 and includes round-trip international airfare, all meals and accommodations, all excursions, guides, and admissions.
AGE OF PARTICIPANTS: The average age of participants is usually 55 to 65.
PERSONS WITH DISABILITIES: All who are physically able to participate are welcome. Castles, archeological sites, and châteaux rarely have elevators. The program also involves a considerable amount of walking.
COMMENTS: Interested students can earn academic credit from Portland State University. Contact Cross-Culture for more information. Most participants are usually from the United States.

▶⇒▶⇒▶

Cuauhnahuac
519 Park Drive
Kenilworth, IL 60043

Phone: (708) 256-7570
Fax: (708) 256-9475

INSTITUTION/ORGANIZATION: Founded in 1972, Cuauhnahuac is a nonprofit Spanish-language school that provides a variety of intensive and flexible programs for those interested in acquiring a functional fluency in Spanish.

PROGRAM: "Intensive Spanish Study." Participants attend six hours of classes daily, which are taught entirely in Spanish. Instructors are all native speakers of Spanish with special training in Cuauhnahuac's teaching methods. The majority hold university degrees. The study of Mexican culture, extra activities, and excursions are also part of the program.
ELIGIBILITY: Applications are accepted from all interested persons.
LOCATION: Cuernavaca, Mexico.
TIME OF YEAR: Options are available throughout the year.
DURATION: Participants may study for any length of time.
ACCOMMODATIONS: Private homes.
COST: The monthly cost is approximately $1,004, which includes registration fee, room, and board. Airfare is not included.
PERSONS WITH DISABILITIES: Cuauhnahuac can accommodate students with most disabilities; classrooms are easily accessible.
COMMENTS: If you are a college/university student, you may be able to receive academic credit for participation. Contact Cuauhnahuac for more information. About 80 percent of the participants are usually from the United States.

▶️⇒▶️⇒▶️

Cultural Folk Tours International
10292 Gumbark Place
San Diego, CA 92131
Phone: (800) 448-0515 or (619) 566-5951

INSTITUTION/ORGANIZATION: Cultural Folk Tours International is a commercial tour operator that has run culturally oriented tours to Turkey since 1979.

PROGRAM: Bora Oskok, the director of Cultural Folk Tours, personally leads group tours, which include seminars on Turkish culture, folk dance, music, and history, as well as opportunities to meet the local people. Oskok has taught Turkish music and folk dance worldwide.

ELIGIBILITY: Applications are accepted from all interested persons.

LOCATION: Istanbul, Bursa, Troy, Izmir, Ephesus, Kusadasi, Pamukkale, Capradocia, Ankara, Tokat, Trabzon, Erzurum, Dogubayazit, Van, and other Turkish cities.

TIME OF YEAR: Spring, summer, and fall.

DURATION: Two to three weeks.

ACCOMMODATIONS: Hotels.

COST: Varies with each tour; generally ranges from $2,000 to $3,500 and includes round-trip international airfare, all travel within Turkey, room (based on double occupancy), two meals a day, and most admission fees and tips.

PERSONS WITH DISABILITIES: Persons with disabilities are welcome as long as a traveling companion can assist them.

AGE OF PARTICIPANTS: The average age of participants is about 50 to 60 years old.

COMMENTS: Most participants are from the United States.

▶➡▶➡▶

Deutsch in Graz

Zinzendorfgasse 30
A-8010 Graz
AUSTRIA
Phone: (43) 316 38 37 47
Fax: (43) 316 38 37 64

INSTITUTION/ORGANIZATION: Founded in 1980, Deutsch in Graz is a nonprofit organization that offers German language courses.

PROGRAMS: Deutsch in Graz offers German language courses for adults from beginner to advanced levels, with an emphasis on oral communication. Classes are small and intensive, and instructors are experienced in teaching German as a foreign language. The institute has also offered courses for persons with a knowledge of German: "German for Trade and Commerce," "German for the Hotel and Service Industries," and "Austrian Literature and Civilization."

ELIGIBILITY: Depends on the course; some require basic knowledge of German (see above).

LOCATION: Graz, Austria.
TIME OF YEAR: Depends on the course; contact Deutsch in Graz.
DURATION: Courses generally run for two weeks, although some are available for three or six weeks.
ACCOMMODATIONS: Hotels or families.
COST: In 1992 the cost for a two-week program ranged from $430 to $560 (5,000 and 6,500 Austrian schillings) for tuition only. Full board with a family or at a hotel is available for an additional charge of about $500.
AGE OF PARTICIPANTS: The average age of participants is usually about 30.
COMMENTS: Funding is available for students, persons from Third World nations, and Eastern Europeans. Contact Deutsch in Graz for more information.

▶➡▶➡▶

Did Deutsch-Institut

Hauptstrasse 26
8751 Stockstadt am Main
GERMANY
Phone: (49) 06027-2009-0
Fax: (49) 06027-2009-13

INSTITUTION/ORGANIZATION: Did Deutsch-Institut is a chain of commercial language institutes specializing in teaching German language.

PROGRAMS: Intensive German courses for adults are taught by instructors with degrees in teaching German as a foreign language. Diploma and vacation courses are also offered for students, children, and adults.
ELIGIBILITY: Applications are accepted from all interested persons.
LOCATION: Destinations include Frankfurt, Munich, Berlin, Mainz, Wiesbaden, Hannover, Hamburg, Düsseldorf, Bonn, Nuremberg, and Würzburg, Germany.
TIME OF YEAR: Options are available throughout the year.
DURATION: Participants have the option to enroll for a two-week minimum and can extend their studies beyond eight weeks if desired.
ACCOMMODATIONS: College dormitories and private homes.

COST: Varies depending on the program; contact Did Deutsch-Institut for more information.
AGE OF PARTICIPANTS: The average age of participants is usually between 20 and 25.
PERSONS WITH DISABILITIES: Persons with disabilities are encouraged to participate.
COMMENTS: Usually about five percent of the participants are from the United States.

➤➤⇒➤➤⇒➤➤

Dillington House

Ilminster, Somerset TA19 9DT
UNITED KINGDOM
Phone: (44) 460 52427
Fax: (44) 460 52433

INSTITUTION/ORGANIZATION: Founded in 1950, Dillington House is a conference and training center with adult education programs.

PROGRAMS: Short residential courses are offered in a variety of areas including calligraphy, painting, music, photography, sewing, philosophy, and languages (French, Italian, and German).
ELIGIBILITY: Applications are accepted from all interested persons.
LOCATION: Ilminster, Somerset.
TIME OF YEAR: Time of year varies.
DURATION: One to seven days.
ACCOMMODATIONS: Participants stay in Dillington House, which dates from the 16th century and was the home of Lord North, George III's prime minister.
COST: Varies; contact Dillington House.

➤➤⇒➤➤⇒➤➤

Dora Stratou Dance Theatre

8 Scholiou Street
Plaka, Athens 10558
GREECE
Phone: (30) 1 3244395

INSTITUTION/ORGANIZATION: Established in 1953, the Dora Stratou Dance Theatre is a nonprofit, cultural institution that performs traditional Greek dances, conducts classes, and houses a research center devoted to Greek music, dances, and costumes.

PROGRAM: The Dora Stratou Dance Theatre sponsors a dance and folk culture program that includes study and training for the ethnography of dance. The program is led by an experienced instructor and includes lectures, tutorials, workshops, and small group discussions. The maximum number of people permitted in each group is 30.
ELIGIBILITY: Applications are accepted from all interested persons.
LOCATION: Athens, Greece.
TIME OF YEAR: Summer and winter.
DURATION: Four weeks.
ACCOMMODATIONS: Participants are responsible for arranging their own accommodations. The theatre office will help arrange accommodations.
COST: $150 per week, which covers tuition only.
AGE OF PARTICIPANTS: The average age of participants is usually about 30.
COMMENTS: About 10 percent of the participants are usually from the United States.

▶⇒▶⇒▶

Dyfed County Council

Theatr Felinfach
Felinfach, Lampeter
Dyfed SA48 8AF
UNITED KINGDOM
Phone: (44) 570 470 005

INSTITUTION/ORGANIZATION: The Dyfed County Council is a nonprofit organization founded in 1980 that teaches and organizes Welsh language classes for adults in Dyfed.

PROGRAM: "Welsh for Adults." Classes are offered at all levels, with an intensive study program offered twice annually. Instructors are experienced teachers and hold a university degree or the equivalent.
ELIGIBILITY: Applications are accepted from all interested persons.
LOCATION: Aberystwyth, Wales.

TIME OF YEAR: Spring and summer.
DURATION: Four to seven days.
ACCOMMODATIONS: College dormitories.
COST: Approximately $56 (32 British pounds) for tuition per session
and $185 (105 British pounds) for full board.
AGE OF PARTICIPANTS: The age of participants ranges from 20 to
60.
COMMENTS: About two percent of the participants are usually from
the United States.

▶▶⇒▶▶⇒▶▶

The Earnley Concourse
Earnley, Chichester
West Sussex P010 7DR
UNITED KINGDOM
Phone: (44) 243 670392
Fax: (44) 243 670832

INSTITUTION/ORGANIZATION: Founded in 1975, The Earnley Concourse is a nonprofit educational trust.

PROGRAMS: The Earnley Concourse offers a wide variety of adult
education courses including several walking tours and classes such as
"Lino Prints and Woodcuts," "Care and Restoration of Antique Fur-
niture," and "Chinese Brush Painting." Music appreciation classes, as
well as beginning to advanced language classes, are also available.
ELIGIBILITY: Applications are accepted from all interested persons.
LOCATION: West Sussex, England, just south of Chichester, with
walking tours in the surrounding areas.
TIME OF YEAR: Options are available throughout the year.
DURATION: Courses take place mainly on weekends, with some last-
ing four days. Seven-day courses are available during the summer.
ACCOMMODATIONS: Single and double rooms are available at the
Concourse, all with private bathroom, and some with showers as well.
Meals are offered in a self-service dining room. Participants are not
required to stay at the Concourse.
COST: To secure a booking, a nonrefundable deposit is required.
Course costs range from $205 to $641 for those staying at the Con-

course and from $123 to $396 for nonresidents. Meals are extra. Airfare is not included.

AGE OF PARTICIPANTS: The average age is usually between 45 and 50.

PERSONS WITH DISABILITIES: Persons with disabilities are welcome, depending on subject. Some specially equipped ground-floor bedrooms are available.

Earth Island Institute

Sea Turtle Restoration Project
300 Broadway, Suite 28
San Francisco, CA 94133
Phone: (415) 788-3666
Fax: (415) 788-7324

INSTITUTION/ORGANIZATION: Founded in 1982, Earth Island is a nonprofit organization that works to protect and restore sea turtle populations worldwide.

PROGRAM: "Sea Turtle Brigades." This outdoor field research project involves assisting scientists who are studying endangered sea turtles, and taking part in sustainable community development programs for these turtles. Brigades are limited to 10 people.

ELIGIBILITY: Applications are accepted from all interested persons.

LOCATION: Nicaragua and Costa Rica.

TIME OF YEAR: Summer and fall.

DURATION: Projects run from 10 to 14 days.

ACCOMMODATIONS: Tents and field stations.

COST: Projects range from $600 to $1,000 and include room, board, and ground transportation. International airfare is additional.

PERSONS WITH DISABILITIES: The Sea Turtle Restoration Project does not discriminate against persons with disabilities, although the program requires strenuous physical work.

COMMENTS: Some funding is available for participants; all interested persons are eligible to apply. Contact the Sea Turtle Restoration Project for more information.

▶⇒▶⇒▶

Earthwatch

Box 403N
680 Mt. Auburn Street
Watertown, MA 02272
Phone: (617) 926-8200
Fax: (617) 926-8532

INSTITUTION/ORGANIZATION: Founded in 1971, Earthwatch is a nonprofit organization that sponsors scholarly field research. Earthwatch ranks with the National Geographic Society and World Wildlife Fund as one of the largest private sponsors of field research expeditions in the world.

PROGRAMS: Earthwatch sponsors 135 projects in more than 50 countries. These scholarly research projects focus on such areas as rain forest conservation and ecology, art and archaeology, geosciences, life sciences, marine studies, and social sciences. Volunteers assist the scientists who lead the expeditions.

ELIGIBILITY: Participants must be at least 16 years old.

LOCATION: Destinations outside the United States include Indonesia, New Zealand, Costa Rica, Switzerland, Iceland, Mexico, Greece, Australia, Papua New Guinea, Canada, Peru, Bahamas, Fiji, Belize, South Africa, Mozambique, Vietnam, Canary Islands, Madagascar, Nepal, Russia, Georgia, China, Ethiopia, Zimbabwe, Spain, Thailand, Chile, Argentina, France, Honduras, Tunisia, Italy, Namibia, Dominican Republic, England, Scotland, South Korea, Ghana, India, Barbados, Bulgaria, Poland, Kenya, Nigeria, Brazil, Hong Kong, and Czechoslovakia.

TIME OF YEAR: Options are available throughout the year.

DURATION: Projects run from two to three weeks.

ACCOMMODATIONS: Vary with the project; participants have lived in hotels/motels, tents, hostels, private homes, and college dormitories.

COST: The cost generally ranges from $800 to $2,000 and includes all expenses except international airfare.

AGE OF PARTICIPANTS: Participants range in age from 16 to 82.

PERSONS WITH DISABILITIES: Individuals are accepted as long as they can do the work.

COMMENTS: Funding is available for high school students and teachers of grades K through 12. Contact Earthwatch for more information. Earthwatch distributes a fact sheet that provides a detailed overview of its activities, as well as a magazine that describes its work in progress and research findings. These publications are free to members.

▸⇒▸⇒▸

Eastern Michigan University

Office of Academic Programs Abroad
333 Goodison Hall
Ypsilanti, MI 48197
Phone: (800) 777-3541
Fax: (313) 487-2316

INSTITUTION/ORGANIZATION: Founded in 1849, Eastern Michigan is a comprehensive state university that is a member of the Council on International Educational Exchange.

PROGRAMS: The programs sponsored by Eastern Michigan University vary, but might include the following:
- "Discover Russia." Focused on Russian history, this travel/ study program takes participants to Russia and Poland. Guided by university-approved faculty, the program includes lectures and small group discussions, with visits to historical sites. The tour runs for three weeks during the summer. Participants stay in hotels. The cost is approximately $3,200, which includes round-trip airfare from New York, room and partial board, ground transportation, excursions, tuition, and fees. Open to all interested persons. To be offered in 1993. Group size is limited to 25 participants.
- "European Travel Study." This study program takes partici- pants to Germany, Austria, and Italy for four weeks during the summer. The focus is on modern European history; EMU faculty provide the instruction. Lectures are combined with small group discussions. Participants stay in hotels. The cost is approximately $3,800, which includes round-trip international airfare from New York, room, all ground transportation, some meals, tuition, fees, and excursions. To be offered in 1993. Group size is limited to 25 participants.
- "Educators' Tour of New Zealand and Australia." This study tour focuses on the educational systems and cultures of New Zealand and Australia. Led by EMU faculty, the program con- centrates on primary education. Lectures are combined with

small group discussions. Participants stay in hotels/motels. In 1992 the cost was approximately $4,500 and included round-trip airfare from Los Angeles, room, most meals, transportation, tuition, fees, and excursions. The program runs for three weeks during the summer. Group size is limited to 20 participants.

- "Art History and Drawing in Spain." Focused on Spanish art history and studio art, this study tour is led by EMU faculty. Lectures, tutorials, and small group discussions are combined with site visits. Participants stay in hotels. In 1992 the cost was approximately $3,000 and included round-trip airfare from New York, room, some meals, transportation, tuition, fees, and excursions. The program takes place for three weeks during the spring. Group size is limited to 25 participants.

ELIGIBILITY: Applications are accepted from all interested persons.

LOCATION: Destinations vary each year. See descriptions above for recent locations.

TIME OF YEAR: Time of year varies; see program descriptions above.

DURATION: Programs vary from three to four weeks.

AGE OF PARTICIPANTS: The average age of participants is usually between 30 and 40.

COMMENTS: Interested participants can be admitted to the university as "guest" students and either audit or receive academic credit for their work.

Ecotour Expeditions

P.O. Box 1066
Cambridge, MA 02238
Phone: (800) 688-1822
Fax: (617) 576-0552

INSTITUTION/ORGANIZATION: Founded in 1988, Ecotour Expeditions is a commercial tour operator that conducts study tours focused on ecology in the tropical forests of Latin America.

PROGRAM: "Tropical Forest Expeditions." Focused on ecological studies, these expeditions provide students with the opportunity to spend time in the forest examining plant and animal life. Forest walks, boat excursions, and clinics in plant and animal identification are conducted. The guides are drawn from many fields, including ornithology, herpetology, and limnology. Teachers and group leaders can tailor the content to suit their particular curricular objectives if desired. Groups are usually no larger than 10 to 15.

ELIGIBILITY: Applications are accepted from all interested persons.

LOCATION: Destinations vary each year. Previous expeditions have taken place in South America.

TIME OF YEAR: Options are available throughout the year.

DURATION: Projects run for one to three weeks.

ACCOMMODATIONS: Participants live in hotels and air-conditioned boat cabins.

COST: In 1992, project costs ranged from $1,650 to $1,950 and included international airfare, room, and board.

➤➤➤

Elderhostel

75 Federal Street
Boston, MA 02110
Phone: (617) 426-7788

INSTITUTION/ORGANIZATION: Founded in 1975, Elderhostel is a nonprofit educational organization that specializes in programs for the 60+ traveler. Elderhostel coordinates a network of more than 1,600 educational and cultural institutions that host their programs.

PROGRAMS: Elderhostel programs are noncredit academic (liberal arts) learning adventures. Program focuses vary depending on the host institution. Instructors are required to be members of the host institution's faculty or staff, or experts in the designated fields. The maximum group size is 40.

ELIGIBILITY: Participants must be at least 60 years old, though a younger spouse or companion may accompany age-eligible participants.

LOCATION: Elderhostel programs take place throughout the United States and in 44 other countries, including Bermuda, Brazil, Canada, China, Costa Rica, England, Scotland, Wales, France, Israel, Italy, Japan, Kenya, Mexico, Portugal, Spain, and Turkey.

TIME OF YEAR: Varies, depending on the host institution.

DURATION: Programs generally run from two to four weeks.

ACCOMMODATIONS: Participants live in hotels, tents, hostels, private homes, or college dormitories.

COST: Program costs generally range from $880 to $5,000 and include round-trip airfare, room, board, classes, admissions, excursions, and all ground transportation.

AGE OF PARTICIPANTS: The average age of participants is usually about 68.

PERSONS WITH DISABILITIES: Some host campuses have facilities to accommodate students with disabilities. Check with Elderhostel.

➤⇒➤⇒➤

Empire State College

International Programs
28 Union Avenue
Saratoga Springs, NY 12866
Phone: (518) 587-2100
Fax: (518) 587-4382

INSTITUTION/ORGANIZATION: Founded in 1971, Empire State College is a nonprofit institution that is part of the State University of New York. The college is a member of the Council on International Educational Exchange.

PROGRAMS:
- "Comparative Public Policy." This study program, designed for those interested in comparative public policy in the United States and the United Kingdom, takes place in England and focuses on such issues as health care, labor, criminal justice, and the environment. Led by faculty from Empire State College, lectures, tutorials, and small group discussions are combined with site visits. Participants also have the opportunity to meet with distinguished British faculty. Excursions include meetings with professionals in the health and social services industries. This program usually runs for about 10 days during the summer. Participants stay in college dormitories in the city of Bristol. The program costs approximately $1,400. The maximum group size is 40, and the average age of participants is usually about 37.
- "International Business in the EEC." Designed for those interested in international business and the European Economic

Community, this program is led by faculty from Empire State College. Lectures, tutorials, and small group discussions are combined with visits to businesses and industrial sites in Europe, as well as economic policy agencies. Meetings with professionals in these areas are arranged. The program runs for about 10 days in the late spring. Destinations vary within the EEC but have included Germany, Italy, and Belgium. Participants stay in hotels or pensions. The approximate cost ranges from $1,200 to $1,500. The maximum group size is 20, and the average age of participants is usually about 37.

ELIGIBILITY: Applications are accepted from all interested persons.

LOCATION: Destinations vary each year. Previous destinations have included England, Germany, Italy, and Belgium.

TIME OF YEAR: Spring and summer.

DURATION: Programs run for about 10 days.

PERSONS WITH DISABILITIES: Empire State will try to accommodate disabled persons whenever possible.

▶⇒▶⇒▶

English Literature Summer Schools

c/o Wilson & Lake International
468 "B" Street, Suite #3
Ashland, OR 97520
Phone: (503) 488-3350

INSTITUTION/ORGANIZATION: Founded in 1978, English Literature Summer Schools is a commercial tour operator that specializes in literary, cultural, historical, and study holidays.

PROGRAM: "The Writer and the Environment." This study holiday, complete with lectures given by university faculty, explores the parts of England that influenced its great writers. Participants discuss the works of the Brontës, Jane Austen, Wordsworth, Coleridge, D. H. Lawrence, Ted Hughes, and Shakespeare, and then make excursions to the places that inspired these writers.

ELIGIBILITY: Applications are accepted from all interested persons.

LOCATION: Program is based in Sheffield, England, with excursions to Grasmere, Stratford, Eastwood, and Newstead Abbey, Haworth and Derbyshire Peak District.

TIME OF YEAR: Summer and fall.

DURATION: The program described above runs for two weeks.

ACCOMMODATIONS: Participants stay in private homes with host families. Hotel accommodations can be arranged for a supplementary charge.

COST: Cost is $1,290 and includes all expenses except airfare to Sheffield.

PERSONS WITH DISABILITIES: Some alternative arrangements can be made for outings.

COMMENTS: Usually about 40 percent of the participants are from the United States. English Literature Summer Schools also offers special programs for professionals, and designs study holidays for groups.

Eurocentres

c/o Council Travel
205 East 42nd Street, 16th Floor
New York, NY 10017
Phone: (212) 661-1450
Fax: (212) 972-3231

INSTITUTION/ORGANIZATION: Eurocentres is a nonprofit organization comprised of 28 language institutes in nine countries offering courses in six languages.

PROGRAMS: Courses in German, French, Japanese, Italian, Spanish, and English are available. Special refresher programs for teachers are offered, along with holiday and intensive courses for beginning to advanced students. All instructors are native speakers of the languages, and classes are usually no larger than 15 students each.

ELIGIBILITY: Applications are accepted from all interested persons.

LOCATION: Germany, Switzerland, France, Japan, Italy, Spain, the United Kingdom, and the United States.

TIME OF YEAR: Options are available throughout the year.

DURATION: Programs range from two to 14 weeks.

ACCOMMODATIONS: Hotels, private homes, and flats.

COST: Varies, depending on the program and length of study. Contact Council Travel for a Eurocentres booklet and course calendar.

PERSONS WITH DISABILITIES: Eurocentres will accommodate persons with disabilities whenever possible, but must be informed of the disability in advance to allow ample time for necessary arrangements.

The following Eurocentres are partially, if not entirely, wheelchair-accessible: Germany (Köln), France (La Rochelle), and England (Cambridge and London Victoria).

COMMENTS: Scholarships are available for people with demonstrated need and who would benefit professionally from language training.

▶⇒▶⇒▶

Farm Tours, Etc.

1150 North Gem Street
Tulare, CA 93274
Phone and fax: (209) 688-2479

INSTITUTION/ORGANIZATION: Founded in 1986, Farm Tours is a commercial tour operator that sponsors agriculture-related study tours and farm visits.

PROGRAM: "French Countryside Wine Tour." This study tour focuses on wine grape growing and wine making and is accompanied by professional farmers and wine makers. Each group is limited to eight participants.

ELIGIBILITY: Participants should enjoy wine. There are no minimum or maximum ages for participation, but those under 18 are not able to sample the wines in some places.

LOCATION: Destinations in France include Paris, Blois, St. Emillion, Beaune, and Epernay.

TIME OF YEAR: Spring, summer, and fall.

DURATION: Two weeks.

ACCOMMODATIONS: Hotels.

COST: The cost is $100 a day, which covers lodging (based on double occupancy), breakfast, dinner, and land transportation. Airfare is additional.

AGE OF PARTICIPANTS: The average age of participants is usually about 50.

PERSONS WITH DISABILITIES: Farm Tours works to facilitate the participation of persons with disabilities.

➤⟹➤⟹➤

Federation of Ontario Naturalists

Canadian Nature Tours
355 Lesmill Road
Don Millis, Ontario
CANADA
Phone: (416) 444-8419
Fax: (416) 444-9866

INSTITUTION/ORGANIZATION: Founded in 1931, Federation of Ontario Naturalists is a nonprofit organization that offers natural history tours across Canada and around the world. Dedicated to exploring and protecting natural areas and wildlife, the Federation chooses destinations carefully for their natural history interest. The organization's goal is to have 10 percent of the cost of each individual's tour fund its environmental work.

PROGRAMS: "Canadian Nature Tours." These tours provide participants with firsthand experience of natural areas and wilderness. Up to 50 different tours are offered, focusing on such areas as birds, botany, hiking, photography, marine life, canoeing techniques, culture/history, conservation issues, geology, and mammals. Led by volunteers knowledgeable in natural history, groups are usually limited to 10 people.

ELIGIBILITY: Participants must be members of the Federation of Ontario Naturalists or of the Canadian Nature Federation; in 1992 annual membership cost $31 (U.S. dollars).

LOCATION: Destinations vary each year. Previous locations have included Canada and France, and the Galapagos Islands.

TIME OF YEAR: Options are available throughout the year.

DURATION: Tours run from one to two weeks.

ACCOMMODATIONS: Participants live in hotels, tents, and boats.

COST: Varies depending on the destination. In 1992 tours cost between $600 and $6,000.

AGE OF PARTICIPANTS: The average age of participants is usually about 53.

▶▶═▶▶═▶▶

Field Studies Council

Central Services
Preston Montford
Montford Bridge
Shrewsbury SY4 1HW
UNITED KINGDOM
Phone: (44) 743 850164 (programs outside the U.K.)
        (44) 743 850674 (programs within the U.K.)
Fax: (44) 743 850178

INSTITUTION/ORGANIZATION: Founded in 1943, the Field Studies Council (FSC) is a British nonprofit organization that conducts courses in the United Kingdom as well as overseas. The Field Studies Council has nine field centers located in England and Wales.

PROGRAMS: FSC sponsors programs in the United Kingdom and other various locations abroad.
- FSC offers short courses at its nine residential centers throughout England and Wales. More than 400 courses are available in a wide range of subjects including natural history, biology and conservation, flowers and other plants, geology, landscape, and climate, archaeology, history, and architecture, painting, drawing, photography, and crafts. The residential teaching staff all have degrees in the appropriate academic subjects. Weekend through one-week courses are available. Participants live at the center.
- "Special Interest Holidays." Sponsored by the Field Studies Council overseas, these holidays are run in various locations throughout the world. Concerned with environmental education, courses include the study of birds, flowers, butterflies, and landscapes, as well as painting and photography, depending on the program location. All tours are led by tutors who are experts in the appropriate subjects. Accommodations vary, depending on the trip. Programs run from one to four weeks. Groups usually consist of 10 to 14 people.

ELIGIBILITY: Applications are accepted from all interested persons.
LOCATION: The Field Studies Centers have nine locations in England and Wales. Destinations vary each year for the special-interest holidays, though many programs are repeated annually. Previous destinations have included Sweden, New Zealand, Galapagos Islands,

Iceland, Malta, Poland, Cyprus, Nepal, England, and Wales, among others.
TIME OF YEAR: Options are available throughout the year.
DURATION: Courses at the Field Studies Centers in England and Wales run from a weekend to one week; special-interest holidays run from one to four weeks.
ACCOMMODATIONS: Vary depending on the program.
COST: For programs in England and Wales, costs range from approximately $130 (75 British pounds) for a weekend to $350 (199 British pounds) for a week, and include room and board, tuition, and transportation during the program. Special-interest holidays range from $880 (500 British pounds) to about $5,275 (3,000 British pounds), depending on the program.
PERSONS WITH DISABILITIES: Persons with disabilities are handled on a case-by-case basis and accepted whenever possible.

➤➤➤

Folkways Institute

14600 SE Aldridge Road
Portland, OR 97236
Phone: (800) 225-4666
Fax: (503) 658-8672

INSTITUTION/ORGANIZATION: Founded in 1984, Folkways Institute is a U.S.-based international education organization and commercial tour operator that offers courses, workshops, and study tours to various overseas and domestic locations.

PROGRAM: "Senior Studies Program." The focus of the trips varies. Some may emphasize natural history; others might focus on cultural exploration. Participants visit historic, cultural, and natural sites, depending on the program focus, and learn through experience, observation, presentations, and lectures given by local experts. Small group discussions are also encouraged. Program directors accompany the group to coordinate and facilitate all activities. Groups vary in size from 16 to 20 people.
ELIGIBILITY: Participants must be at least 55 years old and active.
LOCATION: Previous destinations have included Egypt, China, Nepal, India, Tibet, Bhutan, Myanmar, Thailand, Vietnam, Indonesia, Kenya,

Botswana, Costa Rica, Argentina, Peru, England, Ireland, Switzerland, Austria, Greece, Turkey, Italy, and New Zealand.

TIME OF YEAR: Varies; check with Folksways Institute.

DURATION: Programs generally run from one to four weeks.

ACCOMMODATIONS: Participants live in hotels, tents, lodges, and cabins.

COST: Program costs generally range from $1,500 to $3,800 and cover room, most meals, instruction by program director, lectures, and program preparation materials.

➤⇒➤⇒➤

Footloose & Fancy Free

69-71 Banbury Road
Oxford OX2 6PE
UNITED KINGDOM
Phone: (44) 865 310355
Fax: (44) 865 310299

INSTITUTION/ORGANIZATION: Founded in 1976, Footloose & Fancy Free is a commercial tour operator. It was launched with the idea of traveling on foot through parts of Europe, with luggage transported en route.

PROGRAM: Participants create their own itinerary from five possible locations in England, France, and Italy. They decide where to start and stop as well as where to stay each night. Luggage is transported by Footloose & Fancy Free to each stop. Participants are given a carefully annotated map; a guidebook of recommended places to eat, drink, and find the best local specialties for picnics; a list of background reading on the area; and recommendations on what to bring and what to wear for walking.

ELIGIBILITY: Applications accepted from all interested persons in good health.

LOCATIONS: Châteaux of the Loire, Cinqueterre, the Cotswolds, the Dordogne, and Tuscany-Chianti.

TIME OF YEAR: April to October; other dates available upon request.

DURATION: Trips are arranged according to participants' needs.

ACCOMMODATIONS: Participants stay in hotels and inns in one of three different grades, depending on availability and the traveler's budget.

COST: There is a reservation charge of $300 per person traveling. Cost varies from about $45 to $250 per person per night and includes accommodation in a double room with twin beds. Airfare is not included.

▶=▶=▶

Foreign Language/Study Abroad Programs

5935 SW 64th Avenue
South Miami, FL 33143
Phone: (212) 662-1090 or (305) 662-1090
Fax: (305) 662-2907

INSTITUTION/ORGANIZATION: Founded in 1971 and administered by Louise Harber, this organization offers intensive language programs in Europe, Asia, Latin, and North America.

PROGRAMS: Language offerings include French, Spanish, Portuguese, German, Italian, Russian, Japanese, Mandarin Chinese, and Dutch. Participants have the option to choose from the program types described below:
- "Intensive Contemporary Language Courses." These courses are for all levels from beginner to advanced. Classes are small and intensive; emphasis is placed on the spoken language. Also suited for the person who needs to learn the language for career advancement.
- "Super Intensive Refresher/Review & Special Interest Language Programs." Developed for teachers and other professionals interested in brushing up on language skills and gaining firsthand experience of the political, social, and economic changes occurring in the country of interest. In addition to small classes, participants have the option to receive private tutoring to concentrate on pronunciation, phonetics, conversation, grammar, etc.
- "International Homestays/Home Language Lessons." This program provides the opportunity to experience total language and cultural immersion. Participants stay in a private home and take language lessons in the country and region of their choice. Designed for adults who want to study the language outside of a traditional classroom setting. Adults are placed in the homes of certified teachers who are native speakers. (There is

also a similar program for high school and college students.)

ELIGIBILITY: Applications are accepted from all interested persons.

LOCATION: Destinations include Canada, France, Germany, Austria, Costa Rica, Mexico, Spain, Italy, Portugal, Holland, Russia, Japan, Taiwan, England, Ireland, Scotland, and Argentina.

TIME OF YEAR: Most programs are offered throughout the year.

DURATION: The International Homestays program gives participants the option to study for a minimum of one week; the other programs generally require a minimum of two weeks. Duration beyond the required minimum stay is usually flexible.

ACCOMMODATIONS: Students live in private homes, residence halls, and other facilities if specially requested (e.g., apartments).

COST: Varies, depending on the program, destination, and length of stay. Contact Foreign Language/Study Abroad Programs for more information.

COMMENTS: This organization offers numerous study programs that are primarily designed for the adult learner, although interested students can obtain college credit for participation. Courses in most languages are offered in more than one city and/or country.

▶⇒▶⇒▶

Forum International

91 Gregory Lane, #21
Pleasant Hill, CA 94523
Phone: (415) 671-2900
Fax: (415) 946-1500

INSTITUTION/ORGANIZATION: Founded in 1965, Forum International is a nonprofit educational organization dedicated to ecotourism.

PROGRAM: "Environment, Tourism, Culture." This program includes more than 1,200 vacations focused on exploring nature, culture, and social conditions, with special emphasis on environmental integrity, social responsibility, and human health. Each vacation is limited to 20 participants.

ELIGIBILITY: Applications are accepted from all interested persons.

LOCATION: Worldwide in 135 countries throughout Africa, Asia, the South Pacific, South and North America, and Europe.

TIME OF YEAR: Options are available throughout the year.

DURATION: Eight to 10 days, on the average.

ACCOMMODATIONS: Participants live in hotels, tents, hostels, private homes, and college dormitories.

COST: Varies with the program; generally $50 to $150 per day. This includes transportation within the country, accommodations, food, and instruction.

AGE OF PARTICIPANTS: The average age of participants is usually about 40.

PERSONS WITH DISABILITIES: Special arrangements will be made for groups of persons with disabilities.

▶⟹▶⟹▶

Foundation for Field Research

P.O. Box 2010
Alpine, CA 91903
Phone: (619) 445-9264
Fax: (619) 445-1893

INSTITUTION/ORGANIZATION: Founded in 1982, the Foundation for Field Research is a nonprofit organization that links volunteers to scientists requiring field labor and funds. In this way, members of the public subsidize research projects by volunteering to assist scientists in the field.

PROGRAM: The Foundation looks for volunteers to assist on scientific research expeditions. Focused on archaeology, marine biology, botany, folklore, marine archaeology, and large mammal studies, projects are led by experts in the field. On-site instruction is provided by the researchers. Expeditions are limited to 18 volunteers.

ELIGIBILITY: Applications are accepted from all interested persons.

LOCATION: Grenada, Europe, Mali, Canada, and Mexico.

TIME OF YEAR: Options are available throughout the year.

DURATION: Projects run from five days to three months.

ACCOMMODATIONS: Tents.

COST: The cost ranges between $395 to $1,672 (depending on the project) and includes lodging, meals, transportation during the project, and funds for the researcher.

AGE OF PARTICIPANTS: The average age of participants is usually about 55.

PERSONS WITH DISABILITIES: Some projects can take persons with wheelchairs. Check with the Foundation.

COMMENTS: Interested students have the option to earn academic credit for participation. Some funding is available for students and teachers.

►►⇒►►⇒►►

Foundation for International Education

121 Cascade Court
River Falls, WI 54022
Phone: (715) 425-2718
Fax: (715) 425-5101

INSTITUTION/ORGANIZATION: Founded in 1978, the Foundation for International Education is a nonprofit organization that arranges international work experiences for professionals.

PROGRAMS:
- "Visiting Social Service Worker." This program gives persons in the social service field the opportunity to spend two weeks working in an overseas agency. Individuals are placed continuously throughout the year in most English-speaking countries, including England, Ireland, Scotland, Australia, and New Zealand. Participants live in private homes. The approximate cost is $1,400 for the United Kingdom and includes registration, airfare, room, and board; Australia and New Zealand are approximately $2,100 and cover the same expenses. Interested persons must be experienced social service workers.
- "Visiting Teaching." This program provides teachers with the opportunity to spend three weeks working with their counterparts in overseas schools. Individuals are placed continuously throughout the year in most English-speaking countries, including England, Ireland, Australia, New Zealand, and Scotland. Participants live in private homes. The cost is approximately $1,500 for the United Kingdom and covers registration, transportation, room, and board; Australia and New Zealand are approximately $2,200 and cover the same expenses. Interested persons must be experienced teachers.

ELIGIBILITY: Varies according to program. See program descriptions above.

LOCATION: Most English-speaking countries, including England, Ireland, Scotland, Australia, and New Zealand.

TIME OF YEAR: Options are available throughout the year.

DURATION: Programs vary from two to three weeks.

PERSONS WITH DISABILITIES: The Foundation tries to accommodate persons with disabilities.

COMMENTS: An optional orientation program for those participating in the "Visiting Teaching" program takes place in St. Paul, Minnesota.

▶⇒▶⇒▶

The French-American Exchange

Language Programs in France
313 C Street, NE
Washington, DC 20002
Phone: (202) 546-9612
Fax: (202) 337-1118

INSTITUTION/ORGANIZATION: Founded in 1987, the French-American Exchange is a nonprofit organization that seeks to promote language study abroad for French and American citizens.

PROGRAM: "Intensive Summer Program." Intensive French language courses are available on all levels along with elective courses in French civilization, literature, cinema, business French, and tourism. Instructors are native speakers of the language with university degrees and two years of experience. Instruction is in French and includes lectures, small group discussions, and private tutoring. All programs include a weekend in Paris.

ELIGIBILITY: Interested persons should be at least 18 years of age and have a high school diploma.

LOCATION: Montpellier, France.

TIME OF YEAR: Summer.

DURATION: Students have the option to participate from four to eight weeks.

ACCOMMODATIONS: Private homes, apartments, dormitories, and hotels.

COST: In 1992 the program cost about $2,310 per month, which included tuition, housing, some meals, round-trip airfare from New York, fees, and field trips.

AGE OF PARTICIPANTS: The average age of participants is usually about 21.

PERSONS WITH DISABILITIES: Applicants are considered on a case-by-case basis; accessibility is very limited.

COMMENTS: About 30 percent of the students are usually from the United States.

▶▶═▶▶═▶▶

The French & American Study Center

12.14 Boulevard Carnot
B.P. 176
14104 Lisieux Cedex
FRANCE
Phone: (33) 31312201

INSTITUTION/ORGANIZATION: Founded in 1975, The French and American Study Center is a nonprofit language institute.

PROGRAM: "French in France." French language courses are taught by speakers of Parisian French with diplomas. Lectures and tutorials are combined with small group discussions.

ELIGIBILITY: Applications are accepted from all interested persons.

LOCATION: Lisieux, Normandy, and the French Riviera, France.

TIME OF YEAR: Options are available throughout the year.

DURATION: Participants have the option to study from one to 10 weeks.

ACCOMMODATIONS: Private homes and châteaux.

COST: Approximate cost for one week is $620, which includes tuition, room, board (two meals daily), and excursions on Saturdays.

AGE OF PARTICIPANTS: The average age of participants is usually about 25.

PERSONS WITH DISABILITIES: Persons with disabilities are accommodated if and when possible.

▶▶═▶▶═▶▶

Fudan Museum Foundation

1522 Schoolhouse Road
Ambler, PA 19002
Phone: (215) 699-6448

INSTITUTION/ORGANIZATION: Founded in 1900, the Fudan Museum Foundation is a nonprofit educational organization.

PROGRAM: The Foundation sponsors a study and archaeological excavation program at the Sino-American Field School of Archaeology. With a focus on Chinese cultural history and archaeology, lectures and digs are conducted by experts. Instruction is in English, and participants are given a small stipend or living allowance. The maximum group size is 20.

ELIGIBILITY: Applications are accepted from all interested persons.

LOCATION: Shanghai, Xi'an, and Beijing, China.

TIME OF YEAR: Summer.

DURATION: Five weeks.

ACCOMMODATIONS: College guesthouses.

COST: $3,700, which includes airfare (round-trip from New York), room and board, excursions, and ground transportation.

AGE OF PARTICIPANTS: The average age of participants is usually about 30.

PERSONS WITH DISABILITIES: The Fudan Museum Foundation is open to people with disabilities.

COMMENTS: If you are a student, it is possible to obtain undergraduate or graduate credit for this program.

➤➡⇒➤

Galápagos Travel
P.O. Box 1357
San Juan Bautista, CA 95045
Phone: (800) 969-9014
Fax: (408) 623-2923

INSTITUTION/ORGANIZATION: Founded in 1990, the Galápagos Travel is a commercial tour operator that specializes in trips to the Galápagos Islands and publishes natural history books.

PROGRAM: "Natural History/Photography Workshops in the Galápagos Islands." Participants tour the islands on a chartered 12-passenger yacht, observing and photographing the wildlife. Most tours are led by Barry Boyce, author of *A Traveler's Guide to the Galápagos Islands,* published by Galápagos Travel in 1990. Each evening, participants can attend an informal lecture on Galápagos natural history and photography.

ELIGIBILITY: Applications are accepted from all interested persons.
LOCATION: The Galápagos Islands, Ecuador.
TIME OF YEAR: Every other month throughout the year.
DURATION: Workshops run from 11 to 14 days.
ACCOMMODATIONS: Twelve-passenger yacht.
COST: The cost is $2,350, which includes meals, accommodations, and surface transportation. Airfare is additional.
AGE OF PARTICIPANTS: Most participants are about 35 to 65 years old.
COMMENTS: Participants are usually from the United States.

GATE–Global Awareness Through Experience

936 Winnebago Street
LaCrosse, WI 54601
Phone: (608) 791-0462
Fax: (608) 782-6301

INSTITUTION/ORGANIZATION: GATE, sponsored by the Congregation of the Franciscan Sisters of Perpetual Adoration, a nonprofit organization, has been operating alternative tourism programs for 10 years.

PROGRAM: In cooperation with ecumenical faith communities in the target countries, GATE offers the opportunity to learn from the poor as well as social and political analysts, theologians, and economists. GATE connects participants with the lives of ordinary people. Participants attend lectures and go on visits to local communities. Presenters have advanced degrees.
ELIGIBILITY: Applications are accepted from all interested persons at least 21 years of age.
LOCATION: Mexico, Nicaragua, Guatemala, Germany, Czechoslovakia, Zimbabwe.
TIME OF YEAR: Options are available throughout the year.
DURATION: Usually 10 to 14 days.
ACCOMMODATIONS: Hotels, hostels, and private homes.
COST: Varies according to program. Costs generally range from $400 to $900, not including airfare.
PERSONS WITH DISABILITIES: Accepted if the disability is manageable in the environment.

AGE OF PARTICIPANTS: The average age of participants generally ranges from 35 to 45.

▸⇒▸⇒▸

German Wine Academy

P.O. Box 1705
D-6500 Mainz
GERMANY
Phone: (0) 61 31-28290 or (212) 213-7028 (ask for Monika Neufang)

INSTITUTION/ORGANIZATION: Founded in 1974, the German Wine Academy is a commercial operation that offers seminars in English for persons interested in improving their knowledge of German wine.

PROGRAMS: Wine seminars are offered annually on basic and advanced levels. Also available is a seminar on "Wine and Historical Germany." Instructors include industry professionals, wine merchants, and the program director of the Academy. Lectures and small group discussions are combined with wine tasting. Seminars are limited to about 40 people.

ELIGIBILITY: Applications are accepted from all interested persons.

LOCATION: Destinations in Germany include Kloster Eberbach, the Mosel Valley, the Nahe region, and Rheinhessen region.

TIME OF YEAR: Summer and fall.

DURATION: One week.

ACCOMMODATIONS: Hotels.

COST: The seminars range in cost from approximately $1,028 (1,640 German marks) to $1,757 (2,800 German marks).

AGE OF PARTICIPANTS: The average age of participants is usually between 20 and 30.

PERSONS WITH DISABILITIES: Persons with disabilities are welcome, although seminars include visiting wineries that are not accessible.

COMMENTS: About 70 to 80 percent of participants are usually from the United States.

Global Volunteers

375 East Little Canada Road
St. Paul, MN 55117
Phone: (800) 487-1074
Fax: (612) 482-0915

INSTITUTION/ORGANIZATION: Founded in 1984, Global Volunteers is a nonprofit, nonsectarian voluntary service organization concerned with helping to establish a foundation for peace through mutual international understanding.

PROGRAM: Global Volunteers sponsors short-term service opportunities worldwide. Teams of volunteers work alongside the local people on human and economic development projects. Volunteers work in teams of eight to 12 persons.
ELIGIBILITY: Applications are accepted from all interested persons.
LOCATION: Destinations have included Jamaica, Tanzania, Guatemala, Mexico, Poland, Tonga, and Indonesia.
TIME OF YEAR: Options are available throughout the year.
DURATION: Projects run from two to three weeks.
ACCOMMODATIONS: Hotels, private homes, schools, and churches.
COST: Ranges from $600 to $1,900 and includes room, board, in-country transportation, team leader, administrative fees, and project costs. Airfare is additional.
AGE OF PARTICIPANTS: Participants are generally in their 30s, 40s, or 60s.

Goethe-Institut

Postfach 800727
D-8000 München 80
GERMANY
Phone: (49) 85 41868-200
Fax: (49) 85 41868-202

INSTITUTION/ORGANIZATION: Founded in 1952 and affiliated with the German government, the Goethe-Institut is a nonprofit organization offering instruction in the German language.

PROGRAM: The language institute offers German courses taught by instructors with advanced degrees who have completed a special training program in German as a foreign language. Lectures and tutorials are combined with small group discussions.

ELIGIBILITY: Participants must be at least 18 years old.

LOCATION: Institutes are located throughout Germany in 16 cities.

TIME OF YEAR: Options are available throughout the year.

DURATION: Participants can study for a four- or eight-week session.

ACCOMMODATIONS: Hotels, hostels, private homes, and college dormitories.

COST: Approximately $1,056 (1,750 German marks), which includes instruction only. Rooms usually cost between $210 and $330 (350 and 550 German marks) per month; meals generally range from $3 to $7 (5 to 10 German marks) each.

AGE OF PARTICIPANTS: The average age of participants is usually between about 25 and 30.

PERSONS WITH DISABILITIES: Persons with disabilities will be accepted if at all possible; there are rooms suitable for persons with wheelchairs in Mannheim.

COMMENTS: Interested students can receive academic credit for participation from the University of Connecticut.

➤⇒➤⇒➤

Professor Polly Guerin

c/o Fashion Institute of Technology
FBM Dept.
227 West 27th Street
New York, NY 10001
Phone: (212) 760-7662

INSTITUTION/ORGANIZATION: Polly Guerin, a historian whose specialties are fashion and lace, is an independent commercial tour leader.

PROGRAM: "Costume Museum Tour and Vintage Clothing/Lace Shopping Tour." This independent tour, developed and led by Professor Polly Guerin, focuses on the history of costume, lace, Victoriana, and vintage collectibles. Based in London, the program includes a curatorial tour of fashion exhibitions at the Victoria & Albert Museum. Also included are excursions to the Bethnal-Green Children's Museum, the Friends of Fashion London Museum, and Bath Costume

Museum. Vintage and antique markets are among other places of interest. Lectures are provided by Professor Guerin. This tour is designed for the professional adult and is offered annually.

ELIGIBILITY: Applications are accepted from all interested persons.

LOCATION: Destinations in England include London, Brighton, Worthing-by-the-Sea, Bath, Oxford, and Stratford-upon-Avon.

TIME OF YEAR: July.

DURATION: The tour runs for nine days.

ACCOMMODATIONS: Hotels.

COST: Approximately $3,000, which includes international airfare, room, escorted touring, lectures, and small receptions at museums, lace emporiums, and antique centers. Main meals are additional.

Solomon R. Guggenheim Museum

Art-Study Travel Program
1071 Fifth Avenue
New York, NY 10128
Phone: (212) 423-3500/3600
Fax: (212) 423-3650

INSTITUTION/ORGANIZATION: The Guggenheim Museum is a nonprofit cultural institution that collects, exhibits, preserves, and interprets the visual arts of the 20th century to encourage greater visual literacy, aesthetic perception, and intellectual curiosity.

PROGRAMS: "Art-Study Travel Programs." Programs include tours of museums and seminal monuments of modern art and architecture with curators and directors. Participants attend receptions and view leading private collections. Visits to artists' studios and attandance at gala previews are also included.

ELIGIBILITY: Participants must be adults and members of the Guggenheim at the Fellow Associate level ($250) and above.

LOCATION: Programs primarily take place in major European and American cities and art centers, but there are also some programs offered in Asia and South America.

TIME OF YEAR: Options are available throughout the year.

DURATION: From three to five or 10 to 14 days.

ACCOMMODATIONS: Hotels.

COST: From $2,000 to $5,000 for a domestic program and from

$6,000 to $8,000 for a foreign program, including roundtrip airfare, accommodations, ground transportation, museum entrance fees, most meals, porterage, tipping, and a tax-deductible contribution.

PERSONS WITH DISABILITIES: Programs are open to persons with disabilities but entail much walking and a hectic pace. Also, many foreign institutions, museums, and private collections are not equipped for participants with disabilities.

▶▶⇒▶▶⇒▶▶

Heritage Touring

172 Bellevue Avenue
Newport, RI 02840
Phone: (401) 849-5286
Fax: (401) 849-5878

In the United Kingdom:

754 The Square
Cattistock, Dorchester
Dorset DT2 OJD
UNITED KINGDOM
Phone: (44) 300 20671
Fax: (44) 300 21042

INSTITUTION/ORGANIZATION: Founded in 1988, Heritage Touring is a commercial tour operator that offers short tours focusing on great British authors.

PROGRAMS: Participants take guided tours through the countryside once inhabited by some of England's most famous authors. Each tour focuses on a single author—Thomas Hardy, Jane Austen, Charles Dickens, or Edward Rutherfurd—and leads into often unfamiliar parts of Britain, bringing history and literature to life. Each tour is escorted by a trained, experienced, professional tourist guide, knowledgeable about the author and the area concerned.

ELIGIBILITY: Applications are accepted from all interested persons.
LOCATION: England.
TIME OF YEAR: From May through October.
DURATION: Tours last six days/nights.

ACCOMMODATIONS: Hotels, inns, and well-appointed farmhouses. All rooms have private bathrooms.

COST: About $1,225 per person, which includes six nights accommodation plus full board, a full-time guide, transport on all touring days, and entry fees. Single rooms are available for about $18 extra per person per night. Airfare is not included.

AGE OF PARTICIPANTS: The average age is usually about 50.

PERSONS WITH DISABILITIES: Persons with disabilities are welcome.

Home and Host International

2445 Park Avenue
Minneapolis, MN 55404
Phone: (800) SOVIET U
Fax: (612) 871-8853

INSTITUTION/ORGANIZATION: Founded in 1990, Home and Host International is a commercial tour operator emphasizing cultural exchange. This company customizes homestays and apartment stays plus any special interest activities desired, such as language study and adventure travel.

PROGRAM: Customized homestays are structured to meet the traveler's needs. A variety of options is available, ranging from the deluxe homestay, which provides you with an English-speaking host who acts as your private guide, transfers, all meals, private room, and entrance fees, to a bed-and-breakfast stay that includes a private room in an English-speaking home, transfers, and meals. Home and Host International can also place you with a host who shares your interests and/or area of expertise.

ELIGIBILITY: Applications are accepted from all interested persons.

LOCATION: Homestays can be arranged in Russia, Ukraine, Uzbekistan, Kazakhstan, Byelorussia, Azerbaijan, Georgia, Tadzhikistan, Moldavia, Kirghizia, Lithuania, Armenia, Turkmenistan, Latvia, Estonia, Costa Rica, China, Argentina, and Chile.

TIME OF YEAR: Options are available throughout the year.

DURATION: As long or as short as the traveler wishes.

COST: Generally, $80 per person per day; an escorted homestay costs about $125 per day.

AGE OF PARTICIPANTS: The average age of participants is usually between 40 and 65.

PERSONS WITH DISABILITIES: The organization is pleased to accommodate persons with disabilities.

COMMENTS: Funding is available for students for five to 50 percent of the cost of the homestay.

►►⇒►►⇒►►

Home Language International

Reservations Office
17 Royal Crescent
Ramsgate
Kent CT11 9PE
UNITED KINGDOM
Phone: (44) 843 851116
Fax: (44) 843 590300

INSTITUTION/ORGANIZATION: Home Language International sponsors language/homestay programs in Europe, Asia, and Latin America.

PROGRAMS: These programs provide participants with the opportunity to live with a private teacher while learning a language. All instructors have either a teaching certificate recognized by the state or a university degree; homes are inspected by the organization. Languages taught include French, German, Italian, Spanish, Portuguese, Chinese, Russian, Japanese, and English, and are available on all levels. A special program for executives is also offered.

ELIGIBILITY: Applications are accepted from all interested persons.

LOCATION: France, Germany, Italy, Spain, Argentina, Canary Islands, Portugal, Taiwan, Russia, Japan, Great Britain, Ireland, and Malta.

TIME OF YEAR: Options are available throughout the year.

DURATION: Participants can choose the length of time they wish to study; the minimum is one week.

ACCOMMODATIONS: Private teacher's home.

COST: Varies, but all prices include accommodations, tuition, and meals. Airfare is additional.

PERSONS WITH DISABILITIES: The programs are open to persons with disabilities.

COMMENTS: Participants have the option to share the study program with another person. Home Language can pair them with someone, or they can bring a companion.

▶⟹▶⟹▶

Hope College
Education Department
Holland, MI 49423
Phone: (616) 394-7733

INSTITUTION/ORGANIZATION: Founded in 1866, Hope College is a four-year liberal arts institution.

PROGRAM: "British Theme Teaching." This program concentrates on the "theme" teaching approach used in British schools and emphasizes elementary education. All instructors are professors regularly employed by Froehel College in England. The program includes visits to British schools. Group size is limited to 20 participants.

ELIGIBILITY: Participants should be teachers or prospective teachers at the elementary or middle school level.

LOCATION: The program primarily takes place in London, with excursions to Stratford, Bath, Greenwich, and Windsor.

TIME OF YEAR: Summer.

DURATION: Three weeks.

ACCOMMODATIONS: Participants live in an English manor house.

COST: The cost is approximately $3,200, which includes round-trip airfare from Detroit, room and partial board, field trips, and academic credit.

AGE OF PARTICIPANTS: Most participants are usually either in their early 20s or mid-40s.

PERSONS WITH DISABILITIES: Persons who are unable to walk cannot be accommodated due to the varied school visits and field trips.

COMMENTS: Participants can earn academic credit on the graduate level.

▶⟹▶⟹▶

Hostelling International/American Youth Hostels
P.O. Box 37613
Washington, DC 20013

Phone: (202) 783-6161
Fax: (202) 783-6171

INSTITUTION/ORGANIZATION: Founded in 1934, Hostelling International/American Youth Hostels is a member of Hostelling International, formerly the International Youth Hostel Federation. This nonprofit organization runs educational and recreational travel programs for all ages. Hostelling International American Youth Hostels is a member of the Council on International Educational Exchange.

PROGRAMS: "Discovery Tours" combine vacation adventures with enriching learning experiences, involving hiking, cycling, backpacking, and more. Tours are designed for five different age groups, from teens to the 50 + traveler. The hiking and cycling tours are available on varying levels according to physical ability. Specific tours include the Youth Tour for ages 15 to 18; the Young Adult Tour for ages 17 to 25; the Open Tour for ages 15 and over; the Adult Tour for ages 18 and over; and the 50 + Tour for ages 50 and over. Tour leaders have completed leadership training program. Thirty different tours with numerous departure dates are available. Groups are small: The maximum number of participants is nine.

ELIGIBILITY: Program participants must join Hostelling International American Youth Hostels. Membership costs range from $10 to $35 per year, according to age.

LOCATION: Recent destinations outside the United States include Canada, England, Wales, France, Italy, Switzerland, Scotland, Ireland, Germany, Austria, and the Netherlands.

TIME OF YEAR: Summer.

DURATION: Tours run from one to six weeks.

ACCOMMODATIONS: Tents and hostels.

COST: Ranges from $300 to $3,450, depending on the tour, and includes lodging, group-prepared meals, land transportation, group activities budget, administrative and leadership costs. Airfare is additional.

AGE OF PARTICIPANTS: Tours are designed for specific age groups. See program description above.

▶⟹▶⟹▶

Independent Travel in Asia

1878 South Peach Street
Medford, OR 97501
Phone: (503) 779-8039

INSTITUTION/ORGANIZATION: Founded in 1976, Independent Travel in Asia is a nonprofit organization that conducts organized intensive small-group programs designed to provide beginning travelers with the knowledge, skills, and confidence needed to travel independently, safely, and cheaply throughout the world.

PROGRAM: "Independent Travel in Asia: A Guided Introduction." Participants receive predeparture briefings on travel skills, language acquisition, health maintenance, and cross-cultural communication. Each group of about eight travelers is accompanied by one experienced travel facilitator, who helps orient the group to their environment while in Asia. Ed Kiefer, the program director, accompanies most groups. Kiefer is a former counselor, social worker, and teacher who has led these programs to India and Southeast Asia since 1976. Participants are taught to travel off the beaten track by public transport, to find low-cost accommodations, and to stay healthy while traveling. Special parents' and children's groups can be arranged, as well as programs for women, hikers, senior citizens, and others.

ELIGIBILITY: Participants must be in good health and at least moderate physical fitness.

LOCATION: Indonesia, Singapore, Malaysia, Thailand, Myanmar (Burma), India, Nepal, and Australia.

TIME OF YEAR: Spring and summer.

DURATION: Six weeks.

ACCOMMODATIONS: Hotels, hostels, simple family-run lodgings.

COST: About $3,000, which includes all food, lodgings, surface transportation, fees, and round-trip airfare from the West Coast.

PERSONS WITH DISABILITIES: All participants must be able to cope with rugged and primitive conditions, such as treks through jungles on foot or by local transportation.

AGE OF PARTICIPANTS: Participants range in age from about 25 to 60.

COMMENTS: Usually about 75 percent of the participants are from the United States.

▶▷▶▷▶

Indiana University at Bloomington

School of Continuing Studies
Owen Hall 202
Bloomington, IN 47405
Phone: (812) 855-0225

INSTITUTION/ORGANIZATION: Founded in 1820, Indiana University–Bloomington is a state institution that is a member of the Council on International Educational Exchange.

PROGRAM: IU sponsors a counseling education program on the Stonington campus of Bermuda College. Taught by Indiana University faculty or accredited therapists, lectures and small group discussions are combined with practical experience in the field. This program has been running for more than 20 years.
ELIGIBILITY: Participants must have a bachelor's degree.
LOCATION: Hamilton, Bermuda.
TIME OF YEAR: Summer.
DURATION: Two to four weeks.
ACCOMMODATIONS: Hotels and college dormitories.
COST: Contact the university.
COMMENTS: Although this is primarily a graduate program, it is not necessary to be enrolled in a graduate program in order to participate. Interested persons have the option to enroll on a noncredit basis.

▶▷▶▷▶

Indiana University at Indianapolis

English Department
425 University Blvd., #502L
Indianapolis, IN 46214
Phone: (317) 274-2171
Fax: (317) 274-2347

INSTITUTION/ORGANIZATION: Founded in 1972, Indiana University is a state institution that is a member of the Council on International Educational Exchange.

PROGRAM: "Literary Perspectives in England and Scotland." Participants explore the literary landscapes of English and Scottish writers while comparatively studying English, Scottish, Canadian, and American educational systems. Lectures, tutorials, and small group discussions are combined with visits to authors' homes and schools. Instructors hold doctorates in English. Group size is limited to 25 participants.

ELIGIBILITY: Participants are required to have an undergraduate degree.

LOCATION: In England, destinations include Durham, Ambleside (Lake District), York, London, and Stratford-upon-Avon. In Scotland, participants explore Edinburgh.

TIME OF YEAR: Summer.

DURATION: Five weeks.

ACCOMMODATIONS: College dormitories.

COST: The cost is $3,500, which includes airfare, room, two meals a day, tours to literary heritage centers, theater (Edinburgh, Stratford, and London), private coach transportation in Britain, and lectures. Tuition at the university is additional.

AGE OF PARTICIPANTS: The average age of participants is usually about 35.

PERSONS WITH DISABILITIES: Demands of travel may limit participation of those with physical disabilities.

COMMENTS: Participants can earn six hours of graduate credit from Indiana University. Contact the English Department for more information.

Insight Travel

502 Livermore Street
Yellow Springs, OH 45387
Phone: (513) 767-1102
Fax: (513) 767-7550

INSTITUTION/ORGANIZATION: Founded in 1987, Insight Travel is a commercial tour operator that specializes in pilgrimages to important Buddhist sites.

PROGRAMS: Insight Travel's journeys to the temples, villages, and archaeological remains that mark key locations of ancient Buddhist culture are enriched by meetings with traditional teachers as well as daily meditation. Group leaders have strong academic backgrounds in Buddhist studies, and experience with the practice of meditation. Annual programs include "Pilgrimage to India and Nepal" and "Pilgrimage to Bhutan."

ELIGIBILITY: Applications are accepted from all interested persons.

LOCATION: Bhutan, India, and Nepal.

TIME OF YEAR: Winter.

DURATION: All trips last approximately three weeks.

ACCOMMODATIONS: Hotels and guesthouses.

COST: Programs cost between $2,000 and $4,000, which includes ground and local air transportation, three meals a day, and accommodations.

PERSONS WITH DISABILITIES: Insight Travel does not impose restrictions; however, there is very little wheelchair access in Bhutan, India, and Nepal.

COMMENTS: The average age of participants is usually about 37.

▸⇒▸⇒▸

Institute for Food and Development Policy

145 Ninth Street
San Francisco, CA 94103
Phone: (415) 864-8555

INSTITUTION/ORGANIZATION: This nonprofit research and education organization investigates and analyzes Third World development.

PROGRAM: The Institute's "Kerala Good Life" program takes participants to the southern Indian state of Kerala, where they learn low-consumption living as a means of protecting the environment. Group size is limited to eight people.

ELIGIBILITY: Applications are accepted from all interested persons.

LOCATION: Kerala, India.

TIME OF YEAR: Fall and winter.

DURATION: One month.

ACCOMMODATIONS: Private homes.

COST: A fee of $1,565 covers room, board, and all travel expenses in India.

PERSONS WITH DISABILITIES: Persons with disabilities are welcome.
AGE OF PARTICIPANTS: The average age of participants is usually
about 52.
COMMENTS: About seventy percent of the participants are from the
United States.

▶➡▶➡▶

Institute for Readers Theater

P.O. Box 17193
San Diego, CA 92177
Phone: (619) 276-1948

INSTITUTION/ORGANIZATION: Founded in 1972 and affiliated with
the University of Southern Maine, the Institute for Readers Theater
sponsors international workshops, productions, and script services.

PROGRAM: The "International Readers Theater Workshop" is a study
program that combines all aspects of Readers Theater, including script-
making, staging, and methodology. Instructors are Readers Theater
specialists. The program includes lectures, hands-on activities, and
rehearsals.
ELIGIBILITY: Applications are accepted from all interested persons.
LOCATION: Destinations have included England, Austria, France,
Greece, Italy, and Canada. The 1993 program is scheduled for Rome.
TIME OF YEAR: Summer.
DURATION: Three weeks.
ACCOMMODATIONS: Participants live in hotels, college dormitories,
and flats.
COST: In 1992 the cost was $1,695, which included room, breakfast,
institute fees, instructional facility, and materials. Transportation and
tuition fees for the University of Southern Maine were not included.
AGE OF PARTICIPANTS: The average age of participants is usually
about 35.
PERSONS WITH DISABILITIES: Although the Institute places no restrictions on persons with disabilities, some locations may not be
accommodating. Check with the Institute.
COMMENTS: As part of the program, participants enroll for six undergraduate or graduate credits; however, it is not necessary to be a
college/university student in order to participate. The Institute has
enrolled high school students as well as postprofessional doctorates.

▶⟹▶⟹▶

Institute of China Studies

7341 N. Kolmar Street
Lincolnwood, IL 60646
Phone: (708) 677-0982
Fax: (708) 673-2634

INSTITUTION/ORGANIZATION: Founded in 1979, the Institute of China Studies is a nonprofit organization that promotes Chinese studies.

PROGRAM: "Study and Travel Program." This program combines the study of Chinese language (Mandarin) and culture at Fudan University with eight to 10 days of travel in China. Participants are taught by faculty of Fudan University.
ELIGIBILITY: Applications are accepted from all interested persons.
LOCATION: Destinations include Shanghai (Fudan University), Hangzhou, and Suzhou, with the option to travel to Luoyang, Xi'an, Beijing, Nanchang, Lushan, Juijiang, Quilin, Guangzhou, and Shenzhen.
TIME OF YEAR: Summer.
DURATION: The program runs for about six weeks.
ACCOMMODATIONS: College dormitories and hotels.
COST: The approximate cost is $3,500 and includes round-trip airfare from San Francisco, tuition, room, board, and eight to 10 days of travel in China.
AGE OF PARTICIPANTS: The average age of participants is usually under 40.

▶⟹▶⟹▶

Institute of Noetic Sciences

P.O. Box 909
Sausalito, CA 94966-0909
Phone: (415) 331-5650
Fax: (415) 331-5673

INSTITUTION/ORGANIZATION: The Institute is a nonprofit membership organization dedicated to expanding knowledge of the nature and the potential of the human mind and spirit. This research foundation provides grants for study in the "field of consciousness," publishes books, and organizes conferences and educational travel.

PROGRAMS: The Institute sponsors trips to various countries, focusing on local religions, cultural practices, and healing methods. Group leaders are specialists in the area of the tour focus. While heavy emphasis is placed on interacting with the local people, lectures and small group discussions are also part of the learning experience. Groups are limited to 30 people.

ELIGIBILITY: Applications are accepted from all interested persons.

LOCATION: Destinations include Chile and Easter Island, Egypt, Bali, Wales and Ireland, Brazil, Yucatán and Belize, Australia, Kenya, Bahamas, New Mexico, and Turkey.

TIME OF YEAR: Options are available throughout the year.

DURATION: Two to three weeks.

ACCOMMODATIONS: Hotels.

COST: Prices vary depending on the program; write or call for the travel program catalog, which provides a detailed description of all costs. In 1992 program costs ranged from $3,000 to $5,000.

PERSONS WITH DISABILITIES: Those requiring physical assistance must be accompanied by a companion.

AGE OF PARTICIPANTS: The average age of participants is over 40.

COMMENTS: Most participants are usually from the United States.

▶⇒▶⇒▶

Institute for Shipboard Education

University of Pittsburgh
Semester at Sea
811 William Pitt Union
Pittsburgh, PA 15260
Phone: (412) 648-7490
Fax: (412) 648-2298

INSTITUTION/ORGANIZATION: Founded in 1787, the University of Pittsburgh is a nonprofit institution.

PROGRAM: "Caribbean Seminar at Sea." This educational cruise sails to a number of destinations throughout the Caribbean. Guest faculty from colleges and universities across the country conduct lectures and facilitate discussions to provide participants with an overview of these Caribbean cultures. Political, social, economic, and environmental issues affecting each country are discussed, and Spanish language workshops are conducted. Recreational activities are also an integral part of the cruise program. Each cruise accommodates about 500 participants.

ELIGIBILITY: Applications are accepted from all interested persons.

LOCATION: Destinations include the Bahamas, Puerto Rico, Martinique, Trinidad, Venezuela, Curaçao, and Aruba.

TIME OF YEAR: The cruise takes place in January.

DURATION: Two weeks.

ACCOMMODATIONS: Participants stay aboard the SS *Universe*.

COST: Costs vary depending on the size of cabin you choose; prices range from approximately $1,175 for a budget berth to $2,950 for a deluxe cabin. Fee includes cruise transportation, accommodations, all meals, entertainment, lectures, and services aboard ship. Transportation to port of embarkation (Nassau, the Bahamas), port charges, shore excursions, medical services, bar beverages, and personal expenses are additional.

AGE OF PARTICIPANTS: Participants generally range in age from 30 to 70.

PERSONS WITH DISABILITIES: Disabled persons are accommodated but should be able to manage independently.

▶⇒▶⇒▶

Institut Français des Alpes

Château d'Agnac
34690 Fabregues
Montpellier
FRANCE
Phone: (33) 67 85 13 55
Fax: (33) 67 85 28 20

INSTITUTION/ORGANIZATION: Founded in 1983, the Institut Français des Alpes is a nonprofit organization that combines the teaching of French with skiing on the French Alps.

PROGRAM: "French and Skiing." This program enables participants to study French in the mornings and ski in the afternoons. Instructors have university degrees and are widely experienced in teaching French as a foreign language. On the first day of the program, participants are given an oral and written examination to evaluate their knowledge of French. Participants ski in Megeve, home of Mont-Blanc, which offers a challenging variety of slopes suitable for the novice through the expert skier. Cross-country trails are also available. Megeve is home to one of the best French ski schools.

ELIGIBILITY: Applications are accepted from all interested persons.

LOCATION: Megeve, France.

TIME OF YEAR: January through March.

DURATION: Programs range in length from one to 12 weeks; complete beginners in the French language should attend for at least two weeks.

ACCOMMODATIONS: Hotels.

COST: In 1992 a one-week course cost $890 (4,995 French francs), which included room and board, French lessons, ski pass, and skiing insurance. Airfare is additional.

AGE OF PARTICIPANTS: The average age of participants is usually about 30.

▸⇒▸⇒▸

Institut Mediterraneen d'Initiation à la Culture Française (IMICF)

Château d'Agnac
34690 Fabregues
Montpellier
FRANCE
Phone: (33) 67 85 13 55
Fax: (33) 67 85 28 20

INSTITUTION/ORGANIZATION: Founded in 1963, IMICF is a nonprofit organization that offers French courses to persons of all nationalities.

PROGRAMS: Intensive French courses are taught by university graduates who specialize in teaching French as a foreign language. Courses are available on all levels from beginner to advanced; students also have the option to take private lessons. Classes are combined with socio-cultural activities.

ELIGIBILITY: Applications are accepted from all interested persons.

LOCATION: Fabregues, France.

TIME OF YEAR: Spring, summer, and fall.

DURATION: Participants have the option to study for a minimum of two weeks and can extend their stay beyond six weeks if desired.

Complete beginners are required to stay for a minimum of three weeks.

ACCOMMODATIONS: Students live in double or single rooms in the Château d'Agnac.

COST: Varies depending on the duration of study; the 1992 charge for the four-week course was about $1,620 (9,015 French francs), which included tuition, full board, and excursions. Participants are responsible for arranging their own transportation to and from Château d'Agnac.

AGE OF PARTICIPANTS: The average age of participants is usually about 30.

COMMENTS: About seven percent of participants are usually from the United States.

➤⟹➤⟹➤

Instituto Universal Idiomas

751-2150 Moravia
COSTA RICA
Phone: (506) 23 96 62
Fax: (506) 23 9917

INSTITUTION/ORGANIZATION: Founded in 1981, Instituto Universal de Idiomas offers courses in Spanish and English as a foreign language.

PROGRAM: "Spanish as a Foreign Language." The teaching of conversational Spanish is combined with cultural activities. Courses are taught by university-trained instructors and/or instructors with a minimum of five years experience. Tutorials are combined with small group discussions.

ELIGIBILITY: Participants must have a high school diploma.

LOCATION: San José, Costa Rica.

TIME OF YEAR: Throughout the year, with courses beginning every month.

DURATION: From two weeks up to one month.

ACCOMMODATIONS: Participants live with Costa Rican families.

COST: In 1992 the program cost approximately $630 for four weeks and included tuition and homestay (room, board, and laundry).

AGE OF PARTICIPANTS: The average age of participants is usually about 40.

PERSONS WITH DISABILITIES: The institute does not discriminate against persons with disabilities. The school has elevators.
COMMENTS: Usually about 60 percent of the participants are from the United States.

▶⇒▶⇒▶

Interhostel

University of New Hampshire
6 Garrison Avenue
Durham, NH 03824
Phone: (800) 733-9753
Fax: (603) 862-1113

INSTITUTION/ORGANIZATION: Interhostel is an international educational travel program for physically active adults over 50 who enjoy travel and believe that education is a lifelong process. The University of New Hampshire is a member of the Council on International Educational Exchange.

PROGRAM: Affiliated with the University of New Hampshire, Interhostel sponsors educational tours that include cultural activities designed to increase the knowledge and understanding of the history and people of the country explored. Lecturers are faculty members of the host institutions, or local experts. Tours to museums and other points of interest are included in most programs. Tours are limited to 40 participants.
ELIGIBILITY: Participants must be at least 50 years of age or accompanying someone who is at least that age. Traveling companions must be at least 40 years old.
LOCATION: Program destinations include, among others: Australia, New Zealand, China, Thailand, England, France, Ireland, Scotland, Greece, Italy, Germany, Sweden, Norway, Spain, Portugal, Poland, Czechoslovakia, Hungary, Austria, Switzerland, Mexico, and Guatemala.
TIME OF YEAR: Options are available throughout the year.
DURATION: Usually two weeks.
ACCOMMODATIONS: College dormitories.
COST: The cost ranges from $1,400 to $1,900, which includes room and board, activities, and ground transportation. Airfare is not included.

AGE OF PARTICIPANTS: The average age of participants is usually from the mid to late 60s.

➤➤➤

International Bicycle Fund

4887 Columbia Drive South
Seattle, WA 98108
Phone and fax: (206) 628-9314

INSTITUTION/ORGANIZATION: Founded in 1983, the International Bicycle Fund is a nonprofit organization promoting economic development and international understanding.

PROGRAM: "Bicycle Africa." This outdoor adventure provides participants with the opportunity to experience Africa by bicycling through several major cities and rural areas. The program focuses on cultural, historical, and economic diversity; specialists with a broad knowledge of Africa accompany the group to explain local culture and answer questions. Site visits are combined with small group discussions. Cyclists travel from 20 to 60 miles per day, averaging about 40. Groups are limited to 12 participants.
ELIGIBILITY: Interested persons should be in good health.
LOCATION: Destinations include Tunisia, Senegal, Mali, Togo, Benin, Ghana, Cameroon, Kenya, and Zimbabwe.
TIME OF YEAR: Options are available throughout the year.
DURATION: Trips run for two weeks.
ACCOMMODATIONS: Hotels, hostels, and private homes.
COST: The fee is approximately $990, which covers room, board, and guides. Airfare is additional.
AGE OF PARTICIPANTS: The average age of participants is usually about 37.
PERSONS WITH DISABILITIES: Individuals are handled on a case-by-case basis.

➤➤➤

International Bicycle Tours

7 Champlin Square
P.O. Box 754
Essex, CT 06426

Phone: (203) 767-7005
Fax: (203) 767-3090

INSTITUTION/ORGANIZATION: Founded in 1976, International Bicycle Tours is a commercial tour operator that specializes in tours of Holland but also offers tours to other parts of Europe.

PROGRAMS: In addition to tours of Holland, International Bicycle Tours runs trips through England, France, Germany, and the Netherlands. Tours emphasize exploration of the countries, with frequent stops at sites of interest. The guides are multilingual and knowledgeable about the geography and history of the tour area. Participants ride about 30 miles per day. Special tours are available for the traveler over 50. Groups range in size from 23 to 30 people.

ELIGIBILITY: Participants must be in good health and have the ability to ride 30 miles each day.

LOCATION: The Netherlands, France, England, and Germany.

TIME OF YEAR: April through October, with frequent departures.

DURATION: One to two weeks.

ACCOMMODATIONS: Hotels.

COST: In 1992, costs ranged from $1,260 to $1,600 and included room, most meals, airport transfers, bicycle, tips and taxes, two guides, and a support van. Room costs were based on double occupancy; for a single room there was a supplemental charge ranging from $175 to $275. Airfare was additional.

AGE OF PARTICIPANTS: The average age of participants is over 50.

COMMENTS: Usually about 95 percent of the participants are from the United States.

▶⇒▶⇒▶

International Council for Cultural Exchange

1559 Rockville Pike
Rockville, MD 20852
Phone: (301) 983-9479
Fax: (301) 770-4499

INSTITUTION/ORGANIZATION: Founded in 1982, the International Council for Cultural Exchange (ICCE) is a nonprofit organization established to foster international cultural exchange programs and cultural contacts between persons.

PROGRAMS: ICCE offers a variety of study programs focused on language, culture, and the arts, including:

- "Spanish Language and Culture." This language immersion program takes place in Costa Del Sol in southern Spain and includes classes in language, literature, art, history, and cultural anthropology. Participants live with Spanish families while attending small classes taught by university faculty experienced in teaching foreign students. Tutorials are combined with small group discussions. Participants can enroll for two-, three-, or four-week programs offered throughout the year. In 1992 the program ranged from $1,998 to $2,481 and included round-trip airfare from New York, transfers, room and board, field trips (summer only), and tuition. Many participants are in their mid-20s.

- "Italian Language and Culture." Offered for three to four weeks during the summer, this program is aimed at providing the learner with a comprehensive outline of Italian language and culture. Taught by university faculty, three hours of language study daily (except Sundays) is combined with lectures in literature, history of language, music, and art. Students live in college dormitories and hotels on the Italian Riviera Della Versilia. In 1992 the program cost was $2,659 and included round-trip airfare from New York, room and board, tuition, and excursions. Open to all interested persons. Many participants are in their late 20s.

- "French Language and Culture." Offered for three weeks during the summer, this program combines five hours of language study daily with optional workshops in French art, music, theater, poetry, and photography. Participants live in hotels, private homes, student residence halls, and apartments on the French Riviera. Taught by university professors or high school teachers, lectures are combined with small group discussions and visits to places of cultural interest. In 1992 the program cost was $2,940 and included round-trip airfare from New York, transfers, accommodations, meals, field trips, workshops, and tuition. Open to all interested persons. Many participants are in their mid-20s.

- "Japanese Language and Culture." Focused on presenting a well-rounded picture of different sides of Japanese life, this program takes place in Tokyo for five weeks during the summer. Courses are offered in Japanese language, art, literature, religion, sociology, management, and other areas; participants enroll in two for the term. Taught in English by university faculty, lectures are combined with small group discussions and field trips. Participants live in student residence centers. In 1992 the program was $3,229 and included round-trip airfare from Los Angeles, room, tuition, and cultural field trips. Open to all persons from college age to senior citizens. For Japanese language courses, reading and writing skills in *Haragana* and *Katakana* are useful.

- "Italian Opera Festival: Arena Di Verona and Puccini Torre Del Lago." This program takes participants to two opera festivals in northern Italy, accompanied by a leader with an extensive background in opera production, conducting, or singing. Lectures are combined with small group discussions and critiques of the six opera performances. Participants live in hotels. Offered for two weeks during the summer. In 1992 the program cost was $3,559 and included round-trip airfare from New York, transfers, four-star hotel rooms, meals, tickets to performances and museums, and field trips. The program attracts adults between the ages of about 50 to 80.

- "Britain Theatre Festival." Offered for two weeks during the summer, this program takes participants to theater festivals in London and Edinburgh. Three performances are attended at each festival; participants are accompanied by a leader with a background in theater, literature, and acting. Lectures are combined with small group discussions and critiques of the performances. Participants live in hotels. The approximate cost is $3,000, which includes round-trip airfare from New York, transfers, hotel, meals, tickets to performances and museums, and field trips.

- "Art in Italy: A Practical Course in Painting." Offered for three weeks during the summer, this program takes place in Viareggio and the surrounding area in Tuscany. Participants study art history while sketching and painting in the studio, as well as in the Tuscan countryside. Instruction in watercolor, oils, and marble sculpture is given by university faculty or practicing artists. Participants live in hotels and college dormitories. The approximate cost is $2,398 and includes round-trip airfare from New York, transfers, room, board, class fees, and field trips. Open to all interested persons.

- "France: Art Festival." Offered for three weeks during the summer, this program takes place in Nice and the surrounding area on the Cote d'Azur. Participants study modern French art by visiting the many museums and art studios on the French Riviera. Led by university faculty or practicing artists, lectures are combined with small group discussions. Participants live in hotels. The program cost is approximately $3,000 and covers round-trip airfare from New York, transfers, room, board, and class fees. Open to all interested persons at least 18 years of age.

ELIGIBILITY: Applications are accepted from all interested persons.
LOCATION: Spain, Italy, France, Japan, Britain.
TIME OF YEAR: Time of year varies. See descriptions of programs above.
DURATION: Programs vary from two to five weeks.
PERSONS WITH DISABILITIES: Provisions vary according to the program. Contact ICCE for more information.

▶⇒▶⇒▶

International Executive Service Corps

P.O. Box 10005
Stamford, CT 06904
Phone: (203) 967-6000
Fax: (203) 243-4372

INSTITUTION/ORGANIZATION: Founded in 1964, the International Executive Service Corps is a nonprofit organization that sends highly skilled retired U.S. business people overseas to assist Third World business development.

PROGRAM: "International Executive Service Corps (IESC)." This program enables highly skilled U.S. business people to assist businesses in the developing nations and countries entering into the free market economies. As advisers, these volunteers work with the local people in the hopes of upgrading management skills, improving basic business technologies, and promoting better trade relations around the world. Hundreds of projects are available annually, and volunteers are placed individually. IESC is funded by grants from the U.S. Agency for International Development, client contributions toward project costs, and voluntary contributions from corporations, foundations, and private sponsors in the United States and abroad.

ELIGIBILITY: Interested persons must have proficiency in a skill that Third World businesses can use, such as computer skills, management, or international trade. The program was developed for people who have had a lifetime of experience in their respective industries.

LOCATION: Destinations have included countries throughout Africa, Central and South America, the Middle East, and South, East, and Southeast Asia, as well as Europe.

TIME OF YEAR: Options are available throughout the year.

DURATION: Projects run from two weeks to three months.

ACCOMMODATIONS: Participants live in hotels.

COST: All expenses are paid for executive and spouse.

AGE OF PARTICIPANTS: Though most participants are about 55 to 75 years old, younger persons are welcome to apply.

➤➤⇒➤➤⇒➤➤

International Expeditions

One Environs Park
Helena, AL 35080
Phone: (800) 633-4734
Fax: (205) 428-1714

INSTITUTION/ORGANIZATION: Founded in 1980, International Expeditions is one of the largest and oldest commercial tour operators of ecologically responsible travel, offering programs to more than 25 destinations worldwide. Its "sister" organization, the Amazon Center for Environmental Education and Research (ACEER), located on the Amazon Biosphere Reserve in Peru, is a nonprofit organization that provides accommodations and research facilities for scientists, rain forest workshop participants, and environmentally conscious travelers. ACEER was created to preserve rain forest habitats through education, awareness, and sustainable utilization of rain forest resources.

PROGRAMS: "International Rain Forest Workshops." Focused on the study of rain forest dynamics, wildlife, and culture, these workshops are conducted by 20 leading scientists and naturalists who have either extensive field study experience or academic status. Up to 100 people are permitted in each workshop.

ELIGIBILITY: Applications are accepted from all interested persons.

LOCATION: Peru and Costa Rica.

TIME OF YEAR: Spring.

DURATION: Workshops run for eight days.

ACCOMMODATIONS: Participants live in jungle lodges.

COST: Approximately $1,498, which includes round-trip airfare from Miami, room, board, ground transportation, workbooks, and instruction. Airfare from hometown to Miami is additional.
AGE OF PARTICIPANTS: The average age of participants is usually about 40.
PERSONS WITH DISABILITIES: Trails are only traversable by foot.
COMMENTS: Funding is available to assist participants. Contact International Expeditions for more information.

▸⇒▸⇒▸

International House
c/o CES School of Languages
at the Center for English Studies
330 Seventh Avenue
New York, NY 10001
Phone: (212) 620-0760
Fax: (212) 594-7415

INSTITUTION/ORGANIZATION: Founded in 1966, International House is a commercial language institute that runs more than 100 centers worldwide, including schools in France, Italy, Germany, Austria, Egypt, Brazil, and Spain.

PROGRAMS: Language programs include Spanish, German, French, colloquial Arabic, Portuguese, and Italian. Instructors are all fully trained teachers from the respective countries.
ELIGIBILITY: Applications are accepted from all interested persons.
LOCATION: Destinations include Spain, Germany, Austria, France, Egypt, Brazil, and Italy.
TIME OF YEAR: All programs operate throughout the year except colloquial Arabic in Egypt, which is a summer program only.
DURATION: Participants have the option to enroll for a minimum of two weeks up to a maximum of one year for all programs except colloquial Arabic in Egypt and Italian in Italy, which run for one month.
ACCOMMODATIONS: Hotels, college dormitories, and private homes.
COST: Varies depending on the program and length of stay. Contact CES for specific prices.

▶⇒▶⇒▶

International House Language School

P.O.B. 95
Budapest 1364
HUNGARY
Phone: (36) 1 1154013
Fax: (36) 1 1155275

INSTITUTION/ORGANIZATION: Founded in 1984, International House Language School offers courses in English and Hungarian and serves as a teacher-training institute.

PROGRAM: Hungarian language courses are conducted by certified teachers. Intensive and regular courses are available.
ELIGIBILITY: Applications are accepted from all interested persons.
LOCATION: Budapest, Hungary.
TIME OF YEAR: Options are available throughout the year.
DURATION: Participants have the option to study for a one-month or three-month period. (One-month sessions are offered nine times per year; three-month sessions are offered two to three times per year.)
ACCOMMODATIONS: Private homes.
COST: Varies depending on the length and type of program; cost ranges from $100 to $400 for tuition only.
AGE OF PARTICIPANTS: The average age of participants is usually between about 25 and 35.
PERSONS WITH DISABILITIES: Persons with disabilities are considered on a case-by-case basis.

▶⇒▶⇒▶

International Movement ATD Fourth World

107 Avenue du General Leclerc
95480 Pierrelaye
FRANCE
Phone: (33) 34 64 69 63
Fax: (33) 34 64 12 02

INSTITUTION/ORGANIZATION: Founded in 1957, the Fourth World Movement is a nonprofit organization that runs cultural and educational projects in partnership with extremely poor families around the world. The Fourth World functions based on the belief that "whenever men and women are condemned to live in extreme poverty, human rights are violated. It is our solemn duty to come together to ensure that they are respected."

PROGRAM: "Summer Workshops" provide the opportunity for volunteers from various countries to get together and serve the poor. Projects involve construction, gardening, cooking, typing, packaging greeting cards, or library work. Evenings are reserved for films and discussions on issues facing the impoverished. Group leaders are full-time volunteers who have experience in poor areas of the world.
ELIGIBILITY: Participants are required to have health insurance. Knowledge of French is helpful but not mandatory.
LOCATION: Mery-sur-Oise, France.
TIME OF YEAR: Summer.
DURATION: Two weeks.
ACCOMMODATIONS: Volunteers live in tents and wooden cabins.
COST: About $70 (400 French francs) total, which covers room and baord. Airfare is not included.
AGE OF PARTICIPANTS: The average age of participants is usually about 26.
PERSONS WITH DISABILITIES: Persons with disabilities are not excluded, but they should be able to do light work. The camp is in a mountainous area.
COMMENTS: About 10 percent of the participants are usually from the United States.

International Oceanographic Foundation
4600 Rickenbacker Causeway
Miami, Florida 33149
Phone: (305) 361-4697
Fax: (305) 361-9306

INSTITUTION/ORGANIZATION: Founded in 1953, the International Oceanographic Foundation is a nonprofit organization dedicated to the promotion of ocean science to the layperson.

PROGRAMS: "Educational Travel Programs Abroad." These programs include study, outdoor adventure, and field research opportunities.

Led by university faculty, the trips focus on oceanography and take place in locations throughout the world.

ELIGIBILITY: Participants must be members of the Foundation.

LOCATION: The Bahamas, Costa Rica, Belize, Antarctica, the western Mediterranean, Indonesia, Greenland, the Galápagos Islands, the Caribbean, China, and Eastern Europe.

TIME OF YEAR: Options are available throughout the year.

DURATION: Programs vary from eight to 21 days.

ACCOMMODATIONS: Hotels, hostels, and yachts.

COST: The cost ranges from $1,200 to $7,000 and includes most expenses, but generally does not cover international airfare.

AGE OF PARTICIPANTS: The average age of participants is usually about 50.

PERSONS WITH DISABILITIES: Most programs can accommodate the disabled. Whenever possible, necessary assistance will be provided.

COMMENTS: Interested persons can obtain academic credit for participation. Contact the Foundation for more information.

▶⇒▶⇒▶

International Peace Walk

4521 Campus Drive, #211
Irvine, CA 92715
Phone: (714) 856-0200
Fax: (714) 856-0201

INSTITUTION/ORGANIZATION: Founded in 1986, the International Peace Walk is a nonprofit organization concerned with international conflict resolution through large-scale citizen projects. Adversaries are brought together in a paradigm of how international relations could evolve.

PROGRAM: "International Peace Walk." Citizen delgations from nations with poor relations come together to live, work, and walk in communities throughout a host nation. Focused on politics, sociology, comparative culture, and history, these walks have combined study with outdoor adventure, voluntary service, and field research. The maximum number of participants on a single walk is 250.

ELIGIBILITY: Applications are accepted from all interested persons.

LOCATION: Destinations vary each year. Previous destinations have included Vietnam and Cuba.

TIME OF YEAR: Summer and winter.

DURATION: Walks last for three weeks.

ACCOMMODATIONS: Participants have stayed in hotels, tents, hostels, private homes, and college dormitories, depending on the circumstance.

COST: The cost ranges from approximately $2,000 to $3,500 and includes round-trip airfare from the United States, room, board, transportation, events, and organizing costs.

PERSONS WITH DISABILITIES: The program is open to persons with disabilities.

▸⇒▸⇒▸

International Zoological Expeditions

210 Washington Street
Sherborn, MA 01770
Phone: (508) 655-1461
Fax: (508) 655-4445

INSTITUTION/ORGANIZATION: Founded in 1971, International Zoological Expeditions is a commercial tour operator that runs expeditions focused on wildlife, cave exploring, Mayan ruins, anthropology, fishing, diving, snorkeling, and bird watching.

PROGRAM: "Wildlife Ecology—Rain Forest and Marine Ecology." Guided by instructors with complete knowledge of the neotropical country of Belize, these ecological expeditions take participants throughout the country bird-watching and studying natural history. Also included is a four-day excursion to Guatemala. Groups range from 10 to 35 people.

ELIGIBILITY: Applications are accepted from all interested persons.

LOCATION: Belize and Guatemala.

TIME OF YEAR: Spring, summer, and winter.

DURATION: Programs run from 10 to 21 days.

ACCOMMODATIONS: Hotels, private homes, and field stations.

COST: The cost ranges from $44 to $120 per day and includes room, board, and in-country travel.

COMMENTS: Some funding is available to participants. Contact Zoological Expeditions for more information.

➤➡➤

ISOK (Voor een vreemde taal naar het vreemde land)

Jan-Tooropstraat 4
2225 XT Katwijk Zh.
THE NETHERLANDS
Phone: (31) 01718 13533

INSTITUTION/ORGANIZATION: Founded in 1968, ISOK is a Dutch language institute.

PROGRAM: Participants study the Dutch language while living with a family in Holland. Lessons are adapted to the interests of the participants and can be either private or in groups. ISOK teaches through a total immersion method: Contact with other English speakers is discouraged while the participant is in the program.

ELIGIBILITY: Applications are accepted from all interested persons.

LOCATION: Oegstgeest, Noordwijkerhout, Sassenheim, and Leidschendam.

TIME OF YEAR: Options are available throughout the year.

DURATION: Varies according to the wishes of the participant.

ACCOMMODATIONS: Private homes.

COST: Room, meals, and linguistic help from host families cost approximately $515 per week. Group language sessions cost about $28 per session; private lessons cost about $46 per hour. There is a registration fee of approximately $83. Airfare is not included.

➤➡➤

Israel Antiquities Authority

P.O.B. 586
91 004 Jerusalem
ISRAEL
Phone: (972) 2 292607
Fax: (972) 2 292-628

INSTITUTION/ORGANIZATION: Established in 1948, Israel Antiquities Authority (IAA) is a nonprofit organization that serves as the government authority for supervision of all archaeology activities in Israel. IAA prints an annual list of excavations needing volunteers.

PROGRAMS: Field research/archaeology digs are offered throughout Israel and sponsored by Israeli and/or foreign archaeological institutions and licensed by IAA. Usually no previous experience is necessary.

ELIGIBILITY: Applications are accepted from all interested persons.

LOCATION: Israel.

TIME OF YEAR: Spring, summer, fall.

DURATION: Length varies with the excavation.

ACCOMMODATIONS: Accommodations include hotels/motels, tents, hostels, and college dormitories.

COST: Varies depending upon site. All volunteers are responsible for their own travel expenses; room and board are usually provided.

COMMENTS: IAA itself does not sponsor excavations. The organization provides interested volunteers with information on digs needing volunteers. You must then contact the sponsoring organization/institution.

▶⇒▶⇒▶

Journeys East

2443 Fillmore Street, #289
San Francisco, CA 94115
Phone: (415) 647-9565

INSTITUTION/ORGANIZATION: Journeys East began in 1985 leading small groups of hikers through the Japanese Alps. Specializing in Japan, Journeys East is a commercial tour operator with an emphasis on eco-tourism.

PROGRAMS: Journeys East offers four different packages. "Mountains, Temples, and Hamlets" is a backcountry tour focusing on Japanese wilderness. "From Farmhouse to Teahouse" also takes participants through the backcountry, focusing on folk architecture. "Brushes With the Past and Present" combines glimpses of old and new in city and country. "Inner Japan: From Sumo to Zen" explores the spiritual life of Japan with visits to shrines, temples, and Sumo stables. Leaders are proficient in Japanese language and knowledgeable about the culture and history of Japan. Group size is limited to 16 people.

ELIGIBILITY: Journeys East specifies that applicants should be open-minded.

LOCATION: Typical destinations are Tokyo, Kyoto, Takayama, Niigata, Koyasan.
TIME OF YEAR: Spring and fall.
DURATION: Tours last approximately two weeks.
ACCOMMODATIONS: Traditional Japanese inns and temples.
COST: Tours cost approximately $3,000, which includes all lodging, breakfasts, most dinners, six lunches, and in-country travel. Airfare is not included.
PERSONS WITH DISABILITIES: No restrictions as long as person can carry his/her own luggage.
AGE OF PARTICIPANTS: The average age of participants is usually between 40 and 50.
COMMENTS: About 95 percent of the participants are usually from the United States.

▸⟹▸⟹▸

Kay Pastorius' School of International Cuisine

1075 Dyer Place
Laguna Beach, CA 92651
Phone: (714) 494-1774

INSTITUTION/ORGANIZATION: Founded in 1974, Kay Pastorius' School of International Cuisine is a commercial school that combines international travel with courses in ethnic cooking.

PROGRAM: The study of ethnic cuisine with hands-on cooking lessons is combined with sight-seeing. Excursions are led by Kay Pastorius. Groups are limited to 12 people.
ELIGIBILITY: Applications are accepted from all interested persons.
LOCATION: Destinations vary each year. Recent destinations have included Italy and Costa Rica.
TIME OF YEAR: Spring and fall.
DURATION: 10 to 12 days.
ACCOMMODATIONS: Hotels.
COST: Not available at time of publication; contact the school.
AGE OF PARTICIPANTS: The average age of participants is usually between 45 and 55.

▶⇒▶⇒▶

Kent State University

The College of Continuing Studies
  and Department of Classical Studies
Kent, OH 44242
Phone: (216) 672-3102
Fax: (216) 672-2203

INSTITUTION/ORGANIZATION: Kent State University is a member of the Council on International Educational Exchange. The College of Continuing Studies helps the university reach out to the community as well as the nontraditional student. Outreach activities include programs for professionals, summer students, adult students over 21 years old, those attending evening and weekend classes, as well as business and professional organizations.

PROGRAM: "Classical Studies in Italy: Monuments of the Etruscan Civilization and Ancient Rome." This study program focuses on the rich archaeological sites and museums of Rome, Pompeii, Bologna, and Florence, along with the life and manners of ancient Romans. Led by professors with demonstrated expertise in ancient Roman studies, small group discussions take place on site locations. Instructors are also required to be intensely familiar with modern-day Italy. Groups are limited to 16 participants.

ELIGIBILITY: Participants must have a high school diploma.

LOCATION: Rome, Pompeii, Bologna, and Florence, Italy.

TIME OF YEAR: Summer.

DURATION: The program runs for 20 days.

ACCOMMODATIONS: Hotels.

COST: In 1992 the cost was approximately $2,000, which included tuition (six credit hours), room, most meals, and land travel while in Italy. Airfare was not included.

AGE OF PARTICIPANTS: Participants usually range in age from 18 to 70.

PERSONS WITH DISABILITIES: The program is open to disabled persons if they are able to keep up with the extensive amount of daily walking required.

COMMENTS: This program is offered twice each summer. The first session is designed for college/university students and other adults; the second session is geared toward recent high school graduates and high school teachers. Interested students have the option to earn either undergraduate or graduate credit.

Kibbutz Aliya Desk

27 West 20th Street
New York, NY 10011
Phone: (212) 255-1338
Fax: (212) 929-3459

INSTITUTION/ORGANIZATION: Established in 1968, the Kibbutz Aliya Desk is a nonprofit organization that serves as a representative of the kibbutz movement. They supply information about kibbutz life and promote and assist people who want to settle on kibbutzim.

PROGRAM: "Volunteer on Kibbutz." Participants live and do volunteer work on a kibbutz.
ELIGIBILITY: Participants must be between the ages of 18 and 35 and in good physical and mental health.
LOCATION: Israel.
TIME OF YEAR: Options are available throughout the year.
DURATION: Four weeks (minimum).
ACCOMMODATIONS: Kibbutz.
COST: $115 per month, which includes registration fees, room, board, and insurance.
AGE OF PARTICIPANTS: The average age of participants is usually about 21.
PERSONS WITH DISABILITIES: Persons with disabilities are welcome if they are capable of meeting the requirements of the program.

The Kosciuszko Foundation

15 East 65th Street
New York, NY 10021
Phone: (212) 734-2130
Fax: (212) 628-4552

INSTITUTION/ORGANIZATION: Founded in 1925, The Kosciuszko Foundation is a Polish nonprofit educational and cultural organization.

PROGRAM: The Kosciuszko Foundation has sponsored a summer study program in Poland for 22 years. Lectures on Polish language, history, art, and culture are combined with some travel. Instructors are teachers of Polish language with proficiency in English. The maximum number of participants permitted on each program is 200; instruction is conducted in small groups.

ELIGIBILITY: Applications are accepted from all interested persons.

LOCATION: Warsaw, Cracow, Lublin, and Paznan.

TIME OF YEAR: Summer.

DURATION: Three, four, five, or six weeks.

ACCOMMODATIONS: College dormitories.

COST: Ranges from $600 to $1,100 and includes room, board, and local travel. International airfare is not included.

AGE OF PARTICIPANTS: The average age of participants is usually over 40.

PERSONS WITH DISABILITIES: Open to participation by persons with disabilities, but "Poland has virtually no facilities adapted for the handicapped."

▶▶⇒▶▶⇒▶▶

Language Studies Abroad

249 S. Highway 101
Suite 226
Solana Beach, CA 92075
Phone: (619) 943-0204
Fax: (619) 943-1201

INSTITUTION/ORGANIZATION: Language Studies Abroad serves as the U.S. coordinator for programs sponsored by language institutes in a variety of countries throughout the world.

PROGRAMS: Language Studies Abroad represents language institutes offering intensive programs in Spanish and Italian. In most cases, courses are taught by native speakers holding university degrees. Spanish institutes represented include Centro Internacional de Lengua y Cultura Española (Spain); Cuauhnahuac (Mexico); Forester Instituto Internacional (Costa Rica). Italian institutes include Michelangelo (Florence) and Istituto Italiano (Rome).

ELIGIBILITY: Applications are accepted from all interested persons.

LOCATION: The language institutes are located in San José, Costa Rica; Valencia, Spain; Cuernavaca, Mexico; Rome and Florence, Italy.

TIME OF YEAR: Options are available throughout the year.

DURATION: All institutes offer programs for two weeks or longer except the institute in Florence, which sponsors programs for a minimum of four weeks.

ACCOMMODATIONS: Students in the Spanish language programs live in private homes. Those in the Italian programs live in private homes, hotels, and apartments.

COST: Varies, depending on the institute and length of stay. Contact Language Studies Abroad for more information.

PERSONS WITH DISABILITIES: Individuals are considered on a case-by-case basis.

University of La Verne
Study Abroad Office
1950 Third Street
La Verne, CA 91750
Phone: (714) 593-3511
Fax: (714) 593-0965

INSTITUTION/ORGANIZATION: Founded in 1891, the University of La Verne is an independent, comprehensive institution with emphasis in liberal arts, business, education, and public administration. The university is a member of the Council on International Educational Exchange.

PROGRAMS: The University of La Verne sponsors study travel programs led by experts in the appropriate academic disciplines. Programs are limited to 15 participants each. Recent offerings have included the following:

- "Experiencing British Life and Culture" focuses on political, cultural, and economic institutions, and includes theater trips. The program takes place in London and other cities in the United Kingdom.
- "Comparative Cultures: Russia" emphasizes art, music, dance, and politics; also covers history and economics. The program takes place in Russia and the Ukraine.
- "Study in Cuernavaca, Mexico" involves intensive study of Spanish language and Mexican culture.
- "Comparative Cultures: Africa" is a study of art, music, and dance, but also covers history and politics. Some years the

program takes place in Kenya; other years, in the Gambia.

- "Seminar in Eastern Europe," designed for professional public administrators, focuses on administration and management. (At publication time the itinerary had not been determined).

LOCATION: Destinations vary each year. Previous locations have included the United Kingdom, Eastern Europe, Russia, the Ukraine, Kenya, Senegal and the Gambia, and Mexico.

ELIGIBILITY: There are no prerequisites for any of the programs except for the one in Eastern Europe, which is designed for working or retired public administrators.

TIME OF YEAR: January.

DURATION: Progams run for four weeks.

ACCOMMODATIONS: Participants stay in hotels and private homes.

COST: Program costs range from $2,100 to $2,700 and include round-trip airfare from Los Angeles, room and board, city transfers, some lectures, and site entry fees.

AGE OF PARTICIPANTS: Most participants are usually in their early 20s; those who participate in the Eastern Europe program are usually in their early 40s.

PERSONS WITH DISABILITIES: The university does not discriminate on the basis of disabilities and will try to accommodate persons with disabilities on all programs.

COMMENTS: Students can receive academic credit for participation; most participants are traditional-age undergraduates.

In addition to January programs, La Verne has a full-service educational center in Athens, Greece, offering courses in modern Greek language and culture, as well as a full array of U.S. academic courses for degree-seeking students. Participants must enroll for a minimum of six weeks. A recent study program that may soon be offered again is "Analysis of Pacific Rim Business." Contact the university for more information.

▶▶⇒▶▶⇒▶▶

Learning Alliance: Options for Education and Action

494 Broadway
New York, NY 10012
Phone: (212) 226-7171
Fax: (212) 274-8712

INSTITUTION/ORGANIZATION: Founded in 1985, the Learning Alliance is a nonprofit organization "committed to providing people with the education and resources they need to act on the issues which confront the city and the world."

PROGRAM: Outdoor adventure and study programs are sponsored in Latin and South America. With an emphasis on ecological and community development issues, programs are led by professional educators. Groups are limited to 20 people.

ELIGIBILITY: Applications are accepted from all interested persons.

LOCATION: Destinations include Costa Rica and Peru.

TIME OF YEAR: Summer and winter.

DURATION: Programs vary from 10 to 14 days.

ACCOMMODATIONS: Hotels.

COST: Program costs range from $1,300 to $1,600 and include room, board, guides, and land transportation. International airfare is not included.

AGE OF PARTICIPANTS: The average age of participants is usually about 35.

PERSONS WITH DISABILITIES: The Learning Alliance encourages the participation of persons with disabilities.

▶▶⇒▶▶⇒▶▶

LEX America

68 Leonard Street
Belmont, MA 02178
Phone: (617) 489-5800
Fax: (617) 489-5898

INSTITUTION/ORGANIZATION: Founded in 1981, LEX America, the Institute for Language Experience, Experiment, and Exchange, has dedicated itself to promoting a multicultural and multilingual world. LEX is a nonprofit organization.

PROGRAM: "Adult Exchange to Japan." This homestay program provides participants with the opportunity to live with Japanese families. Participants absorb the customs of the host culture by taking part in daily life, attending workshops, and visiting sites accompanied by their Japanese hosts.

ELIGIBILITY: Interested persons should be at least 21 years old.

LOCATION: Japan (nationwide).
TIME OF YEAR: Spring and fall.
DURATION: Homestays usually run from two to four weeks.
ACCOMMODATIONS: Private homes.
COST: In 1992 prices ranged from $1,900 to $2,800 and included round-trip airfare, all in-country costs except personal expenses, and orientation materials.
AGE OF PARTICIPANTS: The average age of participants is usually about 45.
PERSONS WITH DISABILITIES: LEX does not discriminate on any basis.
COMMENTS: Custom programs are also designed for groups and can be as short as two days.

➤➤➤

The Lisle Fellowship

433 West Sterns
Temperance, MI 48182
Phone: (313) 847-7126
Fax: (419) 537-7719 (Attn: Dr. Mark Kinney)

INSTITUTION/ORGANIZATION: Founded in 1936, The Lisle Fellowship is a nonprofit intercultural education organization encouraging world peace and survival through interpersonal contacts. The organization is a member of the Council on International Educational Exchange.

PROGRAMS: The educational exchange programs described below will be offered in 1993; contact The Lisle Fellowship for the dates. All Lisle programs provide continual opportunity for reflection and discussion.
- "Art and Culture: Community Development in Mexico." Focused on intercultural understanding, this program takes place in Guadalajara, Patzcuaro, and Mexico City. The group will address the question of whether or not ancestral arts and crafts bring humans together or separate them. Mexican artistic expression and processes of production and marketing are discussed. Offered for three or four weeks in mid-December, the program is designed for persons of varied ages. The program

costs approximately $1,650, which includes room (hostel), board, in-country travel, and leadership. Airfare is additional.

- "Sapporo: Adventures in Northern Japan." This summer program, focused on Japanese life-style and culture, takes participants to explore Sapporo and the Japanese island of Hokkaido. Participants live with native families. Offered for three or four weeks during the summer, the program is designed for persons of varied ages. In 1992 the program cost approximately $1,950, which included leadership, room (hostel), board, and in-country travel. Airfare was additional.

- "Indian Realities: The Social and Environmental Dynamics of Change." In cooperation with the Gandhi Peace Foundation, this program is concerned with understanding the global issues involved in creating environmental practices that work. Participants will look at environmental programs developed in rural communities. Designed for persons of varied ages, the program runs for three to four weeks during the summer. Participants explore New Delhi and the surrounding areas. In 1992 the program cost approximately $1,700, which included leadership, room (hostel), board, and in-country travel. Airfare was additional.

- "Costa Rica: Peacefully Combining Ecosystems and Humanity." Offered for three to four weeks during the winter, this program focuses on Costa Rica's complex biological ecosystems. Intercultural understanding and responsible tourism are emphasized. Instructors generally possess college degrees. Participants stay in hostels. The cost is approximately $1,800 and includes leadership, room, board, in-country travel, and other program-related expenses. Airfare is additional. Minimum age for participants is 16; the average age of participants is usually about 34.

- "Bali Beyond Tourism: Attempting Genuine Understanding." Offered for three to four weeks during the summer, this program takes participants to Bali and Java to explore Indonesian culture and life-style. Sponsored in cooperation with the Canti Sena Conference Center, participants take part in community activities, projects, and rituals. Designed for persons of varied ages, the program includes homestays, field visits, and speakers on Balinese history, culture, and education. In 1992 the cost was approximately $1,750 and included leadership, room (hostel), board, and in-country travel. Airfare was additional.

ELIGIBILITY: Applications are accepted from all interested persons who are willing to participate in group sharing and learning.

LOCATION: Mexico, Japan, India, Costa Rica, and Indonesia.
TIME OF YEAR: Time of year varies. See descriptions of programs above.
DURATION: Programs vary from three to four weeks.
PERSONS WITH DISABILITIES: Persons will be assisted as much as possible.
COMMENTS: Scholarships are available to participants; awards are based on need. Contact the Lisle Fellowship for more information.

▶⟹▶⟹▶

University of Louisville

International Center
Brodschi Hall
Louisville, KY 40292
Phone: (502) 588-6602
Fax: (502) 588-7216

INSTITUTION/ORGANIZATION: Founded in 1798, the University of Louisville is a state university with many returning and mature students. The university is a member of the Council on International Educational Exchange.

PROGRAMS: The University of Louisville has offered a broad range of short-term educational vacation overseas, which include the following:
- "Art Therapy." With an emphasis on counseling and social work, participants study the practice of art therapy in Britain. Lectures, tutorials, and small group discussions led by University of Louisville faculty and guest speakers are combined with site visits. Participants stay in college dormitories. Open to practitioners in art therapy, counseling, and social work. Upper-level students in these areas are also eligible to participate. The program runs for two to three weeks during the summer. Group size is limited to 30 participants. Contact the office above for program cost.
- "French Language and Art History in Paris." Participants study French language (on several levels) and art history. Taught by faculty from the University of Louisville as well as international colleagues, lectures and small group discussions are combined with museum and site visits. Participants live in college dormitories. The program takes place for one month during the

summer. Open to persons at least 17 years of age. Contact the office above for program cost. Group size is limited to 40 participants.

- "Pan-African Studies in Ghana." Focused on the study of culture, art, and the history of West Africa, this program takes participants to Accra and Tamale. Led by faculty from the University of Louisville, lectures and small group discussions are combined with site visits. The program runs for one month during the summer; participants stay in hotels. Open to persons at least 18 years of age. Contact the office above for program cost. Group size is limited to 35 participants.

- "Spanish Language and Culture in Segovia." Led by University of Louisville faculty, this program focuses on the study of Spanish language and culture. Homestays and class work in Segovia are combined with excursions to Madrid and Andalucia. Offered during the summer for five weeks, lectures, small group discussions and tutorials are augmented by field visits. Participants live in private homes and hotels. Interested persons must be at least 17 years old and eligible for college. Contact the office above for program cost. Group size is limited to 40 participants.

- "Egypt and Greece: Treasures of Tut and Philip." Focused on classical studies, this program takes participants to the major sites of ancient Greece and Egypt including the cities of Cairo, Luxor, Memphis, and Athens. Offered during the summer for three weeks, the program is led by faculty from the University of Louisville. Participants stay in hotels. Open to persons at least 17 years of age who are in excellent health; the program is quite rigorous. Contact the office above for the program cost. Group size is limited to 35 participants.

- "Education in Australia." With an emphasis on the educational system in Australia (special education in particular), this program takes participants to Melbourne for two weeks during the summer. Led by faculty from the University of Louisville, lectures, tutorials, and small group discussions are combined with site visits to Australian schools. (This program has also gone to Germany and Great Britain; it may be offered in Scotland in 1993.) Contact the office above for the program cost. Group size is limited to 40 participants.

- "Italian Culture, Language and Art in Perugia." Led by faculty from the University of Louisville, this program focuses on the study of Italian language and art history. Offered for four weeks during the summer, participants attend lectures, tutorials, and small group discussions. Excursions are taken to such places as

Florence, Rome, Assisi, Todi, Orvieto, Siena and Spoleto. Participants live in a monastery. Contact the office above for the program cost. To be offered in 1993. Group size is limited to 40 participants.

- "Political Science, Sociology and German." Offered for four weeks during the summer, this program takes place in Saarbrucken and Mainz, Germany. Led by faculty from the University of Louisville, participants study political science, sociology, and German language and culture. Contact the office above for more information. Group size is limited to 35 participants.
- "Nursing in London." Offered for two weeks during the summer, this program is designed for nursing students and professional nurses. The program is focused on guiding participants in making professional choices in daily career dilemmas. Taught by university faculty, lectures, tutorials, and small group discussions are combined with clinical observations. Participants stay in apartments. In 1992 the cost was $2,295 and included round-trip airfare from Louisville, in-state tuition, room, excursions, admissions, and bus and underground passes. (Program has included an optional excursion to Germany.) Group size is limited to 35 participants.

ELIGIBILITY: Varies according to program. See descriptions above.

LOCATION: Destinations vary each year.

TIME OF YEAR: Summer.

DURATION: Programs vary from two to four weeks.

PERSONS WITH DISABILITIES: The University of Louisville does not discriminate based on disabilities, but all participants must be able to function in facilities that are not wheelchair-accessible.

COMMENTS: Interested students have the option to obtain academic credit for participation in any of these programs.

Marine Sciences Under Sails

P.O. Box 3994
Hollywood, FL 33023
Phone: (305) 983-7015

INSTITUTION/ORGANIZATION: Founded in 1976, Marine Sciences Under Sails is a nonprofit organization dedicated to outdoor education of young and old about the life and history of the sea around Florida. Study cruises for adults, families, and groups of students with their teachers take place throughout the year. The areas of study include mangrove islands, barrier islands, shallow seas, coral reefs, and the open ocean.

PROGRAM: Marine cruises are led by licensed U.S. Coast Guard instructors who have had in-field instructing experience, and water safety and first aid (CPR) training. Participants study the sea while sailing and living on it. Cruises are personalized to meet participants' needs. Groups range in size from three to 16 people.

ELIGIBILITY: Persons should be physically fit and active.

LOCATION: Destinations in 1992 included Belize City, Dangriga, and Placentia, Belize; Caracas, Venezuela; San Blas Islands of Panama; the Colorado River in Costa Rica; and the islands of St. Martin, Antigua, Guadeloupe, and Trinidad, among others.

TIME OF YEAR: Options are available throughout the year.

DURATION: Cruises generally run from one day to one week though participants can sail for as long as a month or more.

ACCOMMODATIONS: Participants live on sailboats.

COST: The price ranges from $33 to $50 per person per day and does not include meals. Participants are required to bring their own food.

AGE OF PARTICIPANTS: The average age of participants ranges from about 28 to 45.

Merkure Institut

130, Av. du Club Hippique
13090 Aix-en-Provence
FRANCE
Phone: (33) 42 20 62 06

INSTITUTION/ORGANIZATION: A member of the Federation Européenne des Ecoles, the Merkure Institut offers French classes at all levels.

PROGRAMS: The Merkure Institut has both semi-intensive and intensive courses: the semi-intensive classes are 17½ hours per week, and the intensive ones are 25 hours per week. Modern methods of teaching are employed, including use of videos and audiocassettes. Study periods are supplemented by exposure to day-to-day life in a busy French town and by contact with the local people.

ELIGIBILITY: Applications are accepted from all interested persons over the age of 18.

LOCATION: Aix-en-Provence, France.

TIME OF YEAR: June, July, and August.

DURATION: Courses run for two to three weeks but can be extended to meet participants' needs.

ACCOMMODATIONS: Participants stay at either a local university campus dorm, the home of a local family, or a residential hotel. All are within easy reach of the institute.

COST: Depending on where you choose to stay and the extent of your stay, prices range from about $710 to $1,765, which includes room, partial board, and tuition. Airfare and surface travel to and from the site are not included.

▶=▶=▶

Mexico Study Groups

P.O. Box 56982
Phoenix, AZ 85079
Phone: (602) 242-9231

INSTITUTION/ORGANIZATION: Founded in 1981, Mexico Study Groups sponsors fully escorted special-interest trips and Spanish language immersion programs.

PROGRAMS: "Mexico Study Groups Live and Learn Vacations." These programs combine Spanish language study with the option to take classes in arts and crafts. Weekend excursions are part of the program. Instructors are fully accredited native Mexicans trained in teaching Spanish as a second language. Art instructors are also accredited. The maximum group size is 20.

ELIGIBILITY: Applications are accepted from all interested persons.

LOCATION: Destinations in Mexico include Cuernavaca and San Miguel de Allende.

TIME OF YEAR: Summer, fall, and spring.

DURATION: Programs usually run for 30 days.

ACCOMMODATIONS: Participants have the option to stay in hotels, but private homestays are encouraged to enhance the learning experience.

COST: Varies according to the classes taken: generally ranges from $1,195 to $1,550, which includes ground transportation between the program site and Mexico City; 30 days room and board; tuition and some excursions. Airfare is additional.

AGE OF PARTICIPANTS: The average age of participants is usually over 50.

PERSONS WITH DISABILITIES: Mexico has few provisions for those with walking disabilities; persons are considered on a case-by-case basis.

COMMENTS: Most participants are from the United States.

►⇒►⇒►

Mexi-Mayan Academic Travel

Cultural and Educational Travel
2216 West 112th Street
Chicago, IL 60643
Phone: (312) 233-1711
Fax: (312) 239-1208

INSTITUTION/ORGANIZATION: Founded in 1972, Mexi-Mayan Academic Travel is a nonprofit educational exchange organization.

PROGRAMS: "Study Tours Abroad." Focused on the study of anthropology, archaeology, and ecology, these educational discovery tours are led by experts in the appropriate fields. Small group discussions are an integral part of the programs. Groups are limited to 18 participants.

ELIGIBILITY: Applications are accepted from all interested persons who are in good health.

LOCATION: Guatemala, Mexico, and Indonesia.

TIME OF YEAR: Spring, summer, and winter.

DURATION: Programs vary from 10 days to two weeks.

ACCOMMODATIONS: Hotels and tents.

COST: Tours cost approximately $150 per day and usually include international airfare, accommodations, tuition, and miscellaneous expenses.

AGE OF PARTICIPANTS: The average age of participants is usually about 35.

PERSONS WITH DISABILITIES: Mexi-Mayan will try to accommodate disabled persons whenever possible, but trips can be rugged.

▶▶⇒▶▶⇒▶▶

Michigan State University
Alumni Lifelong Education
8 Kellogg Center
East Lansing, MI 48824
Phone: (517) 355-4562
Fax: (517) 336-2526

INSTITUTION/ORGANIZATION: Michigan State University (MSU) is a member of the Council on International Educational Exchange. Alumni Lifelong Education, the educational unit of the MSU Alumni Association, sponsors noncredit programs for adults.

PROGRAMS: The MSU Alumni Lifelong Education unit sponsors noncredit study/travel programs led by MSU faculty and experts from the host country. Focused on liberal arts and the natural sciences, these programs combine field lectures with tutorials and small group discussions. Programs are limited to 45 participants each.
ELIGIBILITY: Applications are accepted from all interested persons.
LOCATION: Destinations vary each year. Recent destinations have included Mexico, the United Kingdom, Dominican Republic, New Zealand, France, Austria, Italy, and Switzerland.
TIME OF YEAR: Options are available throughout the year.
DURATION: Two weeks.
ACCOMMODATIONS: Hotels and conference centers.
COST: The cost has ranged from $900 to $3,500, which covers room, most meals, activities, ground transportation, educational program, and baggage handling. Airfare is not included.
AGE OF PARTICIPANTS: The average age of participants is usually about 50.
PERSONS WITH DISABILITIES: Persons with disabilities are accommodated whenever possible.
COMMENTS: Participants may receive academic credit if it is arranged as an independent study with a supporting faculty member.

▶▶⇒▶▶⇒▶▶

Michigan State University
Office of Overseas Study
108 International Center
East Lansing, MI 48824

Phone: (517) 353-8920
Fax: (517) 336-2082

INSTITUTION/ORGANIZATION: Founded in 1855, Michigan State University (MSU) is a state university with an enrollment of over 42,000 students. MSU is a member of the Council on International Educational Exchange.

PROGRAMS: MSU's Office of Overseas Study has offered a variety of study/travel programs for the adult learner, including:

- "Food and Agricultural Systems." Focused on the study of natural resources and agriculture, MSU sponsors summer travel programs to Australia, Japan, and Poland. Participants visit production, processing, and marketing sites in Australia and Japan. In Poland, state and private farms are observed, as well as agricultural research facilities. Excursions to places of cultural and historical significance are included in all programs. Guided by MSU faculty, these field trips are combined with small group discussions. Participants live in hotels in Australia and hotels as well as college dormitories in Japan and Poland. Each program runs for four weeks. The 1992 costs were as follows: Australia, $2,000, which included room and most meals, travel expenses on location, tuition, and administrative fees (airfare was not included, and participants were responsible for transportation to the program site); Japan, $2,575, which included the same items listed above for Australia; Poland, $2,000, which included all items listed above. A background in the course of study is very helpful. Group sizes range from 15 to 25 participants.
- "Interior Design and Architecture." This program takes place in various locations throughout Italy and England during the summer, including London, Milan, and Lake Como. (Optional session in Venice is also available.) Led by MSU faculty, the program runs for five weeks and includes field trips and small group discussions. Participants live in hotels and college dormitories. The approximate cost is $2,988, which includes room and most meals, travel expenses on location, tuition, and administrative fees. Participants are responsible for transportation to the program site. (Optional five-day session in Venice costs approximately $1,019.) A background in the course of study is very helpful. Groups range in size from 15 to 25 participants. This program has been running for more than 17 years.

- "English Education in London." Offered every three years, this program focuses on the study of English literature and writing. British educators conduct workshops to assist American elementary, secondary, and college teachers in understanding the teaching of English in Britain. Guided by MSU faculty, field trips are combined with small group discussions. The program runs for one month during the summer. Participants live in college dormitories. In 1992 the program cost $1,975, which included room and partial board, travel expenses on location, tuition, and administrative fees. Airfare was not included, and participants were responsible for transportation to the program location in London. Group size ranges from 15 to 25 participants.

- "Housing and City Development in Japan." This program focuses on the study of urban planning in Tokyo by addressing the technical and cross-cultural aspects of housing and city design critical to building and living in highly urbanized societies. Led by faculty from MSU, field trips and small group discussions contribute to the learning experience. The program takes place for one month in the spring. Participants live in hostels. In 1992 the approximate cost was $2,700, which included room and partial board, travel expenses on location, tuition, and administrative fees. Participants were responsible for transportation to the program site. Group size ranges from 15 to 25 participants.

- "Exploring Adult and Continuing Education in China Today" provides participants with a close look at adult and continuing education in China and enhances their knowledge of China through direct observation, readings, seminars, and independent projects. Visits might include adult education and training centers, a manufacturing factory, and several villages. Guided by MSU faculty, field trips are combined with small group discussions. Destinations include Hong Kong, Shenzhen, Beijing, Xi'an, and Kunming. The program takes place in the summer and runs for three to four weeks. Participants stay in hotels. In 1992 the approximate cost was $2,600, which included room and partial board, travel expenses on location, tuition, and administrative fees. Airfare was not included, and participants were responsible for transportation to the program location. Group size ranges from 15 to 25 participants.

ELIGIBILITY: Applications are accepted from all interested persons.
LOCATION: Destinations vary each year.

TIME OF YEAR: Time of year varies. See descriptions of programs above.

DURATION: Programs vary from three to five weeks.

PERSONS WITH DISABILITIES: MSU is an equal-opportunity institution and makes every effort to encourage participation by persons with disabilities.

COMMENTS: Scholarships are available for participation in all programs; contact the Office of Overseas Study for more information. The "English Education in London" program is available for six or nine graduate credits, although you don't have to be enrolled in a degree program to participate.

The Minneapolis Institute of Arts

2400 Third Avenue South
Minneapolis, MN 55404
Phone: (612) 870-3030
Fax: (612) 870-3004

INSTITUTION/ORGANIZATION: Established in 1911, The Minneapolis Institute of Arts is a nonprofit fine arts museum.

PROGRAM: The Minneapolis Institute offers educational tours with an emphasis on art, culture, and architecture. Tours include visits to private collections and attendance at limited-admission events. A curator often accompanies the groups. The maximum number of participants on each tour is 25.

ELIGIBILITY: Participants must be members of the museum or be accompanied by a member.

LOCATION: Destinations vary each year. Previous locations have included Holland, Belgium, Turkey, Malaysia, Singapore, Thailand, India, and the islands of the western Mediterranean.

TIME OF YEAR: Options are available throughout the year.

DURATION: Varies with the program.

ACCOMMODATIONS: Deluxe or first-class hotels.

COST: Contact the museum.

PERSONS WITH DISABILITIES: Applicants are accepted if tour destination permits.

▶➡▶➡▶

University of Minnesota

The Global Campus
106 Nicholson Hall
216 Pillsbury Drive SE
Minneapolis, MN 55455
Phone: (612) 625-3588
Fax: (612) 626-8009

INSTITUTION/ORGANIZATION: The University of Minnesota is a comprehensive urban university with a strong tradition of education and public service. The university is a member of the Council on International Educational Exchange.

PROGRAM: "Quincentennial Summer Program for Spanish Teachers." This program is designed to familiarize American teachers of Spanish with the social and cultural reality of contemporary Spain and to increase their command of the Spanish language. Academic study of Spanish society and culture is combined with language study and the development of curricular materials for classroom use. Courses are specifically designed for teachers who are interested in graduate-level credits.

ELIGIBILITY: Interested persons must be teachers or graduate students.

LOCATION: Madrid, Spain.

TIME OF YEAR: Summer.

DURATION: Five weeks: four weeks in Madrid are combined with one week of travel to other regions of Spain.

ACCOMMODATIONS: College dormitories.

COST: In 1992 the cost was $3,800, which included tuition, study abroad and registration fees, complete room and board, medical insurance, field trips, and a one-week excursion. Airfare is not included.

PERSONS WITH DISABILITIES: Special arrangements will be made whenever possible. Contact the program sponsor for information on conditions and accessibility of the program site.

COMMENTS: Fellowships have been awarded to participants. In 1992 300 awards of $1,800 each were available. Call or write for a King Juan Carlos Fellowship application.

▶➡▶➡➡▶

University of Minnesota Law School
International Programs
381 Law Center
Minneapolis, MN 55455
Phone: (612) 625-4544

INSTITUTION/ORGANIZATION: The University of Minnesota is a comprehensive urban university with a strong tradition of education and public service. The university is a member of the Council on International Educational Exchange.

PROGRAMS: The following legal programs have been offered by the Law School in France and Sweden:
- "Lyon Summer Program in European and International Law." This French program combines the study of international law with visits to courts, government offices, and business establishments, among other places of interest. Students examine the international business environment in Europe. The program takes place in Lyon, France (Université Jean Moulin School of Law) for about five weeks during the summer. Participants live in dormitories. In 1991 the approximate tuition was $800; airfare, housing, meals, ground transportation, and educational materials were additional. All courses are taught in English by members of the host institution and faculty of Minnesota Law School.
- "Comparative Legal Studies." This Swedish program focuses on the study of comparative law. Students participate in professional visits and a varied social program to combine the elegant and relaxed sides of Swedish culture. The program takes place in Uppsala, Sweden (Uppsala University), and runs for five weeks during the summer. Participants live in dormitories. In 1991 the approximate tuition cost was $800; airfare, housing, meals, ground transportation, and educational materials were additional. All courses are taught in English by members of the host institution and faculty of Minnesota Law School.

ELIGIBILITY: The programs were developed for law students, law graduates, and lawyers. In order to participate, students are expected to have completed at least one year of a law school accredited by the American Bar Association. Graduates are expected to have completed degrees at ABA-accredited institutions.

LOCATION: France and Sweden.

TIME OF YEAR: Summer.

DURATION: Programs run for about five weeks.

PERSONS WITH DISABILITIES: Special arrangements will be made whenever possible. Contact the program sponsor for information on the accessibility of the program site.

COMMENTS: Students can receive three to five graduate credits for participation.

Mir Initiative

P.O. Box 28183
Washington, DC 20038
Phone: (202) 857-8037
Fax: (202) 861-0621

INSTITUTION/ORGANIZATION: Mir Initiative is the U.S. branch of The Cooperation Project, which is a nonprofit international association of independent organizations committed to promoting multicultural perspectives on ecological and social issues.

PROGRAMS: Mir Initiative sponsors language study, voluntary service opportunities, and ecological expeditions. Language offerings include Russian and Japanese; instructors have teaching credentials and facility in English. Voluntary service projects involve construction and renovation work, as well as farm work. Ecological expeditions include cycling and sailing.

ELIGIBILITY: Applications are accepted from all interested persons.

LOCATION: Russia, Japan, and Mongolia.

TIME OF YEAR: Spring and summer.

DURATION: Two to three weeks.

ACCOMMODATIONS: Participants live in tents, hostels, and on campsites.

COST: Varies with the program; contact Mir Initiative.

AGE OF PARTICIPANTS: Participants are generally in their 20s and 30s.

PERSONS WITH DISABILITIES: Inquiries are welcome and are handled on a case-by-case basis.

COMMENTS: About 40 percent of participants are usually from the United States.

▶▷▷

Mobility International USA (MIUSA)

P.O. Box 3551
Eugene, OR 97403
Phone: (503) 343-1284
Fax: (503) 343-5812

INSTITUTION/ORGANIZATION: Founded in 1981, MIUSA is a non-profit organization dedicated to facilitating opportunities for persons with disabilities to participate in international educational exchange and travel. Members receive a quarterly newsletter, a travel information and referral service, news of international workcamp openings, and help in selecting and applying to international educational exchange programs.

PROGRAMS: MIUSA offers study, voluntary service, professional, and outdoor adventure programs. These opportunities usually focus on rights or services for persons with disabilities. Each program is designed for a specific age group. Led by disabled persons, participants engage in small group discussions.

ELIGIBILITY: Varies according to the program; contact MIUSA for more information.

LOCATION: Destinations vary each year. Previous destinations have included China, Germany, England, Italy, and Costa Rica.

TIME OF YEAR: Options are available throughout the year.

DURATION: Programs usually run for two to four weeks.

ACCOMMODATIONS: Private homes and hostels.

COST: Varies according to destination.

AGE OF PARTICIPANTS: The average age of participants is usually between 20 and 40.

PERSONS WITH DISABILITIES: MIUSA actively recruits persons with disabilities and encourages them to participate. Facilities are accessible where possible; on some trips, interpreters for the deaf as well as attendants are provided.

COMMENTS: MIUSA publishes *A World of Options for the 90's: A Guide to International Educational Exchange, Community Service and Travel for Persons with Disabilities,* a resource book for overseas programs. The organization also produces videotapes documenting the experiences of their exchange program participants. These resources are available from the address above. In addition, some funding is available to program participants. Contact MIUSA for more information.

➤➤➤

Mountain Travel-Sobek: The Adventure Co.

6420 Fairmount Avenue
El Cerrito, CA 94530-3606
Phone: (510) 527-8100
Fax: (510) 525-7710

INSTITUTION/ORGANIZATION: Founded in 1967, Mountain Travel-Sobek is a commercial tour operator that sponsors hiking/trekking and river-rafting trips, as well as environmental/educational, natural history, and cultural programs.

PROGRAMS: Mountain Travel-Sobek offers 160 different programs on seven continents. Trips vary greatly, from the "Amazon Jungle Adventure" and the "Rajasthan Camel Safari and Pushkar Fair" to "Exploring Eastern Europe: Poland and Czechoslovakia" and "Paddle Fiji." Leaders have advanced training in wilderness first aid, experience in geographical region, and proficiency in the language of the host country, among other qualifications. Groups are limited to 15 people.
ELIGIBILITY: Applications are accepted from all interested persons. "Trips are designed for flexible, energetic people who have a healthy dose of curiosity and enthusiasm about our world and a spirit of adventure," according to the sponsor.
LOCATION: Trips take place on all seven continents.
TIME OF YEAR: Options are available throughout the year.
DURATION: Trips last from 10 days to five weeks.
COST: Varies according to program but includes all land costs: meals, accommodations, airport transfers, ground transportation, fees, permits, leadership/instruction, guides, camping gear, and so on. Airfare is not included.
AGE OF PARTICIPANTS: The average age of participants is usually over 35. Many participants are in their 40s, 50s, and 60s.
PERSONS WITH DISABILITIES: Each case is reviewed individually; eligibility is determined on a per-case basis.

➤➤➤

Mozart's Europe Tours

RD 1, P.O. Box 1818
Pawlet, VT 05761
Phone: (802) 325-3656

INSTITUTION/ORGANIZATION: Founded in 1984, Mozart's Europe Tours specializes in following the lives of the great composers in Europe.

PROGRAMS: "Mozart's Europe: Following the Great Composer in Europe." These cultural tours take participants to important life sites and integrated world-class concerts. Discussions with musicologists are also part of the tours. The maximum number of participants on each tour is 29.

ELIGIBILITY: Applications are accepted from all interested persons.

LOCATION: Hungary, Austria, Germany, Czechoslovakia, and Italy.

TIME OF YEAR: Spring, fall, and winter.

DURATION: Tours run from seven to 20 days.

ACCOMMODATIONS: Hotels.

COST: Tours range from $1,400 to $3,300 and include room (first-class or deluxe hotels), half board, eight to 10 concerts, guided tours, entrance fees to cultural sites, and so on. International airfare is additional.

AGE OF PARTICIPANTS: The average age of participants is usually between 50 and 60.

PERSONS WITH DISABILITIES: Participants should be able to walk for one hour and climb two to three flights of stairs at a time.

COMMENTS: Most participants are usually from the United States.

▶⇒▶⇒▶

National Central America Health Rights Network

853 Broadway, #416
New York, NY 10003
Phone: (212) 420-9635

INSTITUTION/ORGANIZATION: Founded in 1983, the National Central America Health Rights Network (NCAHRN) is a nonprofit professional organization consisting of 45 U.S. groups concerned with health rights in Central America. Members of NCAHRN work together with health workers in Central America as clinicians, teachers, and researchers. Others are involved in the collection and delivery of medical aid to the people of the region.

PROGRAM: NCAHRN sponsors work/study delegations to Central America focused on health-related concerns.

ELIGIBILITY: Requirements vary depending upon the program; contact NCAHRN for more information.

LOCATION: El Salvador, Guatemala, Nicaragua.

TIME OF YEAR: Options are available throughout the year.

DURATION: Programs run for 10 days.

ACCOMMODATIONS: Hotels and guesthouses.

COST: Programs range from $600 to $800 and include room, two meals per day, translation, and in-country transportation. Airfare is additional.

AGE OF PARTICIPANTS: Most participants are in their 30s.

PERSONS WITH DISABILITIES: NCAHRN does not discriminate and will make an effort to screen hotels for accessibility.

▶▶=▶▶=▶▶

National Outdoor Leadership Schools (NOLS)

288 Main Street
P.O. Box AA
Lander, WY 82520
Phone: (307) 332-6973
Fax: (307) 332-3631

INSTITUTION/ORGANIZATION: Founded in 1965, NOLS is a non-profit outdoor educational school offering courses designed to teach minimum-impact camping, travel techniques, safety, environmental awareness, and expedition dynamics.

PROGRAMS: Major activities are wilderness backpacking, mountaineering, sea kayaking, ocean sailing, horsepacking, skiing, and winter camping. Instructors are certified by NOLS.

ELIGIBILITY: Good physical condition.

LOCATION: Destinations include Argentina, Canada, Chile, India, Kenya, and Mexico.

TIME OF YEAR: Options are available throughout the year.

DURATION: Two weeks to three months.

ACCOMMODATIONS: Tents and branch school dormitories.

COST: Tuition starts at $1,250 and includes housing, meals, and all ground transportation. Equipment and airfare are additional.

AGE OF PARTICIPANTS: The average age is between 20 and 35.

➤➤➤

National Registration Center for Study Abroad (NRCSA)

P.O. Box 1391
Milwaukee, WI 53201
Phone: (414) 278-0631
Fax: (414) 271-8884

INSTITUTION/ORGANIZATION: Founded in 1968, the NRCSA is a consortium of 86 universities, foreign language institutes, adult education colleges, and activity centers.

PROGRAMS: Language study programs, both group and tutorial, are offered in 16 countries. Courses are taught by instructors with university degrees. Languages include French, Spanish, Italian, English, German, Japanese, Portuguese, and Chinese (Mandarin and Taiwanese).

ELIGIBILITY: Applications are accepted from all interested persons.

LOCATION: Argentina, Austria, Britain, Canada, Costa Rica, Ecuador, France, Germany, Guatemala, Italy, Japan, Mexico, Portugal, Spain, Switzerland, and Taiwan.

TIME OF YEAR: Options are available throughout the year, beginning every Monday.

DURATION: Programs range from one to six weeks.

ACCOMMODATIONS: Hotels, private homes, and college dormitories.

COST: Varies depending on the program. Contact the NRCSA for more information.

➤➤➤

National Trust for Historic Preservation

1785 Massachusetts Avenue, NW
Washington, DC 20036
Phone: (202) 673-4138
Fax: (202) 673-4059

INSTITUTION/ORGANIZATION: Founded in 1949, The National Trust for Historic Preservation is a nonprofit organization concerned with educating Americans on U.S. architectural and cultural history.

PROGRAM: "National Trust Study Tours." This program includes more than 25 study tours focusing on architecture, historic preservation, history, art, and culture. Lectures are provided on tour by the study leaders, who are usually university lecturers or architectural historians. Reading lists are sent to participants prior to program departure. Both land and cruise tours are available. Land tours are limited to 30 participants; cruises are limited to 80. The National Trust has been running these study tours for more than 22 years.

ELIGIBILITY: Applications are accepted from all interested persons who are at least 16 years old.

LOCATION: Outside-the-U.S. destinations include Chile, Argentina, Egypt, Jordan, Russia, Australia, Italy, Holland, Belgium, Portugal, Spain, France, the United Kingdom, Norway, Sweden, Finland, Austria, South Africa, Thailand, Cambodia, and Laos.

TIME OF YEAR: Options are available throughout the year.

DURATION: Most tours run from 10 to 14 days.

ACCOMMODATIONS: Participants stay in hotels.

COST: Costs vary depending on the tour, but range from $900 to $8,000 and include accommodations, sight-seeing expenses, and most meals. Airfare is additional.

AGE OF PARTICIPANTS: The average age of participants is usually between 40 and 70.

PERSONS WITH DISABILITIES: Persons with disabilities are accommodated if at all possible.

▸⇒▸⇒▸

National Trust for Places of Natural Beauty and Historic Interest

P.O. Box 12
Westbury, WILTS BA13 4NA
UNITED KINGDOM
Phone: (44) 373 826826

INSTITUTION/ORGANIZATION: The National Trust is the largest conservation charity in Britain, conserving landscapes and famous houses for the benefit of the nation.

PROGRAMS: The National Trust sponsors short-term voluntary service opportunities in education, recreation, environmental conservation, archaeology/fieldwork, and construction. Projects are led by experienced team leaders and National Trust staff. Volunteers serve 35 hours a week.

ELIGIBILITY: Some projects require experience in construction, bio-surveys, or archaeology.

LOCATION: England, Wales, and Northern Ireland.

TIME OF YEAR: Options are available throughout the year.

DURATION: Projects run from one to two weeks.

ACCOMMODATIONS: Volunteers live in base camps with bunks.

COST: Each project costs 34 British pounds (approximately $62) per week and includes room and board.

AGE OF PARTICIPANTS: Minimum age is 18.

PERSONS WITH DISABILITIES: Some projects have been developed for volunteers over 18 years of age with disabilities. Contact the National Trust for more information.

➤➡➤

Natural Gourmet Cookery School

Institute for Food and Health
48 West 21st Street
New York, NY 10010
Phone: (212) 645-5170

INSTITUTION/ORGANIZATION: Founded in 1977, the Natural Gourmet Cookery School is the country's oldest natural foods cooking school.

PROGRAM: "Taste of Chinese Herbal Cuisine." Five days of Chinese herbal study at the Beijing Culinary Academy is combined with a variety of sight-seeing and cultural activities in Chinese cities. The school teaches the relationship between food and wellness, and how to prepare healthy, palatable cuisine. Instructors are master herbalists specializing in Chinese herbal cuisine.

ELIGIBILITY: Applications are accepted from all interested persons.

LOCATION: Beijing, Hangzhou, Suzhou, and Shanghai, China.

TIME OF YEAR: Spring.

DURATION: The program runs for two weeks.

ACCOMMODATIONS: Hotels.

COST: $3,290, which includes round-trip airfare from New York, room, board, tuition, study supplies, and excursions.

PERSONS WITH DISABILITIES: The program is open to all interested persons.

COMMENTS: The first year the program was offered was 1992; it is expected to run annually.

⟫⟹⟫⟹⟫

Natural History Museum of Los Angeles County
900 Exposition Boulevard
Los Angeles, CA 90007
Phone: (213) 744-3350
Fax: (213) 747-6718

INSTITUTION/ORGANIZATION: Founded in 1913, the Natural History Museum is a nonprofit cultural institution. Dedicated to expanding its educational opportunities and providing its members with an increased global awareness, the "Museum Travel Program" includes unique destinations and unusual adventures worldwide.

PROGRAM: "Museum Travel Program." With an emphasis on the study of natural history, this program has taken participants to Asia, Africa, Europe, and Latin America. Led by museum curators, lectures are combined with hands-on experience and touring. Fifteen different trips are offered throughout the year. The maximum number of participants permitted on each excursion ranges from 24 to 100, depending on the program.

ELIGIBILITY: Participants must be members of the museum.

LOCATION: Destinations have included the Netherlands, Guatemala, Antarctica, Mexico, Micronesia, Ecuador, Morocco, and Greece.

TIME OF YEAR: Options are available throughout the year.

DURATION: Programs vary from one to three weeks.

ACCOMMODATIONS: Hotels.

COST: Usually $800 to $6,800, but varies according to the destination. Contact the museum for more information.

AGE OF PARTICIPANTS: Participants usually range in age from 40 to 75.

PERSONS WITH DISABILITIES: Necessary accommodations and adaptations can be made.

▸⇒▸⇒▸

Nature Expeditions International
P.O. Box 11496
Eugene, OR 97401
Phone: (503) 484-6529

INSTITUTION/ORGANIZATION: Founded in 1973, this commercial tour operator offers wildlife and cultural study tours worldwide.

PROGRAMS: Programs include East African wildlife safaris, Australian natural history tours, a cultural and natural history tour of Bhutan, and many more. Expeditions are graded according to the level of exertion required: easy, comfortable, moderate, and challenging. Guides have college-level teaching experience and advanced degrees in anthropology or natural science. Groups are limited to 16 people.
ELIGIBILITY: Applications accepted from all interested persons.
LOCATION: Africa, Asia, Oceania, North and South America.
TIME OF YEAR: Options are available throughout the year.
DURATION: Programs run from nine to 30 days.
ACCOMMODATIONS: Hotels and traditional inns.
COST: Approximately $1,490 to $4,590, including all land costs. Airfare is additional.
AGE OF PARTICIPANTS: Participants range in age from 20 to 70.

▸⇒▸⇒▸

Network of Educators on Central America
1118 22nd Street SW
Washington, DC 20037
Phone: (202) 429-0137
Fax: (202) 429-9766

INSTITUTION/ORGANIZATION: Founded in 1986, the Network of Educators on Central America is a nonprofit educational organization for elementary and secondary educators.

PROGRAM: "Educators Tour to El Salvador." This program focuses on elementary and secondary education in El Salvador. Participants observe urban and rural elementary and secondary schools in session and meet teachers, students, and their parents, as well as community and educational leaders. Community projects are also observed. Groups are limited to 20 participants.

ELIGIBILITY: Applications are accepted from all interested persons.

LOCATION: San Salvador and one rural community in El Salvador.

TIME OF YEAR: Summer.

DURATION: Tours run for 10 days.

ACCOMMODATIONS: Hotels and rural private homes.

COST: The tour costs approximately $1,200 and includes round-trip international airfare, room, board, and transportation within the country.

AGE OF PARTICIPANTS: Participants range in age from about 25 to 50.

PERSONS WITH DISABILITIES: Disabled persons are considered on a case-by-case basis. Contact the organization to discuss the options available.

▶⇒▶⇒▶

University of New Orleans

International Study Programs
Metro College
New Orleans, LA 70148
Phone: (504) 286-7484
Fax: (504) 286-7317

INSTITUTION/ORGANIZATION: Founded in 1956, the University of New Orleans (UNO) is a public four-year institution that offers postgraduate programs. UNO is a member of the Council on International Educational Exchange.

PROGRAMS: UNO has sponsored a variety of summer programs for adults abroad, including the following:
  • "Edinburgh International Arts Festival." Sponsored in conjunction with the Council on International Educational Exchange, this program takes participants to one of the world's greatest arts events. The Edinburgh Arts Festival in Scotland features plays, exhibitions, opera, concerts, and recitals by major artists from all over the world. While the program focuses on the performing arts, professors also give lectures on Scotland and the Edinburgh Festival. The program runs for 10

days. Participants stay in college dormitories. In 1991 the cost was approximately $1,400, which included room, breakfast daily, tickets to five performances, excursions, lectures, social events, and group accident insurance. Airfare was additional. Groups are limited to 30 people.

- "UNO in Bath, England: Seminars for Educators." Focused on comparative education and curriculum development in the United States and the United Kingdom, this program includes courses on special education and curriculum and instruction. Lectures, seminars, and small group discussions are combined with visits to British schools. All instructors hold doctorates in education. The program runs for three weeks, and participants live in college dormitories. In 1992 the cost was $1,195, which included room, tuition, field trips, visits to British schools twice a week, and group accident insurance. Participants should be teachers, college juniors or seniors majoring in education, or graduate students. Although this is a credit-bearing program, interested persons do have the option to audit; check with UNO for more information. Louisiana residents can apply for tuition reimbursement if eligible. Groups are limited to 40 people.

- "The European Centre." This adult study program in Innsbruck, Austria, offers liberal arts, fine arts, and business classes. Courses are available for credit or for enrichment and are taught by experienced educators with advanced degrees. Social, cultural, and educational activities are combined with weekend travel. The program runs for three weeks and participants stay in college dormitories at the University of Innsbruck. In 1992 the cost was $2,395, which included room, most meals, tuition, lectures, field trips, social events, and group accident insurance. Groups are limited to 50 people.

- "Interhostel." Designed specifically for travelers over 50 years of age, this program is sponsored in conjunction with the University of New Hampshire and takes place in Innsbruck, Austria. Focused on the study of central European culture, lectures are given by experts and combined with group excursions. The program runs for two weeks, and participants live in college dormitories. In 1991 the cost was $1,350 and included group educational activities, admission fees, room, board, ground transportation to group events, and airport transfers. Interested persons must be at least 50 years old. Groups are limited to 40 people.

ELIGIBILITY: Varies according to program. See descriptions of programs above.
LOCATION: Destinations vary each year.
TIME OF YEAR: Summer.
DURATION: Programs vary from 10 days to three weeks.
PERSONS WITH DISABILITIES: Participants must be ambulatory (for all UNO programs), as extensive walking is required. Applicants are considered on a case-by-case basis.

The New York Botanical Garden

Southern Boulevard
Bronx, NY 10458
Phone: (212) 220-8647
Fax: (212) 220-6504

INSTITUTION/ORGANIZATION: Founded in 1891, The New York Botanical Garden is a nonprofit cultural institution that focuses on education and horticulture, and conducts scientific research.

PROGRAMS: The Botanical Garden offers natural history tours and/or volunteer-assisted research expeditions. The natural history tours focus on the study of plants and sometimes of birds, while the expeditions concentrate on plant collecting and ecological and pollination studies. The maximum number of participants on each tour varies from eight to 18.
ELIGIBILITY: Participants must be in good physical condition for research expeditions.
LOCATION: Destinations include Brazil (Amazon area), French Guiana, Venezuela, and Ecuador (Galápagos Islands).
TIME OF YEAR: Varies with the destination.
DURATION: Programs vary from eight to 16 days.
ACCOMMODATIONS: Boats, hammock shelters, small guesthouses, and ranches.
COST: Varies with the destination, but ranges from $1,700 to $3,500 and includes round-trip international airfare, room, and board.
AGE OF PARTICIPANTS: Participants range in age from 20 to 70; the average is 40 to 50.
PERSONS WITH DISABILITIES: Because of somewhat strenuous activities, trips are not recommended for persons with disabilities.

▶️═▶️═▶️

New York University

Gallatin Division
715 Broadway, 8th Floor
New York, NY 10003
Phone: (212) 998-7371
Fax: (212) 998-7351

INSTITUTION/ORGANIZATION: New York University is a member of
the Council on International Educational Exchange. The Gallatin Division, a college of NYU, has an interdisciplinary great books curriculum.

PROGRAM: "Gallatin Abroad: Humanities Seminars in Florence,
Italy." This study program offers courses in the art and literature of
the Italian Renaissance and includes readings from Dante, Boccaccio,
and art history texts, as well as visits to museums, churches, and other
cultural sites. Instructors have strong teaching backgrounds and advanced degrees. Course work is on the graduate level.
ELIGIBILITY: Applications are accepted from all interested persons
who have graduated from high school. Though all participants must
take the program for academic credit, it is not necessary to secure
admission to NYU to participate.
LOCATION: Florence, Italy.
TIME OF YEAR: Summer.
DURATION: The program runs for three weeks.
ACCOMMODATIONS: Hotels.
COST: In 1992 the program cost approximately $2,200, which in-
cluded room and breakfast daily, tuition for four credits, and fees.
Airfare was not included.
AGE OF PARTICIPANTS: Most people are between about 18 and 25
years old, although older students always participate.
PERSONS WITH DISABILITIES: Though few provisions have been
made, tape recorders are permissible, and elevators are available in
the buildings.

▶️═▶️═▶️

Los Niños

9765 Marconi Drive
Suite 105
San Ysidro, CA 92173

Phone: (619) 661-6912
Fax: (619) 661-1363

INSTITUTION/ORGANIZATION: Founded in 1974, Los Niños is a non-profit educational organization that works with communities and orphanages in Mexico. Providing community development services in the areas of literacy, early education, nutrition/health, and family gardens/forestation, Los Niños works to foster independence for Mexican families. In addition, U.S. volunteers are educated about development work and Mexico.

PROGRAMS: Los Niños sponsors a volunteer internship program during the summer, which involves teaching in the morning and attending educational workshops focused on development issues in the afternoon. Also available is a development education program, which strictly involves attending educational workshops. Instructors or lecturers are experts in various areas of development education. The maximum number of participants permitted on each program is 20.

ELIGIBILITY: Participants should be mature, cross-culturally aware, and sensitive to Mexican culture.

LOCATION: Tijuana, Mexico.

TIME OF YEAR: The internship program takes place during the summer; the education program takes place from October to May.

DURATION: The internship program runs for six weeks; the education program ranges from two to 10 days.

ACCOMMODATIONS: College dormitories.

COST: The education program costs $95 for a weekend; $190 for a week. The internship program costs $900 for the summer. These costs include room and board, activities, and transportation in Tijuana. Airfare is not included.

AGE OF PARTICIPANTS: The average age of participants is usually about 21.

PERSONS WITH DISABILITIES: The program is open to anyone interested in applying.

COMMENTS: Most participants are high school and college students, but people of all ages are encouraged to apply.

➤⇒➤⇒➤

Northern Illinois University

International and Special Programs
Lowden Hall 203
DeKalb, IL 60115
Phone: (815) 753-1988
Fax: (815) 753-1488

INSTITUTION/ORGANIZATION: Founded in 1895, Northern Illinois University sponsors a broad range of short-term educational programs overseas. The university is a member of the Council on International Educational Exchange.

PROGRAMS: "Short-Term Foreign Study Programs." Northern Illinois University offers programs with a broad range of educational focuses, including art, history, culture, literature, film and media studies, science, languages, and business. Conducted by university professors, lectures are included on most programs. Group sizes range from 15 to 20 participants.
ELIGIBILITY: Applications are accepted from all interested persons.
LOCATION: Previous destinations have included China, Japan, Great Britain, Ireland, France, the Netherlands, Greece, Czechoslovakia, and Venezuela.
TIME OF YEAR: Summer and winter.
DURATION: Programs vary from two to four weeks.
ACCOMMODATIONS: Hotels, dormitories, and private homes.
COST: Program costs range from approximately $2,000 to $3,900 and include room, board, one to two meals per day, land transportation, and admission fees. Airfare is additional.
PERSONS WITH DISABILITIES: The university complies with the state and U.S. laws regarding persons with disabilities, and with the foreign law when abroad. Special arrangements are handled on a case-by-case basis.

➤⇒➤⇒➤

Oceanic Society Expeditions

Fort Mason Center, Building E
San Francisco, CA 94123
Phone: (800) 326-7491 or (415) 441-1106

INSTITUTION/ORGANIZATION: Founded in 1972, Oceanic Society Expeditions (OSE) is a nonprofit organization concerned with providing opportunities for individuals to learn about the natural world through participating in educational eco-tours. OSE conducts eco-tours with a noninvasive approach to viewing wildlife and wilderness exploration.

PROGRAMS: OSE has sponsored a variety of expeditions, including research projects that offer the lay participant the chance to assist scientists with dolphin- and whale-watching. Other expeditions have included worldwide scuba-diving trips accompanied by marine naturalists; natural history and snorkeling; rain forests and astronomy; African safaris; and archaeological digs.

ELIGIBILITY: Participants should be in good health. Water programs require basic swimming ability.

LOCATION: Destinations vary each year. Previous locations have included South America and Antarctica, Central America, Africa, and Asia (including Siberia).

TIME OF YEAR: Options are available throughout the year.

DURATION: Expeditions generally run from one to two weeks.

ACCOMMODATIONS: Participants live in hotels and lodges, or on ships.

COST: The cost generally ranges from $1,000 to $2,000 and includes room, board, and land transportation. International airfare is included on some programs.

PERSONS WITH DISABILITIES: Individuals are considered on a case-by-case basis.

➤⇒➤⇒➤

Offshore Sailing School

16731 McGregor Boulevard, Suite 110
Fort Myers, FL 33008
Phone: (800) 221-4326
Fax: (813) 454-1191

INSTITUTION/ORGANIZATION: The Offshore Sailing School is a commercial tour operator that has offered sailing lessons for more than 27 years.

PROGRAM: "Learn to Sail." This course includes intensive class and on-water experience spanning beginner through intermediate levels

of sailing skills. An introductory classroom session is held prior to departure. Instructors have coast guard licenses or equivalent experience. Prior to the start of the course, participants receive a text on sailing written by Steve Colgate, owner of the school.
ELIGIBILITY: Applications are accepted from all interested persons.
LOCATION: Destinations include the British Virgin Islands.
TIME OF YEAR: Options available throughout the year.
DURATION: Three to seven days.
ACCOMMODATIONS: Packages that include hotel accommodations are available.
COST: Ranges from $415 to $695 for tuition only.
AGE OF PARTICIPANTS: A wide range of ages participates.

➤⇒➤⇒➤

The Ohio State University
Office of Study Abroad
308 Dulles Hall
230 West 17th Avenue
Columbus, OH 43210
Phone: (614) 292-9660
Fax: (614) 292-4725

INSTITUTION/ORGANIZATION: Founded in 1870, The Ohio State University is a state institution with an enrollment of more than 52,000 students. The university is a member of the Council on International Educational Exchange.

PROGRAM: "The Structures of Colloquial Spanish." This workshop provides high school Spanish teachers with an opportunity to analyze and practice Spanish language in a natural linguistic and cultural context. Taught by faculty from Ohio State University, lectures are combined with small group discussions and out-of-class projects.
ELIGIBILITY: Participants should be high school Spanish teachers.
LOCATION: Cuernavaca, Mexico.
TIME OF YEAR: Summer.
DURATION: Two weeks.
ACCOMMODATIONS: Private homes.
COST: In 1991 the cost was $579, which included tuition, room and board with a Mexican family, excursions, and transportation from

Mexico City to Cuernavaca (and return). International airfare was not included.

PERSONS WITH DISABILITIES: Permission and arrangements must be worked out with Cemanhuac Educational Community, the host institution in Mexico.

COMMENTS: Funding is available for teachers in Franklin County, Ohio, that covers the cost of tuition. Contact the Office of Study Abroad for further information. Participants can earn academic credit.

Ohio University

Office of Continuing Education
Memorial Auditorium
Athens, OH 45701
Phone: (614) 593-1776
Fax: (614) 593-0388

INSTITUTION/ORGANIZATION: Founded in 1804, Ohio University is a state institution with an enrollment of more than 16,000 students. The university is a member of the Council on International Educational Exchange.

PROGRAMS: Study tours, ranging in focus from art to marine biology, are administered by the Office of Continuing Education. Sponsored either solely by the university or in combination with Travelearn, a travel broker specializing in developing learning vacations for adults, these excursions are usually led by university faculty.

ELIGIBILITY: Applications are accepted from all interested persons.

LOCATION: Destinations include Norway, Greece, Ecuador, Egypt, Kenya, China, and Nepal.

TIME OF YEAR: Options are available throughout the year.

DURATION: From one to four weeks, depending on the destination.

ACCOMMODATIONS: Facilities include college dormitories, hotels, private homes, and hostels.

COST: Varies, depending on the destination. Contact the Office of Continuing Education.

AGE OF PARTICIPANTS: The average age of participants is usually between 30 and 40.

Oideas Gael

Ulster Cultural Institute
Glencolmcille, Co. Donegal
IRELAND
Phone: (353) 1 213566 (Dublin)
Fax: (353) 73 30123 (Glencolmcille)

INSTITUTION/ORGANIZATION: Founded in 1984, Oideas Gael is a nonprofit organization established to promote Irish language and culture.

PROGRAMS: Courses in Irish language and culture include all levels of Gaelic as well as classes in dance, painting, music, and hill walking. Instructors are college and university lecturers, and language teachers.
ELIGIBILITY: Applications are accepted from all interested persons.
LOCATION: Glencolmcille, County Donegal, Ireland.
TIME OF YEAR: Spring, summer, and fall.
DURATION: Seven days.
ACCOMMODATIONS: Hotels, hostels, and private homes.
COST: Tuition is approximately $121 (75 Irish pounds) plus $56 to $160 (35 to 100 Irish pounds) for accommodations, depending on the type chosen; contact Oideas Gael for more information.
AGE OF PARTICIPANTS: The average age of participants is usually about 35.
PERSONS WITH DISABILITIES: Ulster Cultural Institute is a modern, accessible building.

University of Oklahoma

Continuing Education and Public Service
1700 Asp Avenue
Norman, OK 73037
Phone: (405) 325-1931 (Academic Programs)
       (405) 325-3488 (Elderhostel)
Fax: (405) 325-7698 (Academic Programs)
     (405) 325-7679 (Elderhostel)

INSTITUTION/ORGANIZATION: The University of Oklahoma is a member of the Council on International Educational Exchange.

The Continuing Education and Public-Service division administers academic programs to enhance degree programs in off-campus locations, including international programs and programs for older citizens.

PROGRAMS: The following study tours are offered:
- "Continuing Education Academic Programs." These study opportunities are available in a variety of subjects, including languages, culture, history, the arts, and humanities. Lectures, tutorials, and small group discussions led by university professors are combined with field tours. Destinations include France, Italy, Japan, Mexico, Czechoslovakia, Russia, and Spain. Programs run from four days to six weeks, and participants live in hotels and college dormitories. The cost varies with the program. Some programs require language facility or university admission; others have no prerequisites. Students can obtain academic credit; contact the office above for information. Groups range in size from 20 to 50 participants, depending on the program.
- "Elderhostel: A Cultural Overview." This program is sponsored in cooperation with Elderhostel, a Massachusetts-based organization that specializes in programs for travelers at least 60 years of age (see page 142 for more information). Focused on the study of language and culture, this program takes participants to Saltillo, Mexico, for eight days. Lectures and small group discussions are combined with field trips to museums. Participants have the opportunity to mingle with the native people. The program has been offered from three to six times a year in the spring, summer, winter, and fall. Participants live in hotels. The 1992 costs ranged from $650 to $750 and included room, board, field trips, admission to museums and special events, classroom materials and instruction, and airport transfers. International airfare is not included. Participants must be at least 60 years old and in reasonably good health. Groups are limited to 25 participants.

ELIGIBILITY: Varies according to the program; see descriptions of programs above.

LOCATION: Previous destinations have included Japan, Mexico, Czechoslovakia, Russia, France, Italy, and Spain.

TIME OF YEAR: Time of year varies. See descriptions of programs above.

DURATION: Programs vary from four days to six weeks.

PERSONS WITH DISABILITIES: The program accepts persons with disabilities; applicants are handled on an individual basis.

COMMENTS: Interested students can earn academic credit for participation on the "Continuing Education Academic Programs."

The Old Corner House, Woebley

The Old Corner House
Broad Street
Woebley, Herefordshire HR4 8SA
UNITED KINGDOM
Phone: (44) 544 318548

INSTITUTION/ORGANIZATION: Founded in 1982, this residential painting center offers a wide range of painting courses.

PROGRAM: "Watercolor Weeks at Woebley." Painting and drawing courses, studio-based as well as on location, are taught by highly qualified instructors. Lectures and tutorials are combined with demonstrations. Thirty courses are offered per year. The maximum number of students in each course is 18.

ELIGIBILITY: Applications are accepted from all interested persons.

LOCATION: Woebley, a medieval village.

TIME OF YEAR: Courses take place during the spring, summer, and fall.

DURATION: Each course runs for about one week.

ACCOMMODATIONS: Participants live in private rooms in the Old Corner House.

COST: Approximately $420 (239 British pounds) plus $79 (45 pounds) tax includes tuition, studio facilities, room, breakfast and evening meals.

AGE OF PARTICIPANTS: The average age of participants is usually about 30 to 50.

PERSONS WITH DISABILITIES: Persons with disabilities are welcome. Individuals are handled on a case-by-case basis.

COMMENTS: Approximately five percent of participants are usually from the United States.

▶➡▶➡

OPA Tours Greece

9345 Glory Avenue
Tujunga, CA 91402
Phone: (818) 352-4526

INSTITUTION/ORGANIZATION: OPA is a commercial tour operator
that organizes educational tours to Greece, with an emphasis on art,
archaeology, unique itineraries, and personal involvement.

PROGRAM: "Ancient Civilizations." Focused on ancient art, archae-
ology, and culture, tours explore the Minoan, Mycenaean, Classical,
and Byzantine civilizations of Greece on the mainland and the islands.
Tour leaders are required to have at least a bachelor's degree and a
minimum of three years touring experience. Groups are limited to 25
people.
ELIGIBILITY: Applications are accepted from all interested persons.
LOCATION: Numerous locations in Greece.
TIME OF YEAR: Spring and fall.
DURATION: Three weeks.
ACCOMMODATIONS: Hotels.
COST: Varies. The average cost is $3,000 and includes room (based
on double occupancy), most meals, and round-trip airfare from New
York.
AGE OF PARTICIPANTS: The average age of participants is usually
about 60.

▶➡▶➡

Opera Education International/OEI & OEI Tours

400 Yale Avenue
Berkeley, CA 94708
Phone: (415) 526-5244

INSTITUTION/ORGANIZATION: The primary purpose of Opera Education International (OEI), founded in 1965, is to prepare Bay Area
audiences for upcoming productions by the San Francisco Opera. In
addition, this commercial operation offers educational opera tours
worldwide.

PROGRAMS: OEI sponsors opera tours abroad that seek to educate
participants on performances attended throughout the tour. Led by

Dr. Michael Barclay, a world-known cultural historian, daily lectures are provided on the performances and other topics such as languages, literature, art and cultural history, and the modern world of international opera production. The maximum number of participants on each tour ranges from 12 to 19.

ELIGIBILITY: Applications are accepted from all interested persons.

LOCATION: Destinations include Vienna, Austria; Munich, Germany; Florence, Italy; and London, England, among others.

TIME OF YEAR: Spring, summer, winter.

DURATION: Tours vary from 12 to 19 days.

ACCOMMODATIONS: Hotels.

COST: Varies depending on destination, but can be as high as $8,500. Prices include daily tickets to opera performances (the best available), lectures, room, breakfast daily, gala welcome and farewell dinners, and most surface transportation. Airfare is not included.

AGE OF PARTICIPANTS: Participants are usually in their 60's and 70's.

PERSONS WITH DISABILITIES: OEI tries to accommodate all who are interested, though an accompanying attendant or helper may be required.

▸═▸═▸

Our Developing World

13004 Paseo Presada
Saratoga, CA 95070
Phone: (408) 379-4431

INSTITUTION/ORGANIZATION: Founded in 1974, this nonprofit educational organization is designed to bring the realities of the Third World to North Americans through programs, curricula, and study tours.

PROGRAMS: Tours focus on people and development, visits to grassroots empowerment projects, health, education, law reform, and other issues. The codirectors, Vic and Barby Ulmer, lead the group and provide instruction, although the learning is largely experiential. The Ulmers are retired teachers with experience in high school as well as college. Groups are limited to 12 people.

ELIGIBILITY: Applications are accepted from all interested persons 18 and over.

LOCATION: Destinations vary each year. Previous destinations have included El Salvador and Nicaragua, Mozambique and Zimbabwe, and South Africa.
TIME OF YEAR: Summer.
DURATION: Two to three weeks.
ACCOMMODATIONS: Hotels, hostels, local facilities.
COST: Varies, depending on destination. Contact Our Developing World for more information.
AGE OF PARTICIPANTS: Ages within each group vary greatly.
COMMENTS: Interest-free loans may be available to assist participants. Inquire when you request program information.

Paris en Cuisine

49, rue de Richelieu
Paris 75001
FRANCE
Phone: (33) 1 42 61.35.23
Fax: (33) 1 42 6039.96

INSTITUTION/ORGANIZATION: Founded in 1975, Paris en Cuisine is an ambulatory commercial cooking school that uses France's top restaurants and food shop kitchens as classrooms.

PROGRAM: Paris en Cuisine sponsors a culinary program that includes gastronomic weeks, which provide participants with pastry classes and an introduction to French food today. Instructors are accomplished chefs in fine French restaurants, or quality producers of high quality cheese, wine, and other food products. Lessons are translated into English.
ELIGIBILITY: Applications are accepted from all interested persons.
LOCATION: Paris and various provinces of France.
TIME OF YEAR: Options are available throughout the year.
DURATION: From a 2½-hour class to a one-week pastry program.
ACCOMMODATIONS: Participants are responsible for arranging their own lodging.
COST: Varies; contact the school.
PERSONS WITH DISABILITIES: All are welcome, but many classes and activities are conducted in facilities that are not accessible.

COMMENTS: About 90 percent of participants are usually from the United States. A nine-month program is also available.

▸⇒▸⇒▸

The Partnership for Service-Learning

815 Second Avenue
Suite 315
New York, NY 10017
Phone: (212) 986-0989
Fax: (212) 949-6781

INSTITUTION/ORGANIZATION: Founded in 1982, The Partnership for Service-Learning is a nonprofit educational organization providing programs of structured learning and extensive community service in international/intercultural settings. The Partnership is a membership organization comprised of colleges, universities, service agencies, and related organizations in higher education, as well as individuals.

PROGRAM: "Service-Learning." Participants combine study of another culture with direct experience in that culture through doing extensive community service work. All instruction is given by on-site college/university faculty from the host country and includes such subjects as history, language, literature, and sociology. The service opportunities include teaching, health care, and community development projects. Placement of students is made by the Partnership in cooperation with the host-nation placement officers. Group size ranges from 20 to 25 people.

ELIGIBILITY: Participants must be at least 18 years of age. For programs in France, Ecuador, and Mexico, interested persons should have two years of high school or one year of college-level French or Spanish.

LOCATION: Destinations include Ecuador, England, France, India, Jamaica, Mexico, and the Philippines.

TIME OF YEAR: Options are available throughout the year.

DURATION: Programs vary from three weeks to one year, depending on the location.

ACCOMMODATIONS: Private homes, college dormitories, and service agencies.

COST: Varies depending on the program and the time frame; generally ranges from about $2,500 to $4,000 and covers all in-country or program-site costs, including room, board, instruction, orientation, and administrative fees. Airfare and books are additional.

AGE OF PARTICIPANTS: The average age of participants is usually between 22 and 25, although persons over 60 have participated.

PERSONS WITH DISABILITIES: Applicants are considered on a case-by-case basis.

COMMENTS: Interested students can earn academic credit for participation. Contact the Partnership for more information.

▸⇒▸⇒▸

Photo Adventure Tours

2035 Park Street
Atlantic Beach, NY 11509-1236
Phone: (516) 371-0067
Fax: (516) 371-1352

INSTITUTION/ORGANIZATION: Founded in 1986, Photo Adventure tours is a commercial tour operator.

PROGRAM: A variety of photo tours is available, including camel safaris, special-interest tours, horseback riding tours, and camping-photo tours. Guides are experienced photographers. Groups are limited to 15 people.

ELIGIBILITY: Applications are accepted from all interested persons. Participants must bring their own photographic equipment.

LOCATION: China, Iceland, India, and Greenland.

TIME OF YEAR: Spring, fall, and summer.

DURATION: Tours range in length from about 10 to 27 days.

ACCOMMODATIONS: Hotels and tents.

COST: Varies, depending on the tour; contact Photo Adventure Tours for more information.

AGE OF PARTICIPANTS: The average age of participants usually ranges from 30 to 40.

COMMENTS: Interested students can receive college credit from the University of Puerto Rico's Photography Department.

Plantagenet Tours

85 The Grove
Moordown, Bournemouth BH9 2TY
UNITED KINGDOM
Phone: (44) 202 521 895

INSTITUTION/ORGANIZATION: Founded in 1982, Plantagenet Tours is a commercial tour operator that specializes in historical, cultural, and literary tours to Europe.

PROGRAMS: Organized around historical, cultural, and literary themes, these tours take participants off the beaten tourist paths to numerous countries in Europe. Tours are led by Professor Peter Gravgaard, an expert in English literature and founder of Plantagenet Tours. Past tours have included "Isabella Tour To Moorish Andalucia," "Joan of Arc Tour from Lorraine to Normandy," "Christmas in Denmark," and the "Elizabeth I Tour to Renaissance England," among numerous others. Plantagenet also arranges special interest group tours upon request.

ELIGIBILITY: Applications are accepted from all interested persons.

LOCATION: England, Ireland, Germany, Italy, Spain, Portugal, France, Hungary, Austria, the Baltic States, Russia, Denmark, Sweden, and Norway.

TIME OF YEAR: Throughout the year.

DURATION: Tours vary from 10 to 21 days.

ACCOMMODATIONS: Hotels.

COST: In 1992 tour costs ranged from approximately $1,300 to $2,200 and included room, breakfast and dinner daily, and in-country transportation. Round-trip airfare was additional.

AGE OF PARTICIPANTS: The average age is usually between 50 and 60.

COMMENTS: Students may be able to receive academic credit for participation. Contact Plantagenet for more information.

Plowshares Institute

P.O. Box 243
809 Hopmeadow Street
Simsbury, CT 06070

Phone: (203) 651-4304
Fax: (203) 651-4305

INSTITUTION/ORGANIZATION: Founded in 1981, Plowshares Institute is a nonprofit organization involved in education, service, and research on relations between America and Asia, Africa, and Latin America, with a goal of a more just, sustainable, and peaceful world community.

PROGRAM: "Traveling Seminars." The goal of the seminars is to enable participants to reach their own conclusions about issues in North American relations with countries of the South or Third World. Following an intensive orientation, a representative delegation of North Americans responds to the invitation of religious and civic leaders from host countries to live as guests among their people. Participants have direct contact with religious, business, academic, government, and grass-roots leaders. Seminars are limited to 25 participants.

ELIGIBILITY: Participants must agree to prepare in advance by reading and viewing the resources recommended by the Plowshares staff; live in the life-style of the hosts; and share learnings upon return.

LOCATION: Destinations have included Brazil, Southern Africa, Hong Kong and China, Czechoslovakia, Hungary, Germany, Uganda and Kenya.

TIME OF YEAR: Options are available throughout the year.

DURATION: Usually two to three weeks.

ACCOMMODATIONS: Private homes, hostels, and church guesthouses.

COST: Varies, depending on the destination. In 1992 the seminars cost approximately $3,200 and included international airfare, room, and board.

AGE OF PARTICIPANTS: Participants in some seminars are 45 to 50 years old; other groups consist mainly of graduate students in their mid-20's.

PERSONS WITH DISABILITIES: Access to buildings in Africa, Asia, and Latin America are often restrictive, and the Plowshares Institute has no control over this.

COMMENTS: The program is quite intensive, so all participants need stamina and good health.

▸⟹▸⟹▸

Podere Le Rose-Centro Pontevecchio
Poggio S. Polo
2-Lecchi-Gaiole-Si
ITALY
Phone: (39) 0577 74 61 52
Fax: (39) 055 23 96 887

INSTITUTION/ORGANIZATION: Founded in 1987, Podere Le Rose-Centro Pontevecchio is a school of Italian language and cooking.

PROGRAM: "Chianti in Tuscany." Courses in Italian language are designed for language learners at all levels. Participants can choose the number of class hours they wish to study per week; individual intensive courses are available. Cooking and wine, painting, and gardening classes are also offered. Instructors are specialists in their respective areas. The maximum class size is 10 students.
ELIGIBILITY: Applications are accepted from all interested persons.
LOCATION: Poggio San Polo, Gaiole in Chianti, Italy.
TIME OF YEAR: Spring, summer, and winter.
DURATION: Participants can study for one week or longer.
ACCOMMODATIONS: Hotels and flats.
COST: Language courses cost approximately $210 (260,000 lire); cooking courses cost approximately $330 (410,000 lire). Accommodations cost about $225 (280,000 lire).
AGE OF PARTICIPANTS: Minimum age is 18.
PERSONS WITH DISABILITIES: Applicants are considered on a case-by-case basis.

▸⟹▸⟹▸

Portland State University
Summer Session
P.O. Box 751
Portland, OR 97207
Phone: (503) 725-4081
Fax: (503) 725-4840

INSTITUTION/ORGANIZATION: Founded in 1946, Portland State University (PSU) is a state institution with an enrollment of more than 14,000 students. PSU is a member of the Council on International Educational Exchange.

PROGRAMS: Summer session offerings have included the following:
- "The Natural History of Belau." This on-site field study of Belau's Western Pacific marine ecosystems takes place in Micronesia and focuses on the cultural factors that affect the fragile coral islands. Instructors are experts in their fields. Lectures, tutorials, and small group discussions are combined with hands-on fieldwork, which includes snorkeling and rugged hiking. Field studies take place for 10 days each during the winter and summer (two sessions each season). Participants live in hotels and tents. The cost is approximately $2,800, which includes round-trip airfare from San Francisco, room, partial board, tuition, fees, permits, some local transportation, instruction, boat work, and gratuities. Group size is limited to 22 participants per session. Participants range in age from 17 to 86. The average age of participants in the winter session is usually about 45; for the summer session it is closer to 35.
- "Virgin Islands Natural History Program." On-site study of tropical marine ecosystems in the United States and British Virgin Islands. With an emphasis on biology and geography, this program concentrates on the near-shore/underwater ecosystems and the human factors that affect them. Lectures by experts are provided in the morning; fieldwork, which includes snorkeling and rugged hiking, takes place in the afternoon. The program runs for nine days during the summer. Participants live in hotels. The program costs $1,198, which includes tuition/fees, room, local transportation, gear and instruction, permits, gratuities, boat work, and informational literature. Airfare to and from St. Thomas is additional. Groups are limited to 20 to 25 participants. The average age of participants is usually about 30.

ELIGIBILITY: Applications are accepted from all interested persons.
LOCATION: Japan, Belau, and the British Virgin Islands.
TIME OF YEAR: Summer.
DURATION: Programs vary from nine days to four weeks.
PERSONS WITH DISABILITIES: PSU will accommodate persons with disabilities if at all possible. Contact the university for information on specific programs.
COMMENTS: Some funding is available for programs in Palau and the Virgin Islands. Contact PSU for more information.

▶⟹▶⟹▶

Program of Conscientization for North Americans

1306 East 29th Street
Austin, Texas 78722
Phone: (512) 474-8503

INSTITUTION/ORGANIZATION: Founded in 1976, the Program for Conscientization for North Americans (PCNA) is a Christian non-profit organization coordinated by a joint Mennonite-Catholic team. With an emphasis on Christian faith, PCNA seeks to educate people from the advanced industrialized nations on development issues facing Latin America.

PROGRAM: "PCNA's Latin American Workshop." With an emphasis on "liberation theology," this workshop includes lectures, field trips, interviews, and group reflection. Latin American social and political conditions are analyzed and interpreted from the standpoint of a commitment to liberation and the implications it proposes for the Christian faith. Participants meet with priests, pastors, campesinos, journalists, embassy personnel, and workers. The workshop is conducted on a university academic level.

ELIGIBILITY: Interested persons should be at least college age.

LOCATION: Bogotá and the nearby rural communities of Colombia.

TIME OF YEAR: Summer.

DURATION: One month.

ACCOMMODATIONS: Private homes.

COST: The approximate cost is $710, which includes room, board, and tuition. Airfare is additional.

PERSONS WITH DISABILITIES: Individuals are considered on a case-by-case basis.

COMMENTS: Between 80 and 90 percent of participants are usually from the United States.

▶⟹▶⟹▶

Project RAFT

2855 Telegraph Avenue
Suite 309
Berkeley, CA 94705

Phone: (510) 704-8222
Fax: (510) 704-8322

INSTITUTION/ORGANIZATION: Founded in 1987, Project RAFT (Russians and Americans for Teamwork) is a nonprofit organization that utilizes the wilderness as an educational forum for cross-cultural education and team building.

PROGRAM: "Citizen's Katun Expedition." Focused on cross-cultural education and community building, this program brings Americans together with Russians to navigate the white-water River Katun. Expeditions are led by guides with a minimum of 10 years river guiding experience, as well as training in CPR and first aid. In-depth coverage of river-related safety training is provided. Guides have facility in English and Russian. Expeditions are limited to 30 participants.
ELIGIBILITY: Participants must be enthusiastic.
LOCATION: Russia.
TIME OF YEAR: Summer.
DURATION: The program runs for 15 days.
ACCOMMODATIONS: Tents and private homes.
COST: The cost is approximately $2,500, which includes room, board, river equipment, and guides. International airfare is not included.
AGE OF PARTICIPANTS: The average age of participants is usually about 35.
PERSONS WITH DISABILITIES: Individuals are considered on a case-by-case basis.

▶▶⟹▶▶⟹▶▶

Purdue University

Division of Continuing Education Administration
Study Tours
Stewart Center
West Lafayette, IN 47907
Phone: (317) 404-2975
Fax: (317) 404-0567

INSTITUTION/ORGANIZATION: Founded in 1869, Purdue University is a nonprofit institution.

PROGRAM: "Study Tours." Purdue's Continuing Education division has conducted study tours worldwide for more than 12 years. These tours focus on a range of academic disciplines, including art, culture, agriculture, and archaeology. Programs specifically designed for teachers are also available. Led by experts in the appropriate areas, lectures are combined with small group discussions. Guest speakers from the countries visited are also an integral part of the programs. Groups generally do not exceed 40 people.

ELIGIBILITY: Applications are accepted from all interested persons for most programs. Some tours may require language facility.

LOCATION: Destinations vary each year. Previous destinations have included Guatemala, Ecuador, Argentina, Kenya, Germany, France, Austria, Denmark, the Netherlands, England, Wales, Scotland, Greece, Italy, Russia, and Japan.

TIME OF YEAR: Programs take place throughout the year, though many are run during the summer.

DURATION: Programs usually run for less than three weeks.

ACCOMMODATIONS: Participants stay in hotels and college dormitories.

COST: Program costs vary, but generally range from about $2,200 to $3,200 and include round-trip airfare, room, ground transportation, museum entrance fees, tuition, taxes, and tips.

AGE OF PARTICIPANTS: The average age of participants is usually about 40.

PERSONS WITH DISABILITIES: Tours are open to persons with disabilities. Applicants are considered on a case-by-case basis.

COMMENTS: Interested persons can arrange to receive academic credit for participation.

▶⇛▶⇛▶

Queen Elizabeth's Foundation for the Disabled

Lulworth Court
25 Chalkwell Esplanade
Westcliff on Sea
Essex SSO 8JQ
UNITED KINGDOM
Phone: (44) 702 431725

INSTITUTION/ORGANIZATION: Established more than 30 years ago, Lulworth Court is a holiday center for physically disabled men and women. As a registered charity, this specially adapted seaside home provides the opportunity for disabled people 16 years and older to take an unaccompanied vacation. The full-time staff, along with volunteers, supply round-the-clock nursing care. Social activities and entertainment are provided.

PROGRAM: The Foundation looks for volunteers to help with the personal care (washing, dressing, feeding, and toileting) of severely disabled guests. Assistance is also needed with social activities and outings. This type of service is suitable for persons looking for practical experience in the social science or health fields.
ELIGIBILITY: Applications are accepted from all interested persons.
LOCATION: Southend-on-Sea, Essex, England.
TIME OF YEAR: Late January through mid-December.
DURATION: Volunteers serve for one to two weeks.
ACCOMMODATIONS: Cottages.
COST: Room and board are provided; volunteers are responsible for their own transportation costs. A small stipend is included.
AGE OF PARTICIPANTS: Volunteers are usually under 35 years of age.
PERSONS WITH DISABILITIES: Because of the heavy physical nature of the work, it may not be suitable for physically disabled persons.
COMMENTS: Most volunteers are British.

➤➤➤

Questers Tours and Travel

257 Park Avenue South
New York, NY 10010-7369
Phone: (212) 673-3120
Fax: (212) 473-0178

INSTITUTION/ORGANIZATION: Founded in 1973, Questers is a commercial tour operator that runs nature tours worldwide.

PROGRAM: Natural history tours include visits to national parks and lectures on plants, animals, birds, and geology. Tours are conducted by instructors educated in the natural and biological sciences.
ELIGIBILITY: Applications are accepted from all interested persons, though participants should be in fairly good health as the tours involve a large amount of walking.
LOCATION: Africa, Asia, Europe, Oceania, North and South America.
TIME OF YEAR: Options are available throughout the year.

DURATION: Varies.
ACCOMMODATIONS: Hotels.
COST: Varies; contact Questers for their detailed program catalog.
AGE OF PARTICIPANTS: The average age of participants is usually about 50. Tours cater to a mature age group.

➤⇒➤⇒➤

Ramapo College of New Jersey

Study Abroad Office
505 Ramapo Valley Road
Mahwah, NJ 07430
Phone: (201) 529-7463
Fax: (201) 529-7508

INSTITUTION/ORGANIZATION: Founded in 1972, Ramapo College is a four-year state college specializing in international education. Ramapo is a member of the Council on International Educational Exchange.

PROGRAMS:
- "Archaeological Excavation at Tel Hadar, Israel." Focused on field and biblical archaeology, this program involves the excavation of an 11th-century B.C. Geshurite stronghold along the eastern shore of the Sea of Galilee. The teaching staff is supplied by the New Jersey Archaeological Consortium, an organization of New Jersey state colleges, and Tel Aviv University. Daily instruction is given on the methods, techniques, principles, and problems of field archaeology. Participants live on a kibbutz. In 1992 the approximate cost for the five-week dig was $2,800 and included round-trip airfare to Israel from New York, an eight-day guided tour of Israel with room and two meals per day, room and board while on the dig, tuition and fees, orientation, excursions, and lectures. Shorter programs for teachers and other adults are also available; contact the Study Abroad Office for more information. Group size is limited to 25 people. The average age of participants is usually about 30.
- "Introduction to the Study of Tropical Ecosystems." Focused on tropical ecosystems in Costa Rica, this program provides participants with the opportunity to experience a variety of

tropical ecosystems while undertaking basic ecological field research. Instructors hold advanced degrees in the physical sciences and have experience leading groups abroad. Participants stay in hotels and field station dormitories. The program runs for two weeks in the summer. In 1992 the approximate cost was $2,000 and included round-trip airfare to San José from Newark, transportation while in Costa Rica, room and most meals, orientation, and excursions. Group size is limited to 15 people. The average age of participants is usually about 25.

• "Intensive Study and Appreciation of Italian Language and Culture." This program takes place in the Renaissance city of Urbino, Italy, and includes an intensive study of the Italian language for beginners to advanced students. Courses are also available in modern Italian and Renaissance studies, as well as philosophy. Taught in English and Italian by professors from Ramapo College and the universities of Urbino and Pisa, classes are held five days a week. The program runs for six weeks during the summer, and participants live in college dormitories. In 1992 the program cost $2,700 and included round-trip airfare from New York to Italy, airport transfer, room, most meals, excursions, tours, tuition, and fees. (For Ramapo College students, the price was $2,600 and included the items listed above.) Group size is limited to 40 people. The average age of participants is usually about 30.

ELIGIBILITY: Applications are accepted from all interested persons.
LOCATION: Israel, Costa Rica, and Italy.
TIME OF YEAR: Summer.
DURATION: Programs vary from two to six weeks; see descriptions above.
COMMENTS: Academic credit can be granted for participation on any of these programs.

Recursos de Santa Fe

826 Camino de Monte Rey A-3
Santa Fe, NM 87501
Phone: (505) 982-9301
Fax: (505) 989-8608

INSTITUTION/ORGANIZATION: Founded in 1984, Recursos de Santa Fe is an educational nonprofit organization that sponsors seminars, study tours, and literary events that explore contemporary issues in the arts, culture, geography, and natural history of the Americas.

PROGRAMS: Recursos de Santa Fe offers Spanish and colonial architecture and natural history programs in Mexico and Costa Rica. Usually led by college faculty, the programs combine lectures with small group discussions. Groups are limited to 25 people.

ELIGIBILITY: Applications are accepted from all interested persons.

LOCATION: Mexico and Costa Rica.

TIME OF YEAR: Options are available throughout the year.

DURATION: Two weeks.

ACCOMMODATIONS: Hotels.

AGE OF PARTICIPANTS: The average age of participants is usually between 50 and 65.

PERSONS WITH DISABILITIES: Programs are open to disabled persons providing that the itineraries are not too rough.

COMMENTS: Some funding is available. Students may be able to arrange academic credit through the University of New Mexico. Contact Recursos de Santa Fe for more information.

▸⇒▸⇒▸

Red Coat Tours

1115—8 Avenue South
Lethbridge
Alberta T1J 1P7
CANADA
Phone: (403) 328-9011
Fax: (403) 329-1517

INSTITUTION/ORGANIZATION: Founded in 1990, Red Coat Tours is a commercial tour operator that sponsors programs that take participants on the routes of early western explorers using original journals.

PROGRAM: "In the Footsteps of Peter Fidler." This outdoor adventure focuses on history as participants follow the explorer Peter Fidler's footsteps through Alberta and the Canadian Rockies. Lectures are combined with small group discussions. Groups are limited to 14 people.

ELIGIBILITY: Applications are accepted from all interested persons.
LOCATION: Alberta and the Canadian Rockies.
TIME OF YEAR: Summer.
DURATION: The program runs for seven days.
ACCOMMODATIONS: Hotels.
COST: The approximate cost is $950, which includes room, board, and travel expenses once participant arrives at program site. Transportation to and from program site is not included.
AGE OF PARTICIPANTS: The average age of participants is usually about 60. The program is designed for the traveler over 55.
COMMENTS: About 10 percent of the participants are usually from the United States.

▶⟹▶⟹▶

Rockland Community College
Study Abroad Programs
145 College Road
Suffern, New York 10901
Phone: (914) 574-4205
Fax: (914) 356-1529

INSTITUTION/ORGANIZATION: Rockland Community College is a nonprofit two-year institution of the State University of New York, a member of the Council on International Educational Exchange.

PROGRAMS: Rockland Community College is offering the following study tours in 1993.
- "Comparative Education in China." Focused on the Chinese educational system, this summer program is led by Rockland Community College faculty. Small group discussions are combined with visits, seminars, and tours. The program runs for 15 days. The approximate cost is $2,200 and includes round-trip airfare (from New York), hotel accommodations, lunch and dinner daily, excursions, and tuition for three credits. Open to educators, students, and other interested persons. The program is limited to 20 participants.
- "Painting Seminar in Greece." Focused on painting and drawing, this seminar combines individualized instruction with visits, tours, and small group discussions. Led by Rockland Community College faculty, the program takes place for two

weeks during the summer. The approximate cost is $1,900 and includes round-trip airfare (from New York), hotel accommodations, tuition for three credits, and excursions. Applications are accepted from all interested persons. The program is limited to 20 participants.

- "Wintersession in London." This program runs for two weeks in January. Participants enroll in one course from the following offerings: criminal justice, nursing, art and architecture, drama, literature, psychology, international business, or broadcasting. Led by Rockland Community College faculty, the seminars, tours, and site visits are combined with small group discussions. The program costs approximately $1,300 and includes round-trip airfare (from New York), hotel accommodations, tuition for three credits, and excursions. The program is limited to 20 participants. Open to all interested persons.

- "Ancient Mayans of the Yucatan." This two-week program takes place in Mexico. Led by Rockland Community College faculty, participants explore the ancient Mayan culture, focusing on its history and anthropology. Seminars and tours are combined with small group discussions. The approximate cost is $1,200 and includes round-trip airfare (from New York), hotel accommodations, tuition for three credits, and excursions. Applications are accepted from all interested persons. The program is limited to 20 participants and scheduled to take place either in the summer or the winter.

- "Comparative Nursing Seminar in Israel." This two-week summer program, focused on nursing and nursing education, introduces participants to the health care system of Israel. Led by Rockland Community College faculty, small group discussions are combined with seminars and tours. The approximate cost is $2,000 and includes round-trip airfare (from New York), hotel accommodations, tuition for three credits, and excursions. The program is limited to 20 participants involved in the health care professions or health care education (including students).

ELIGIBILITY: Varies according to program. See descriptions of programs above.

LOCATION: China, Greece, England, Mexico, and Israel.

TIME OF YEAR: Time of year varies. See program descriptions above.

DURATION: Programs run for approximately two weeks.

▶▶=▶=▶

La Romita School of Art

1712 Old Town Road NW
Albuquerque, NM 87104
Phone: (505) 243-1924
Fax: (505) 243-1924

INSTITUTION/ORGANIZATION: Founded in 1966, La Romita School of Art is a nonprofit institution with its own facilities in Italy.

PROGRAMS: La Romita offers workshops in watercolor painting as well as cooking. Generally, the painting workshops are combined with Italian art history and offered to artists on all levels. The cooking workshops emphasize Italian cuisine. Instructors have extensive experience in their respective fields. Site visits to museums, churches, and the hill country are usually included in the workshops. Note: Programs vary in length and emphasis each year, so be sure to write for the current brochure.
ELIGIBILITY: Applications are accepted from all interested persons.
LOCATION: Based in Terni, Italy, with excursions to outside towns.
TIME OF YEAR: Summer and early fall.
DURATION: Programs vary from two to four weeks.
ACCOMMODATIONS: La Romita School (a renovated monastery).
COST: The cost is $1,500 for two weeks; $2,500 for four weeks. These prices include all expenses except art supplies and round-trip airfare to Rome.
AGE OF PARTICIPANTS: The average age of participants is usually about 45.
PERSONS WITH DISABILITIES: Persons with disabilities that restrict motion cannot be cared for adequately.
COMMENTS: La Romita will be happy to provide applicants with the names of past participants for reference. About 95 percent of participants are usually from the United States.

▶▶=▶=▶

La Sabranenque

c/o Jacqueline C. Simon
217 High Park Boulevard
Buffalo, NY 14226
Phone: (716) 836-8698

INSTITUTION/ORGANIZATION: Founded in 1969, La Sabranenque is a nonprofit organization concerned with the preservation of rural architecture and habitats in the villages of southern France and Italy. The goal of this organization is not only to restore and reconstruct, but also to reuse and revitalize abandoned historic sites.

PROGRAM: "Summer Volunteer Restoration Projects." Volunteers work on restoration projects in villages and on small monuments, often dating back to the Middle Ages. Volunteers are recruited from all over the world and work in groups of 12. These projects have been running for more than 20 years.

ELIGIBILITY: Applications are accepted from all interested persons.

LOCATION: Several sites near Saint Victor la Coste (near Avignon), France; Gnallo (northern Italy), and Settefonti (near Bologna), Italy.

TIME OF YEAR: Summer.

DURATION: Projects run for two to three weeks.

ACCOMMODATIONS: Village houses.

COST: The cost is $490 for a two-week session, which includes room, full board, activities, and excursions. Round-trip airfare is not included.

PERSONS WITH DISABILITIES: Projects would be difficult for severely disabled individuals.

COMMENTS: About 40 percent of participants are usually from the United States.

➤➡➤

St. Olaf College

Office of Continuing Education
1520 St. Olaf Avenue
Northfield, MN 55057
Phone: (507) 663-3066
Fax: (507) 663-3549

INSTITUTION/ORGANIZATION: St. Olaf College is a member of the Council on International Educational Exchange. The Office of Continuing Education offers multiple programs for the life-long learner, including short courses and travel-study programs.

PROGRAM: "Continuing Education Study-Travel Program." Designed for the lifelong learner and traveler, two to three different study tours are offered each year that focus on such topics as culture, politics, education, and business. Led by St. Olaf faculty members, the programs combine lectures with small group discussions and are designed for the traveler who is a few years beyond college age. Programs are limited to 15 participants.

ELIGIBILITY: Applications accepted from all interested persons.

LOCATION: Previous destinations have included France, Germany, Greece, Thailand, and the United Kingdom.

TIME OF YEAR: Summer.

DURATION: Two to three weeks.

ACCOMMODATIONS: Hotels and private homes.

COST: The cost has ranged from $2,500 to $3,900 and includes room, most meals, airfare (round-trip from Minneapolis), travel within the country, fees, gratuities, instructional materials, and continuing education credit.

AGE OF PARTICIPANTS: The average age of participants is usually about 43.

PERSONS WITH DISABILITIES: Persons with disabilities are accommodated whenever possible.

COMMENTS: Countries and itineraries change from year to year.

▶⇒▶⇒▶

San Diego Natural History Museum

P.O. Box 1390
San Diego, CA 92116
Phone: (619) 232-3821
Fax: (619) 232-0248

INSTITUTION/ORGANIZATION: Founded in 1874, the museum is a nonprofit organization dedicated to collecting, researching, and offering educational exhibits and programs involving the natural history of the southwest United States and Baja, California. The San Diego Natural History Museum is the second oldest scientific institution west of the Mississippi.

PROGRAMS: Two to four expeditions are offered per year. Programs focus on geology, botany, bird and marine life, paleontology, and other natural sciences. Some programs to be offered in 1993 are a natural history expedition to Costa Rica in April, and a whale-watching expedition in Baja in February/March. A voluntary-service paleontology dig may be offered in the future. Guides are experts in the appropriate fields.

ELIGIBILITY: Participants must be members of the museum; the annual membership fee is $30. Most programs have a minimum age of 15.

LOCATION: Varies from year to year.

TIME OF YEAR: Spring.

DURATION: Usually two weeks.

ACCOMMODATIONS: Participants usually stay in hotels; for the upcoming Baja trip, however, participants will stay on a boat.

COST: Cost varies from year to year.

AGE OF PARTICIPANTS: Participants are usually senior citizens.

San Diego State University

Extended Studies
5630 Hardy Avenue
San Diego, CA 92182
Phone: (619) 594-2645
Fax: (619) 594-7080

INSTITUTION/ORGANIZATION: Founded in 1897, San Diego State University is a nonprofit institution and a member of the Council on International Educational Exchange.

PROGRAMS: Programs offered in 1993 include the following:
- "Spanish Language Immersion in San José, Costa Rica." This three-week intensive language program takes place in the summer. Taught by San Diego State University faculty, small group discussions are combined with tutorials. Participants stay with Costa Rican families. The program fee is approximately $2,185 and includes round-trip airfare from San Diego, room with laundry service, two meals daily, tuition, and fees. The maximum group size is 30, and the average age of participants is usually about 40.
- "Annual Journey to Switzerland in the Fall." Focused on the study of Swiss history and culture, this program is led by experts in the appropriate academic areas. Leisure travel is combined with lectures as participants travel throughout Switz-

erland. The program runs for about two weeks, and participants stay in hotels. The cost is approximately $3,000 and includes round-trip airfare from California, hotel accommodations, two meals daily, admission fees, tips, and porterage. The maximum group size is 30, and participants usually range in age from about 55 to 70.

LOCATION: Costa Rica and Switzerland.
ELIGIBILITY: Applications are accepted from all interested persons.
TIME OF YEAR: Summer and fall.
DURATION: Programs vary from two to three weeks.

San Francisco State University

Extended Education
814 Mission Street, Suite 201
San Francisco, CA 94103
Phone: (415) 338-1372
Fax: (415) 973-6107

INSTITUTION/ORGANIZATION: Founded in 1899, San Francisco State is a four-year public university and a member of the Council on International Educational Exchange.

PROGRAMS: The Extended Education division runs study tours, field research/archaeological digs, and language programs focused on art, business, geography, Spanish, French, Italian, and Japanese. Instructed by university faculty and other qualified lecturers, small group discussions are combined with lectures. In 1992 program offerings included "Explore Egypt"; "Tokyo: Japanese Language and Civilization"; "Doing Business in Europe," which took participants to various countries throughout Europe; "The Côte d'Azur and Picasso," which took participants to the south of France; and "London/Paris Cultural Arts."

ELIGIBILITY: Applications are accepted from all interested persons.
LOCATION: Destinations vary each year. Previous destinations have included Egypt, Japan, France, Ireland, Italy, Germany, England, Spain, the Galápagos Islands, and Ecuador.
TIME OF YEAR: Summer and winter.
DURATION: Programs vary from two to six weeks.
ACCOMMODATIONS: Participants stay in hotels, private homes, college dormitories, and apartments.

COST: Varies with program, but generally includes international airfare, accommodations, breakfasts, tuition, and transfers.

AGE OF PARTICIPANTS: Participants usually range in age from 25 to 45.

PERSONS WITH DISABILITIES: San Francisco State will accommodate disabled persons and make necessary air, bus, and hotel arrangements whenever possible.

➤⇒➤⇒➤

San Francisco State University
Wildlands Studies
3 Mosswood Circle
Cazadero, CA 95421
Phone: (707) 632-5665

INSTITUTION/ORGANIZATION: Founded in 1899, San Francisco State University is a state institution with an enrollment of more than 28,000 students. The university is a member of the Council on International Educational Exchange.

PROGRAM: "Wildlands Studies." Projects concentrate on environmental and cultural studies investigating critical ecological/developmental problems in other cultures. Participants join backcountry study teams as working field associates and help researchers investigate environmental issues. Led by persons with graduate school training in the project field, these programs endeavor to solve critical problems facing wildlands and wildlife populations. Each project is limited to 12 to 14 participants.

ELIGIBILITY: As some projects involve extensive hiking in mountainous terrain, a statement of health is required of all applicants.

LOCATION: Thailand, Nepal, New Zealand, Canada, Mexico, and China.

TIME OF YEAR: Options are available throughout the year.

DURATION: Projects range from three to 10 weeks.

ACCOMMODATIONS: Tents.

COST: Ranges from $385 to $1,900; contact Wildlands Studies for more information.

AGE OF PARTICIPANTS: The average age of participants is usually about 22.

PERSONS WITH DISABILITIES: Applications from persons with disabilities are reviewed on a case-by-case basis.

COMMENTS: Students can obtain academic credit for participation. Contact the office above for more information.

Santa Barbara Museum of Art

Special Programs
1130 State Street
Santa Barbara, CA 93101
Phone: (805) 963-4364
Fax: (805) 966-6840

INSTITUTION/ORGANIZATION: Founded in 1941, the Santa Barbara Museum of Art is a nonprofit institution that houses diverse collections of artwork.

PROGRAMS: "SBMA Travel Program." Focused on the study of art, architecture, gardens, and the performing arts, these programs have a cultural emphasis. Leaders have degrees in the history or art history of the country visited, and lectures are combined with small group discussions and site visits. Some programs combine cruises with land excursions. Groups are limited to 26 people.

ELIGIBILITY: Participants must be members of the museum. The annual membership fee is $40.

LOCATION: Destinations for 1993 include Russia and the Baltic states, Egypt, Morocco, Spain, Portugal, and France.

TIME OF YEAR: Options are available throughout the year.

DURATION: Programs generally run from five to 22 days.

ACCOMMODATIONS: Participants stay in hotels and on cruise ships.

COST: Programs range from approximately $650 to $5,800; the average price is about $3,000.

AGE OF PARTICIPANTS: The average age of participants is usually about 50.

PERSONS WITH DISABILITIES: Handled on a case-by-case basis.

➤⟹➤⟹➤

Saskatchewan Archaeological Society

#5-816 1st Avenue North
Saskatoon, Saskatchewan S7K 1Y3
CANADA
Phone: (306) 664-4124
Fax: (306) 665-1928

INSTITUTION/ORGANIZATION: Founded in 1963, the Saskatchewan Archaeological Society is a nonprofit membership organization dedicated to actively promoting and encouraging the study, preservation, and proper use of the archaeological resources of the area.

PROGRAMS: Focused on the study of archaeology, the Society offers a certification program that includes seminars and training opportunities designed to provide participants with a means of improving their knowledge and technical skills. Groups are limited to 30 participants. An archaeological dig needing volunteers is also offered. Groups for the dig are limited to 20 volunteers. Both programs are led by professional archaeologists.

ELIGIBILITY: Participants should speak English.

LOCATION: Various locations throughout Saskatchewan, Canada.

TIME OF YEAR: The certification program is offered throughout the year; the dig takes place during the summer.

DURATION: The certification program ranges from one to three days. The dig is four days per session; there are two sessions, and volunteers have the option to prticipate in one or both digs.

ACCOMMODATIONS: Participants in the certification program are responsible for finding their own accommodations. Dig volunteers live in cabins, lodges, or tents reserved by the society.

COST: For both programs there is a $10 (Canadian dollars) registration fee. Participants are responsible for all other expenses, including accommodations, meals, and transportation.

AGE OF PARTICIPANTS: The average age of participants is usually about 30.

PERSONS WITH DISABILITIES: Persons with disabilities may participate in the certification program. For the digs, arrangements must be made beforehand, and every effort will be made to accommodate interested persons.

➤⇒➤⇒➤

Scandinavian Seminar

24 Dickinson Street
Amherst, MA 01002
Phone: (413) 253-9736
Fax: (413) 243-5282

INSTITUTION/ORGANIZATION: Founded in 1941, the Scandinavian Seminar is a nonprofit educational organization offering study-abroad opportunities in Scandinavian folk schools as well as the Elderhostel program for persons at least 60 years of age. Sandinavian Seminar is a member of the Council on International Educational Exchange.

PROGRAMS: "Elderhostel." This program is sponsored in cooperation with Elderhostel, an organization that specializes in programs for the traveler over 60 (see description on pages 141–142). A typical Scandinavian Seminar/Elderhostel program takes participants to folk schools in three countries and focuses on cultural studies. Instructors are folk school teachers, and lectures are combined with small group discussions. In 1992, 50 different study tours were offered. The maximum group size ranges from 30 to 45 people.

ELIGIBILITY: Participants must be at least 60 years old.

LOCATION: Destinations include Austria, Belgium, Czechoslovakia, Denmark, Finland, France, Germany, Hungary, the Netherlands, Norway, Poland, Sweden, and Switzerland.

TIME OF YEAR: Options are available throughout the year.

DURATION: Programs run for three weeks.

ACCOMMODATIONS: Dormitories.

COST: The cost ranges from $2,800 to $3,500 and includes round-trip airfare from the United States (Los Angeles or New York), transportation between program sites, room, board, academic program, and excursions.

AGE OF PARTICIPANTS: The average age of participants is usually about 67.

PERSONS WITH DISABILITIES: Contact Scandinavian Seminar to find out whether the sites are accessible.

COMMENTS: Participants must register through Elderhostel, Inc., 75 Federal Street, Boston, MA 02110. Some scholarships are available. Contact Scandinavian Seminar for more information.

▸⇒▸⇒▸

School Year Abroad

Samuel Phillips Hall
Phillips Academy
Andover, MA 01810
Phone: (508) 749-4420
Fax: (508) 749-4425

INSTITUTION/ORGANIZATION: Phillips Academy is an nonprofit independent secondary school.

PROGRAM: "School Year Abroad Teacher Workshop." Designed for teachers of French and Spanish languages, these workshops focus on language and culture. Instructors are seasoned professionals who have worked for Phillips Academy for many years. Lectures are combined with small group discussions. Groups are limited to 15 participants.
ELIGIBILITY: Participants must have language facility in French or Spanish.
LOCATION: France and Spain.
TIME OF YEAR: Summer.
DURATION: Two weeks.
ACCOMMODATIONS: Private homes.
COST: In 1992 the program in Spain cost $750; France cost $950. Both included room, board, instruction, and travel in Spain and France. International airfare was additional.
PERSONS WITH DISABILITIES: Accessibility at both program sites is very limited.

▸⇒▸⇒▸

Sea Quest Expeditions/Zoetic Research

P.O. Box 2424
Friday Harbor, WA 98250
Phone: (206) 378-5767

INSTITUTION/ORGANIZATION: Founded in 1989, Sea Quest Expeditions is a nonprofit environmental organization that conducts scientific research.

PROGRAM: "Sea of Cortez by Seakayak and Snorkel." This sea kayak adventure takes participants to uninhabited islands in the Sea of Cortez. Snorkeling, whale watching, birding, hiking, and fishing are all part of the expedition. Leaders hold degrees in natural science fields and have had years of kayaking experience in Mexico. Expeditions include no more than 12 people.

ELIGIBILITY: Persons should be healthy enough to hike, bike, and swim.

LOCATION: Baja California, Mexico.

TIME OF YEAR: Spring and winter.

DURATION: Expeditions run from five to seven days.

ACCOMMODATIONS: Tents.

COST: Approximately $499 for the five-day program and $599 for a week, which includes all equipment (except clothing, sleeping bag, and snorkeling gear) and food. Participants are responsible for airfare.

AGE OF PARTICIPANTS: The average age of participants is usually between 30 and 50.

▶⇒▶⇒▶

Seniors Abroad International Homestay

12533 Pacato Circle North
San Diego, CA 92128
Phone: (619) 485-1696

INSTITUTION/ORGANIZATION: Founded in 1984, Seniors Abroad is a nonprofit organization that brings active persons over 50 years of age to share homestays with persons of the same general age from other countries.

PROGRAMS: "International Homestay." This program examines aging as a life experience and how it varies among cultures. Participants stay in the homes of their hosts, who teach them about the life-style of older persons in that country. During the program, each participant stays with three different hosts. Upon arrival in each country, the group stays at a hotel for a two-day orientation. Program offerings include "Homestays in New Zealand/Australia," "Homestays in Scandinavia," and "Homestays in Japan."

ELIGIBILITY: Participants must be over 50 years old.

LOCATION: Destinations include cities in Australia, Denmark, Japan, New Zealand, Norway, and Sweden.

TIME OF YEAR: Options are available throughout the year.

DURATION: Homestays run for three to four weeks.

ACCOMMODATIONS: Private homes.

COST: In 1991 the program costs ranged from $2,425 for Japan to $2,700 for New Zealand/Australia and included international airfare from Los Angeles and hospitality with all hosts, hotel, breakfasts, and transportation between cities and countries. Hospitality is voluntary on the part of the host.

AGE OF PARTICIPANTS: The average age of participants is usually about 66.

COMMENTS: Seniors Abroad also looks for U.S. hosts to accommodate international visitors. Hospitality is voluntary and not compensated by Seniors Abroad.

▶▶═▶▶═▶▶

Service Civil International/International Voluntary Service USA

Innisfree Village
Route 2, Box 506
Crozet, VA 22932
Phone: (804) 823-1826

INSTITUTION/ORGANIZATION: Founded in 1920, Service Civil International (SCI) is a nonprofit, nongovernmental organization committed to the promotion of peace and international understanding.

PROGRAM: SCI organizes short- and medium-term voluntary workcamp projects in the United States and abroad. Volunteers come together from various countries to do community service work—"to share cooking and cleaning, to solve problems, to work together, and to have fun," according to the sponsor. The maximum number of participants permitted on each project ranges from eight to 15.

ELIGIBILITY: Generally there are no requirements for participation, but knowledge of a foreign language is necessary for some camps.

LOCATION: Destinations vary each year. Previous workcamps have taken place in Austria, Belgium, Bulgaria, Czechoslovakia, Denmark, Finland, France, Germany, Greece, Greenland, Hungary, Ireland, Italy, the Netherlands, Northern Ireland, Norway, Poland, the former Soviet Union, Spain, Sweden, Switzerland, Turkey, the United Kingdom, and Yugoslavia.

TIME OF YEAR: Most camps are offered during the summer.

DURATION: Two to three weeks.

ACCOMMODATIONS: Simple living arrangements: tents, dormitories, or one large room for all volunteers.

COST: The cost is $75, which includes room, board, and supplemental accident/health insurance. Airfare is not included.

AGE OF PARTICIPANTS: The average age of participants is usually between 16 and 20, though the workcamps are not designed specifically for youth.

PERSONS WITH DISABILITIES: SCI encourages persons with disabilities to apply; some workcamps are open on a case-by-case basis.

COMMENTS: Generally one to two volunteers per camp are from the United States.

▶⟹▶⟹▶

Sierra Club Outings

730 Polk Street
San Francisco, CA 94109
Phone: (415) 923-5630

INSTITUTION/ORGANIZATION: Founded in 1892, the Sierra Club is a nonprofit organization dedicated to preserving and protecting the natural environment. Since 1901 the Club has offered a variety of outdoor wilderness adventures throughout the United States and abroad.

PROGRAMS: "Sierra Club Outings." Offered annually, these excursions are run with the goal of raising Club members' awareness of and concern for conservation issues. Programs are available for those interested in hiking, camping, backpacking, biking, and kayaking. On some trips participants camp in remote areas; on others, they are accommodated in guesthouses or hotels. Participants often learn about the host country's conservation problems through meetings with local environmentalists. Trips are conducted by experienced leaders. Groups are no larger than 20 people.

ELIGIBILITY: Leader approval is required for all trips.

LOCATION: Destinations outside the United States include Kenya, Zimbabwe, Botswana, China, Nepal, Thailand, the United Kingdom, Czechoslovakia, Austria, Germany, Switzerland, Greece, Costa Rica, Guatemala, Belize, Mexico, Peru, Ecuador, Argentina, New Zealand, and Russia.

TIME OF YEAR: Options are available throughout the year.

DURATION: Overseas trips usually range from two weeks to a month.

ACCOMMODATIONS: Tents, guesthouses, or hotels.

COST: Varies, depending on destination. Overseas trips are tier-priced, which means the cost is dependent on the number of participants and includes all on-trip expenses. Airfare is not included in package prices. Contact Sierra Club for current price list.

PERSONS WITH DISABILITIES: Persons with disabilities are welcome if they can handle the physical requirements of the trip.

Skidmore College

Office of the Dean of Special Programs
Palamountain Hall
North Broadway
Saratoga Springs, NY 12866-1632
Phone: (518) 584-5000 x 2264
Fax: (518) 584-3023

INSTITUTION/ORGANIZATION: Founded in 1903, Skidmore is a private, coeducational four-year liberal arts college. The college is a member of the Council on International Educational Exchange.

PROGRAM: "Study/Vacation in Florence, Italy." This program enables participants to explore the art and culture of Italy past and present through lectures, readings, and field trips in Florence and around Tuscany. Instructors are recruited through a host institution in Italy. Group size is limited to 20 people.

ELIGIBILITY: Applications are accepted from all interested persons 18 and over.

LOCATION: Florence, Siena, San Gimignano, and Pisa, Italy.

TIME OF YEAR: Spring.

DURATION: Two weeks.

ACCOMMODATIONS: Hotels.

COST: From $3,200 to $3,345, which includes tuition, housing, round-trip airfare, excursions, and guided tours.

AGE OF PARTICIPANTS: The average age of participants is usually about 60.

▶︎⟹▶︎⟹▶︎

Smithsonian Odyssey Tours/Saga Holidays

120 Boylston Street
Boston, MA 02116
Phone: (617) 451-6808
Fax: (617) 423-4258

INSTITUTION/ORGANIZATION: The Smithsonian Institution, the national museum, in combination with Saga Holidays, offers educational tours to destinations worldwide. The Smithsonian is a nonprofit organization, and Saga Holidays is a commercial tour operator.

PROGRAMS: "Smithsonian Odyssey Tours." These study tours are usually taken by coach and led by experts in a variety of fields pertaining to the region traveled to. Largely focused on art, history, or geology, the tours include lectures and informal discussions. Thirty different programs are available. The maximum number of participants permitted on each excursion is 40.

ELIGIBILITY: Participants must be members of the Smithsonian Institution. Membership is $20 annually.

LOCATION: In 1992, destinations included Mexico, Venezuela, Belize, Guatemala, Honduras, Hong Kong, Thailand, Malaysia, Indonesia, New Zealand, Australia, Great Britain, Ireland, Italy, Greece, France, Spain, Portugal, and Morocco.

TIME OF YEAR: Spring, summer, and fall.

DURATION: Tours vary from 10 to 24 days.

ACCOMMODATIONS: Hotels.

COST: Varies, depending on destination. Generally programs range from $150 to $300 per day, including international airfare, most meals, accommodations, study materials (books and lecture handouts), transfers, insurance, and taxes. Transportation between participant's home and the departure airport is additional.

AGE OF PARTICIPANTS: The average age of participants is usually about 60.

PERSONS WITH DISABILITIES: Individuals are considered on a case-by-case basis depending upon the suitability of the tour.

▸⟹▸⟹▸

State University of New York at Oswego

International Education Office
102 Rich Hall, Bldg #14
Oswego, New York 13126
Phone: (315) 341-2118
Fax: (315) 341-2477

INSTITUTION/ORGANIZATION: Founded in 1861, SUNY at Oswego is a state institution with an enrollment of more than 8,200 students. SUNY is a member of the Council on International Educational Exchange.

PROGRAM: "Academic Study Tour of Significant Historical Sites in England, Scotland, and Wales." Offered annually, this study tour is guided by professors from SUNY Oswego. Included are visits to museums, castles, cathedrals, monuments, and archaeological sites. Participants are asked to keep a travel journal. Tours are limited to 25 to 30 participants.

ELIGIBILITY: Applications are accepted from all interested persons.

LOCATION: United Kingdom: Bath, Stratford-upon-Avon, London, York, Caernafon, Chester, and Edinburgh.

TIME OF YEAR: Summer.

DURATION: From two to three weeks.

ACCOMMODATIONS: Participants stay in hotels and bed and breakfasts.

COST: Approximately $1,293, which includes room, some meals, in-country travel, and a British Heritage admission pass to historical sites. Airfare is not included.

AGE OF PARTICIPANTS: The average age of participants is usually about 45.

PERSONS WITH DISABILITIES: The university will try to make necessary accommodations.

COMMENTS: Participants should be in good physical shape, as the tour involves extensive walking. It is possible to obtain academic credit for participation. Check with the office above.

▸⇒▸⇒▸

Storyfest Journeys

3901 Cathedral Avenue NW, #608
Washington, DC 20016
Phone and fax: (202) 364-6143

INSTITUTION/ORGANIZATION: Founded in 1980 by Robert and
Kelly Wilhelm, Storyfest Journeys is a commercial tour operator that
runs travel seminars exclusively devoted to the stories and legends of
the places visited.

PROGRAMS: "Storyfest Journeys." All groups are accompanied by the
owners, Dr. Robert Bela Wilhelm (a professional storyteller) and Dr.
Mary Jo Kelly Wilhelm (an expert in travel and leisure studies). Places
visited are generally far removed from the tourist track and rich in
history, folklore, and storytelling. Examples of tours are "Christmas
Storytelling: A Winter Celebration" in Bermuda; "Storytelling in the
Welsh Hills," a study of the Roman influence on Wales and of the
Mabinobion; "Pilgrims to Italy with Francis and Clare," an exploration
of the stories of St. Francis and St. Clare in Assisi, Italy; and "Irish
Traditions and Sacred Stories," in which Celtic history is examined
through evening storytelling. Groups are generally small, with no more
than 20 people.
ELIGIBILITY: Applications are accepted from all interested persons.
LOCATION: Ireland, England, Wales, and Italy.
TIME OF YEAR: Options are available throughout the year.
DURATION: One to two weeks.
ACCOMMODATIONS: According to the sponsor, "lodgings are dis-
tinctive residences that are owner-managed."
COST: Generally ranges from $700 to $2,000 and includes room,
board, coach, and admissions.
PERSONS WITH DISABILITIES: All are welcome.
AGE OF PARTICIPANTS: The average age of participants is usually
between 40 and 60.
COMMENTS: Participants are usually from the United States, Canada,
and Australia.

➤➡➤

Studio Art Centers International

Institute of International Education
U.S. Student Programs
SACI Coordinator
809 United Nations Plaza
New York, NY 10017
Phone: (212) 984-5525
Fax: (212) 984-5325

INSTITUTION/ORGANIZATION: Studio Art Centers International is a nonprofit educational organization founded for students seeking excellence in studio art instruction and liberal arts subjects in Italy. The Institute of International Education is a member of the Council on International Educational Exchange.

PROGRAMS: "SACI/Florence." This program offers an educational experience in Italy that draws upon the rich past of Florence and its resources in museums, architecture, and a wide range of cultural offerings, while presenting contemporary developments in Italian art and culture. SACI courses include drawing, painting, sculpture, photography, graphic and interior design, printmaking, batik, weaving, jewelry, and ceramics, as well as nonstudio courses in art history, Italian language, and history of Italian cinema. Students are taught by highly qualified faculty.

ELIGIBILITY: The program is open to artists for noncredit participation. Undergraduates with a minimum GPA of 2.5, in good standing at any college, university, or art school, are also welcome.

LOCATION: Florence, Italy.

TIME OF YEAR: Spring and summer.

DURATION: The late spring term runs for six weeks; the summer term runs for four weeks.

ACCOMMODATIONS: Student apartments.

COST: The late spring term costs approximately $4,050, which covers tuition, housing, and activity fees. All other expenses are additional. The summer term costs approximately $2,800 and covers the same items mentioned above for the spring.

COMMENTS: Scholarships are available to undergraduate and graduate students. Also available is a visual arts program at the Wimbledon School of Art in the United Kingdom, which runs for more than six weeks. Contact the office above at the Institute of International Education for more information.

➤➤➤➤

Syracuse University

Division of International Programs Abroad
119 Euclid Avenue
Syracuse, NY 13244
Phone: (315) 443-9420
Fax: (315) 443-4593

INSTITUTION/ORGANIZATION: Founded in 1870, Syracuse University is an independent institution with an enrollment of more than 17,000 students. Syracuse University is a member of the Council on International Educational Exchange.

PROGRAM: "Azahar: The Art of the Islamic Conquest and the Gothic Renaissance Art of the Reconquists." This intensive interdisciplinary traveling seminar focuses on the humanities. Guided by a Syracuse University faculty member, lectures are given at artistic and historical sites, including mosques, cathedrals, and synagogues. Group size is limited to 25 participants.

ELIGIBILITY: A bachelor's degree is required.

LOCATION: Destinations have included Toledo, Cordoba, Sevilla, Granada, and Madrid, Spain.

TIME OF YEAR: Summer.

DURATION: Two weeks.

ACCOMMODATIONS: Hotels.

COST: In 1992 the cost was approximately $3,000, which included room, field trip transportation, museum entrance fees, tuition, and other program-related activities. Airfare is not included.

PERSONS WITH DISABILITIES: The Division of International Programs Abroad complies with federal regulations and does not discriminate based on disabilities. Persons are considered on a case-by-case basis.

COMMENTS: Participants have the option either to enroll in the program for academic credit or to audit. Though 1992 was the first year the program was offered, the Division of International Programs has offered similar programs for a number of years and expects to continue to do so.

Taleninstituut Regina Coeli B.V.
Martinilaan 12,
Vught
THE NETHERLANDS
Phone: (31) 73 570200
Fax: (31) 73 563455

INSTITUTION/ORGANIZATION: Founded in 1962, Taleninstituut Regina Coeli B.V. is a language institute offering tailor-made intensive courses for professional adults.

PROGRAMS: Intensive language courses are offered in Dutch, French, English, German, Spanish, and Italian. All teachers are native speakers, and courses are adapted to the students' needs.
ELIGIBILITY: English and French courses are available to advanced learners only. A high school education is required.
LOCATION: Vught, The Netherlands.
TIME OF YEAR: Options are available throughout the year.
DURATION: Courses are available for one to two weeks, with the possibility of a follow-up class.
ACCOMMODATIONS: Private homes and hotels.
COST: Approximately $970 (1,800 guilders), which covers the cost of the course only. Full room and board are available at $240 (445 guilders) per week.
AGE OF PARTICIPANTS: The average age of participants is usually about 40.

Tamu Safaris
P.O. Box 247
West Chesterfield, NH 03466
Phone: (800) 766-9199

INSTITUTION/ORGANIZATION: Founded in 1987, Tamu Safaris is a small, commercial tour operator that specializes in educational programs in six African countries: Kenya, Tanzania, the Seychelles, Madagascar, Botswana, and Zimbabwe. The founders, Costas and Sally Christ, have both spent more than a decade working and living in

Africa as wildlife researchers and anthropologists. Costas and Sally also design private tours.

PROGRAM: "Kenya Natural History Tour." This three-week educational program focuses on Kenya's natural history, highlighting its unique cultural heritage. Lectures, field guides, and local experts join the group and create the core of the educational program. Instructors are required to hold advanced degrees. The travel itinerary is designed to bring you in close contact with the richness of Kenya's flora and fauna, as well as its cultural heritage. Ample time is allotted for visiting local villages and meeting the people of Kenya. Groups are limited to 16 people.
ELIGIBILITY: Applications are accepted from all persons 16 and over who are in good health.
LOCATION: Nairobi, rural villages, and national parks in Kenya.
TIME OF YEAR: The program is offered three times a year in the summer, fall, and winter.
DURATION: 21 days.
ACCOMMODATIONS: Hotels, tents, and hostels.
COST: $2,990, which includes room, board, the educational program, and land travel (in-country). International airfare is additional.
AGE OF PARTICIPANTS: The average age of participants is usually about 40 to 50.
PERSONS WITH DISABILITIES: Wherever possible, persons with disabilities are encouraged to participate. The sponsor has accommodated individuals who are hearing-impaired or mildly physically disabled.
COMMENTS: Tamu Safaris attempts to be ecologically sensitive. Recyclable goods are used wherever possible; large overland vehicles that exacerbate soil erosion are generally not used; and noise levels are kept to a minimum to avoid harassing the animals.

➤➡➡➤

The Texas Camel Corps at the Witte Museum
PO Box 2601
San Antonio, TX 78299
Phone: (512) 820-2167
Fax: (512) 820-2109

INSTITUTION/ORGANIZATION: Founded in 1985, The Texas Camel Corps (TCC) is the Witte Museum's nonprofit adventure travel and field research support group.

PROGRAMS: Outdoor adventure and field research trips focused on anthropology, archaeology, natural history, culture, and ornithology are offered. Orientations are provided by tour leaders, faculty, and museum curators. A general manager accompanies the group, and local experts provide lectures.

ELIGIBILITY: The Texas Camel Corps is a club, with annual dues, but most programs are open to nonmembers. Membership dues range from $25 to $160.

LOCATION: In 1993 destinations will include East Africa, England, Tunisia, Greenland, Nova Scotia, and the Galápagos Islands.

TIME OF YEAR: Options are available throughout the year.

DURATION: Programs run from five days to three weeks.

ACCOMMODATIONS: Hotels, tents, hostels, and private homes.

COST: Varies, but generally ranges from $100 to $200 per day and includes most expenses except occasional meals and personal items. Airfare is not included.

AGE OF PARTICIPANTS: The average age of participants is usually about 50.

PERSONS WITH DISABILITIES: TCC will accommodate persons with disabilities whenever possible.

▸⟹▸⟹▸

The Textile Museum

2320 South Street NW
Washington, DC 20008
Phone: (202) 667-0442

INSTITUTION/ORGANIZATION: Founded in the late 1950s, the Textile Museum is a nonprofit institution dedicated to the exhibition and conservation of rugs and textiles.

PROGRAM: "Travel Program: Study Tours Around the World." Focused on rugs, textiles, and all fiber arts, these tours are led by university faculty or museum curators to destinations worldwide. The maximum number of participants on each tour is 30.

ELIGIBILITY: Participants must be members of the museum. The annual membership fee is $50 for residents of the Washington area and $45 for those outside the area.

LOCATION: Destinations have included Portugal and Moorish Spain, Ecuador, Scandinavia, Switzerland, Turkey, and the United Kingdom.

Destinations for 1993 include India, Spain, Ecuador, Switzerland, and France.
TIME OF YEAR: Options are available throughout the year.
DURATION: Tours run from one to three weeks.
ACCOMMODATIONS: Hotels.
COST: Ranges from $3,500 to $8,000, depending on the program, and includes all air and land travel from gateway city, room, most meals, and daily excursions.
AGE OF PARTICIPANTS: Participants usually range in age from about 45 to 80.
PERSONS WITH DISABILITIES: Applicants will be considered on a case-by-case basis.

▸⇒▸⇒▸

Torre Di Babele

Centro di Lingua e Cultura Italiana
Via Bixio 74
00185 Rome
ITALY
Phone: (39) 6 7008434
Fax: (39) 6 7577067

INSTITUTION/ORGANIZATION: Founded in 1984, Torre Di Babele is a language school that specializes in the teaching of Italian as a foreign language.

PROGRAMS: Torre Di Babele sponsors a variety of Italian language programs that all include cultural and extracurricular activities. Tours, lectures, seminars, and film showings cover a wide variety of fields of interest, including art history, architecture, music, literature, cinema, cooking, and wines. Also available is a special program for tour operators and hotel employees, which focuses on the skills needed for effective communication in these fields. The maximum number of students per class in all programs is 10.
ELIGIBILITY: Applications are accepted from all interested persons.
LOCATION: Rome and Pisciotta, Italy.
TIME OF YEAR: Options are available throughout the year.
DURATION: Programs vary from two to 12 weeks.
ACCOMMODATIONS: Private homes and apartments.

COST: Varies depending on the program and length of study; contact Torre Di Babele.

PERSONS WITH DISABILITIES: Torre Di Babele welcomes all students to apply, although its courses are not appropriate for the deaf.

Travelearn

P.O. Box 315
Lakeville, PA 18438
Phone: (717) 226-9114
Fax: (717) 226-6912

INSTITUTION/ORGANIZATION: Founded in the mid-1970s by Professor Edwin Williams, Travelearn is a commercial tour operator that sponsors educational study tours for adult learners. This company coordinates a network of educational and cultural institutions nationwide that have agreed to offer Travelearn programs and recruit participants.

PROGRAMS: Travelearn sponsors more than 10 study tours annually. A sample of its programs include the following:

- "Russia and the Ukraine." Focused on historic and contemporary Russia, this program runs for two weeks during the summer and is led by college professors experienced in teaching about historic and contemporary Russia. Small group discussions are combined with site visits in Moscow, St. Petersburg, Kiev, and Yalta. The approximate cost is $3,225 and includes round-trip airfare (from New York), academic guide, land and air transportation in Russia and the Ukraine, hotel accommodations, services of a bilingual guide-interpreter, and excursions. Visa fees and departure taxes are additional.
- "A Kenya Adventure." Focused on Kenyan wildlife and bird-life, this safari is escorted by college professors and includes seminars and lectures provided by some of East Africa's foremost wildlife researchers. Participants also have the opportunity to explore Kenyan culture. The program includes visits to each of the three major game reserves of Kenya: Samburu, Masai Mara (Northern Serengeti Plains), and Amboseli (Mount Kilimanjaro). This safari runs for two weeks during the sum-

mer. The cost is approximately $4,125 and includes round-trip airfare (from New York), accommodations (hotels and lodges), most meals, lectures and seminars, transfers and safari transportation, sight-seeing and park entrance fees, tips, and taxes.

- "A China Adventure." Focused on historical China and contemporary issues facing the country, this program is led by college professors and designed for educators. Participants spend two weeks in residence at Zibo Teachers' College, where they are instructed by American and Chinese college professors from a variety of disciplines. Visits to cultural, industrial, historical, and educational sites are an integral part of the itinerary. The program runs for three weeks during the summer, and the approximate cost is $2,925. Included are round-trip airfare (from San Francisco), hotel accommodations, meals, escorts, transportation within China, and excursions.

ELIGIBILITY: Applications are accepted from all interested persons.

LOCATION: Russia and the Ukraine, Kenya, and China. In addition to the programs described above, study tours are also offered in Morocco, Nepal, Patagonia/Chile, Eastern Europe, Ireland, Galápagos Islands and Ecuador, the Dominican Republic, Egypt, China, Brazil, Costa Rica, and Australia.

TIME OF YEAR: Options are available throughout the year.

DURATION: Generally two to three weeks.

▶➡▶➡▶

Trinity College

Elderhostel Programs in Italy
Box 1307
Hartford, CT 06106
Phone: (203) 297-2166
Fax: (203) 297-5305

INSTITUTION/ORGANIZATION: Founded in 1823, Trinity College is a nonprofit liberal arts institution and a member of the Council on International Educational Exchange.

PROGRAMS: "Elderhostel Programs in Italy." Designed for participants at least 60 years of age, these programs concentrate on art history and music. Experts in these fields combine lectures with site visits and other excursions. Groups are limited to 42 participants.

ELIGIBILITY: Open to persons at least 60 years of age. Participants' spouses of any age are welcome. Other companions of age-eligible participants must be at least 50.
LOCATION: Italy.
TIME OF YEAR: Programs take place in the spring, fall, and winter; 80 programs run annually.
DURATION: Programs run for two weeks.
ACCOMMODATIONS: Hotels.
COST: The cost ranges from $2,172 to $2,882 and includes round-trip airfare (from New York), airport transfers, room, board, excursions, and course-related entrance fees.
AGE OF PARTICIPANTS: The average age of participants is usually about 69.
PERSONS WITH DISABILITIES: Participants are considered on a case-by-case basis and asked to submit a letter describing their particular needs before enrolling in the program.

▶▶⇒▶▶⇒▶▶

Tulane University

Summer School
125 Gibson Hall
New Orleans, LA 70118
Phone: (504) 865-5555
Fax: (504) 865-5562

INSTITUTION/ORGANIZATION: Founded in 1832, Tulane University is a private research university and a member of the Council on International Educational Exchange.

PROGRAM: "Summer in Paris." This program includes courses in art, history, music, and French language. Students are required to enroll in two. Instructors are experts in the appropriate fields, and lectures are combined with excursions to cultural sites. The maximum group size is 25.
ELIGIBILITY: Open to all interested persons at least 18 years of age. College students should have at least a 2.0 GPA.
LOCATION: France.
TIME OF YEAR: Summer.
DURATION: Six weeks.
ACCOMMODATIONS: Hotels.

COST: The approximate cost in 1992 was $3,300, which included room, excursions and museum entrance fees, medical insurance, and tuition (eight credit hours). Airfare was additional.

AGE OF PARTICIPANTS: The average age of participants is usually about 23, though there is generally a good age mix in the group.

PERSONS WITH DISABILITIES: The program will try to accommodate persons with disabilities as much as possible.

▶▶⇒▶▶⇒▶▶

The University Museum of Archaeology and Anthropology

University of Pennsylvania
33rd and Spruce Streets
Philadelphia, PA 19104
Phone: (215) 898-9202
Fax: (215) 898-0657

INSTITUTION/ORGANIZATION: Founded in 1887, The University Museum is an internationally known museum and research facility for archaeology as well as anthropology. The University of Pennsylvania is a member of the Council on International Educational Exchange.

PROGRAM: "The Tour Program," established in 1964, primarily includes excursions that have an archaeological and anthropological emphasis, led by curators from the museum and professors at the University of Pennsylvania. Destinations include unusual places not found in most standard travel brochures. Groups range in size from 15 to 25 participants, depending on the program.

ELIGIBILITY: Participants must be members of the museum. Membership rates range from $30 to $1,000, depending on the category.

LOCATION: Previous destinations have included Southeast Asia, Canada, Mexico, India, Guatemala, Sicily, and the Lipari Islands (Italy), and Costa Rica.

TIME OF YEAR: Spring, fall, and winter.

DURATION: Two to three weeks.

ACCOMMODATIONS: Hotels.

COST: In 1992 program costs ranged from $3,500 to $5,500 and included room, board, and entrance fees. Airfare is additional.

AGE OF PARTICIPANTS: The age range of participants is usually between 40 and 75.

▶⟹▶⟹▶

University Research Expeditions Program (UREP)

University of California
Berkeley, CA 94720
Phone: (503) 642-6586
Fax: (503) 643-8683

INSTITUTION/ORGANIZATION: Founded in 1976, University Research Expeditions Program provides the general public with educational field research opportunities while supporting vital research projects in the natural and social sciences. The University of California is a member of the Council on International Educational Exchange.

PROGRAMS: UREP supports field research projects in the natural and social sciences worldwide. Projects involve helping to preserve the earth's dwindling resources; working on programs to improve the lives of people in developing nations; and doing excavation work on archaeological sites. Led by faculty or doctoral candidates from the University of California system, hands-on field experience is combined with on-site discussions.

ELIGIBILITY: Participants should be flexible, enthusiastic, willing to work as part of a team, and interested in the field of study.

LOCATION: Expeditions take place throughout the world. Previous destinations have included Ecuador, France, Portugal, Mongolia, Indonesia, Bolivia, and East Africa.

TIME OF YEAR: Options are available throughout the year.

DURATION: Two to three weeks.

ACCOMMODATIONS: Participants live in hotels, shared apartments, pensions, and tents, depending on the project.

COST: Tax-deductible contributions range from $700 to $1,600 and include room, board, field expenses, and ground transportation. Airfare is additional.

AGE OF PARTICIPANTS: The average age of participants is usually about 35 to 45.

PERSONS WITH DISABILITIES: Project leaders review applications on a case-by-case basis to determine whether or not the individual can meet the rigors of the expedition. Some projects require less strenuous activity than others—documenting culture in an urban setting, for example. (One of the project leaders is wheelchair-bound.)

COMMENTS: Limited scholarships are available to students and K-12 teachers. Contact UREP for more information.

▶⟹▶⟹▶

University Vacations
9602 NW 13th Street
Miami, FL 33172
Phone: (800) 792-0100
Fax: (305) 591-1738

INSTITUTION/ORGANIZATION: University Vacations is a cultural institution that operates 40 vacation seminars for adults at Trinity College Dublin, Cambridge and Oxford Universities in England, and Paris University–Sorbonne.

PROGRAMS: A variety of cultural, literary, and historical programs is offered, including a tour of "Welsh Castles in the Mist" at Oxford and South Wales; a seminar of Cambridge modern mystery writers; a tour of some of England's greatest gardens; a program on the history and heritage of Ireland that includes a tour of the Irish countryside; the Oxford world of the landscape novel that features a special excursion to the Wessex of Thomas Hardy; and many more.
ELIGIBILITY: Applications are accepted from all interested persons 18 years and over.
LOCATION: Ireland, England, Wales, Scotland, France, Italy, and Belgium.
TIME OF YEAR: Programs are offered in the spring, summer, and fall.
DURATION: One to two weeks.
ACCOMMODATIONS: Hotels and college dormitories.
COST: $1,675 and up, which includes private room, some meals, lectures, and field trips. Airfare is not included.
AGE OF PARTICIPANTS: The average age of participants is usually about 45.
PERSONS WITH DISABILITIES: Persons with disabilities are asked to give advance notice so that accommodations can be made for them.

▶⟹▶⟹▶

University of Utah
Center for Adult Development
1195 Annex Building
Salt Lake City, UT 84112
Phone: (801) 581-3228
Fax: (801) 581-3165

INSTITUTION/ORGANIZATION: The University of Utah is a member of the Council on International Educational Exchange. The Center for Adult Development assists adults in career and educational transitions, facilitates access to quality education, and promotes research toward greater understanding of the adult learner.

PROGRAM: "Adults Abroad: Beijing Teacher's College, Beijing, China." This travel/study program is designed for adults and includes courses in history, language, art, and cooking. Participants attend classes in the morning taught by Beijing's Teacher's College faculty and have afternoons free to explore Beijing with a student guide. Group size is limited to 30 participants. This program was first offered in 1992.

ELIGIBILITY: Applications are accepted from all interested persons.

LOCATION: Beijing, China.

TIME OF YEAR: Summer.

DURATION: Two to four weeks depending on choice of term; two terms are offered per summer.

ACCOMMODATIONS: Hotels.

COST: In 1992 the two-week term cost $2,250; the four-week term cost $2,810. These prices included round-trip airfare from Salt Lake City to Beijing, room, board, courses, evening programs, special events, and airport transfers.

PERSONS WITH DISABILITIES: In keeping with the university's policy of equal access, provisions are made on a case-by-case basis.

COMMENTS: Interested persons have the option to earn academic credit. Contact the Center for Adult Development for more information.

▶⟹▶⟹▶

University of Utah

International Center
159 University Union
Salt Lake City, Utah 84112
Phone: (801) 581-5849
Fax: (801) 581-5914

INSTITUTION/ORGANIZATION: Founded in 1850, the University of Utah is a state institution with an enrollment of more than 23,000 students. The university is a member of the Council on International Educational Exchange.

PROGRAMS: The International Center sponsors a variety of programs, including the following:
- The University of Utah sponsors an annual field research program to the Galápagos Islands, Ecuador. Guided by university faculty, participants can observe, study, and photograph the animals and plants, as well as swim and snorkel. The program runs for 11 days in the spring, and participants live on boats. The approximate cost in 1991 was $2,400, which included round-trip air and land transportation, hotel in Quito (three nights), chartered boats in Galápagos (bunk and meals), and a field handbook. There are no prerequisites for interested adults; university students need to have taken a course in biology or evolution. Groups are limited to 32 people.
- "The University of Cambridge International Summer School." Offered annually, this program provides participants with the opportunity to live in historic Cambridge, England, while taking courses related to English life and culture, including politics, history, literature, business, the arts, and architecture. All lectures are given by University of Cambridge faculty or professors from other British universities. Courses run for two, four, or six weeks. Participants live in college dormitories and private homes. In 1991 the costs for applicants were as follows: two weeks, $1,800; four weeks, $2,650; six weeks, $4,150. This included bus transportation from the airport to Cambridge, tuition, room, and board (breakfast and dinner). Not included: airfare, books, health insurance (required), lunch, special beverages with meals, and optional excursions. University students should have completed their sophomore year prior to program departure with a minimum grade point average of 3.0. Other adults need only complete the application.
- "Russian Study Tour." Offered annually, this tour focuses on contemporary education in Russia. Included is an extensive study of Russian institutions, history, and culture as reflected in Moscow and St. Petersburg. Guided by faculty from the University of Utah, lectures are combined with small group discussions. The tour is offered in the spring for 11 days. Participants live in hotels. In 1991 the cost was $2,340, which included round-trip air and land transportation, room, board, guidebooks, tour notes, excursions, and a visa. Most participants are university students, but other adults also participate.

ELIGIBILITY: Applications are accepted from all interested adults. There are some requirements for students; check with the university.
LOCATION: Galápagos Islands, England, and Russia.
TIME OF YEAR: Time of year varies. See descriptions of programs above.
DURATION: Programs vary from 11 days to six weeks.
PERSONS WITH DISABILITIES: The University of Utah will accommodate persons with disabilities if possible.
COMMENTS: Participants have the option to obtain academic credit for all programs. Grants are available to University of Utah students for the field research program in the Galápagos Islands; awards are based on need. For high school teachers, National Science Foundation grants are available for the Galápagos Islands. Contact the International Center for more information.

Venceremos Brigade

P.O. Box 673
New York, NY 10035

INSTITUTION/ORGANIZATION: Founded in 1969, Venceremos Brigade is a nonprofit organization that promotes the normalization of relations with Cuba. Trips to Cuba are sponsored annually for U.S. activists.

PROGRAM: The annual tour to Cuba includes lectures given by members of the Cuban government and leaders of mass organizations. Visits to schools, medical facilities, and other institutions are also included. Participants have the opportunity for informal dialogue with the Cubans. The maximum number of participants permitted on any one tour is 200; all are U.S. residents.
ELIGIBILITY: Applications are accepted from all interested persons.
LOCATION: Havana, Cuba.
TIME OF YEAR: Spring.
DURATION: Two weeks.
ACCOMMODATIONS: International camp barracks.
COST: $950 to $1,100, which covers travel to and from Cuba. The trip is hosted by the Cubans once in Cuba, relieving participants of hotel and meal expenses.

AGE OF PARTICIPANTS: Most participants are in their 30s.

PERSONS WITH DISABILITIES: Participants with disabilities are welcome; however, the trip is not completely accessible.

COMMENTS: Tour cost is based on a sliding scale according to what the prospective participant can afford to pay. Some financial assistance is available.

Volunteers for Peace, Inc.

43 Tiffany Road
Belmont, VT 05730
Phone: (802) 259-2759
Fax: (802) 259-2922

INSTITUTION/ORGANIZATION: Founded in 1982, Volunteers for Peace is a nonprofit membership organization that places American volunteers in international workcamps in 33 countries.

PROGRAMS: "International Workcamps." This program places volunteers on environmental, archaeological, and historic renovation projects. Many of the projects are educationally oriented.

ELIGIBILITY: Applications are accepted from all interested persons.

LOCATION: The workcamps are located in 33 countries, including all of Western and Eastern Europe, the former Soviet Union, Turkey, Japan, Tunisia, Morocco, and Ghana.

TIME OF YEAR: Summer and fall.

DURATION: Most workcamps run for either two or three weeks.

ACCOMMODATIONS: Hostels.

COST: $100 per session, which covers full room and board and the program expense; airfare is not included.

AGE OF PARTICIPANTS: Most volunteers are between 20 and 35 years old.

PERSONS WITH DISABILITIES: About 20 percent of the camps accept volunteers with disabilities. Programs are modified to accommodate those with special needs.

COMMENTS: Participants are recruited from countries around the world. Only three to four from any one country work on each project.

Voyagers International

P.O. Box 915
Ithaca, NY 14851
Phone: (607) 257-3091
Fax: (607) 257-3699

INSTITUTION/ORGANIZATION: Founded in 1982, Voyagers International is a commercial tour operator that organizes worldwide natural history trips for leading nonprofit nature and conservation organizations throughout the United States. With an emphasis on ecotourism, programs are sponsored in cooperation with museums, educational institutions, and professional organizations, among others.

PROGRAMS: Voyagers International operates all types of nature and cultural trips to destinations around the world. Trips focus mainly on birding, outdoor photography, and natural history. Guides have professional experience in the appropriate fields. Groups are usually limited to 15 people.

ELIGIBILITY: Applications are accepted from all interested persons in good health.

LOCATION: Kenya, Tanzania, Botswana, Namibia, Ecuador, Costa Rica, Belize, Indonesia, and Malaysia, along with many others.

TIME OF YEAR: Options are available throughout the year.

DURATION: Two to three weeks.

ACCOMMODATIONS: Hotels, lodges, and tent camps.

COST: Between $1,500 and $4,500, which includes round-trip air and land transport, accommodations, most meals, leaders' expenses, taxes, and fees.

AGE OF PARTICIPANTS: The majority of participants are about 40 to 70 years old.

PERSONS WITH DISABILITIES: Applicants can decide themselves if they are able to participate.

COMMENTS: Students may be able to obtain academic credit for participation in some programs. Contact Voyagers International for more information.

▶=▶=▶

Westchester Community College

International Studies
Science Building, Room 362
75 Grasslands Road
Valhalla, New York 10595
Phone: (914) 285-6843
Fax: (914) 285-6565

INSTITUTION/ORGANIZATION: Founded in 1946, Westchester Community College is a two-year nonprofit institution. The college is affiliated with the State University of New York, a member of the Council on International Educational Exchange.

PROGRAMS:

- "Summer Study in Italy: Studio Arts." Focused on the study of studio arts, this program includes courses in art history, painting, drawing, fresco, etching, ceramic restoration, and photography. Led by university graduates with a minimum of 10 years teaching experience, workshops include lectures, tutorials, and small group discussions. This program runs for two and four weeks during the summer. In 1992 the approximate cost for the two-week program was $1,145; the four-week program cost $2,255. Costs included room (shared student apartment), tuition and fees, local sight-seeing excursions, and instruction. Airfare and meals were additional. Groups are limited to 25 participants. Applications are accepted from all interested persons, and programs are available for audit or credit.

- "Special Three-Week Program for Teachers of Art." Designed for art teachers and prospective teachers of art, this summer program takes place in Italy and includes workshops in art history, watercolor painting, and drawing. In addition, participants have the opportunity to meet Italian art teachers and discuss differences in teaching approaches in the United States and Italy. Led by university graduates with a minimum of 10 years teaching experience, lectures and tutorials are combined with small group discussions. In 1992 the approximate cost was $2,255 and included room (shared student apartment), tuition and fees, local sight-seeing excursions, and instruction. Airfare and meals were additional. In-service teaching credit is available on this program.

- "Summer Study in Italy: Italian Language, Civilization, and Culture." This four-week study program takes place in Florence during the summer. Included is an intensive study of the Italian language for beginning to advanced learners, combined with the study of Italy's civilization and culture, or art history. Led by university graduates with a minimum of 10 years teaching experience, lectures and tutorials are combined with small group discussions. In 1992 the program was approximately $1,440 and included housing, tuition and fees, local sightseeing excursions, two meals, and instruction. Airfare and most meals were additional. Applications are accepted from all interested persons.

ELIGIBILITY: Varies according to program. See descriptions of programs above.

LOCATION: Florence, Italy.

TIME OF YEAR: Summer.

DURATION: Programs vary from two to four weeks.

▶⇒▶⇒▶

Western Michigan University

Office of International Affairs
2090 Friedmann Hall
Kalamazoo, MI 49008
Phone: (616) 387-3951
Fax: (616) 387-3962

INSTITUTION/ORGANIZATION: Established in 1981, the Office of International Affairs provides leadership for the international activities of Western Michigan University. Activities include links with foreign universities, study-abroad programs, study tours, and faculty and student exchanges. The university is a member of the Council on International Educational Exchange.

PROGRAMS: The following programs are available:
- "Africa: Journey of Discovery." This outdoor adventure study/tour to East Africa (Kenya and Tanzania) includes all major ecological areas. Guided by an experienced leader with knowledge of the host countries, participants camp, snorkel, and mountain-climb. Destinations include Nairobi, Mount Kenya, Mombasa, Mount Kilimanjaro, and major game parks. The program is offered for three weeks during the summer. Participants live in hotels and tents. The cost is approximately

$3,000, which includes round-trip airfare to Kenya; room and most meals; some equipment (e.g., tents); tuition for four credits (or audit); insurance and local transportation. Interested persons must be physically fit; participants usually range in age from 25 to 35 years old. Group size is limited to 25 participants.

- "Egyptian Odyssey." This study tour focuses on ancient and modern Egyptian art, architecture, and history. Lectures are provided by professors of Middle Eastern history and local experts. Destinations include Cairo, Luxor, Aswan, and Alexandria. Offered in March for 10 to 11 days. Participants live in hotels. The approximate cost is $2,400, which includes round-trip airfare, room and board, local guides, Nile cruise, admissions, insurance, and administrative fee. Group size is limited to 30 participants.

- "Mediterranean Institute." This ship-based study tour focuses on the ancient, medieval, and modern history and cultures of the Mediterranean. Led by professors of history, lectures are combined with small group discussions. Destinations include Italy, Egypt, Israel, Greece, and Cyprus. Offered for three weeks during the summer. Participants stay on a cruise ship and in hotels. The approximate cost is $2,800, which includes round-trip airfare, cruise ship, land tours, all meals on ship, two meals per day on land, insurance, administrative fee, and tuition for three to four credits (or audit). Group size is limited to 40 participants.

- "Russian Adventure: Summer in Russia." This study tour focuses on Russian language, history, culture, and politics and is led by experts who are fluent in Russian. On-site lectures are provided. Destinations include Russia, the Baltic republics, Central Asia, and Czechoslovakia. The program runs for three weeks during the summer, and participants stay in hotels. The approximate cost is $2,900, which includes round-trip airfare, room and board, excursions, lectures, admissions, tuition for four credits (or audit), insurance, and administrative fees. Knowledge of Russian language is helpful but not required. Group size is limited to 30 participants.

- "The Oxford Seminar." Offered biennially in odd-numbered years, this program takes place in Oxford and London, England. While residing at one of the historic Oxford colleges, participants study English literature and culture. The program includes lectures, discussions with Oxford fellows, and excursions to Stratford, Stonehenge, Salisbury, and Edinburgh, Scotland. The program is led by a university professor of literature.

Offered for four to five weeks during the summer. In 1991 the cost was $3,650, which included round-trip airfare, tuition (six credit hours), room and two meals per day, field trips and excursions, admissions, insurance, and administrative fee. (An optional tour to Continental Europe follows at additional cost.) Interested persons should have at least two years of college/university education. Group size is limited to 30 participants.

- "London Tour." Focused on British history, culture, and theater, this study tour takes participants to the United Kingdom. Led by professors specializing in British history, literature, or politics, the tour includes three or four theater performances. Offered for nine to 10 days in March. Participants stay in hotels. The approximate cost is $1,100, which includes round-trip transatlantic airfare, room, breakfast, city tour, tickets to the theater, insurance, and a professional guide. This study tour has been running annually for more than 17 years. Group size is limited to 30 participants.

ELIGIBILITY: Varies according to program. See descriptions of programs above.

LOCATION: Destinations include Kenya and Tanzania, Egypt, Russia, Italy, Greece, Israel, and England.

TIME OF YEAR: Time of year varies. See descriptions of programs above.

DURATION: Programs vary from 10 days to five weeks.

AGE OF PARTICIPANTS: The average age of participants is usually between 20 and 30.

PERSONS WITH DISABILITIES: The university does not discriminate based on disabilities. Applicants are handled on a case-by-case basis, depending on the program requirements.

COMMENTS: Students can earn academic credit for participation in the programs that take place in Africa and Egypt. Tuition is additional.

➤⇒➤⇒➤

Western Washington University

Department of Communication
Bellingham, Washington 98225
Phone: (206) 676-3298
Fax: (206) 647-6818

INSTITUTION/ORGANIZATION: Founded in 1893, Western Washington University is a state institution with an enrollment of more than

9,000 students. The university is a member of the Council on International Educational Exchange.

PROGRAM: "Shakespeare at Stratford." The purpose of this program is to enhance appreciation and understanding of Shakespearean poetry and drama through interpretive readings, lectures, and discussions, as well as attendance at the Royal Shakespeare Theater. Led by Dr. Arthur Solomon, a retired emeritus professor of the university, lectures are also presented by other Shakespearean experts from the United Kingdom. Visits to Shakespeare Properties, historic sites relating to the Elizabethan and Tudor periods, the English countryside, and a day in London are also included. The program has been running since 1979.

ELIGIBILITY: Applications are accepted from all interested persons.

LOCATION: Stratford-upon-Avon (with excursions to surrounding areas) and London, England.

TIME OF YEAR: Summer.

DURATION: Two weeks.

ACCOMMODATIONS: Guesthouses.

COST: The program costs approximately $2,500, which includes round-trip airfare from Seattle, room, and all other expenses except lunches.

COMMENTS: Students can obtain academic credit for this program from Western Washington University by writing a brief response paper.

▸⇒▸⇒▸

Western Washington University

Dr. Marian J. Tonjes
College of Education
Bellingham, WA 98225
Phone: (206) 676-3337

INSTITUTION/ORGANIZATION: Founded in 1893, Western Washington University is a state institution with an enrollment of more than 9,000 students. The university is a member of the Council on International Educational Exchange.

PROGRAM: "Summer Study in England." Offered annually for more than 18 years, this program focuses on the study of elementary and secondary education. Participants live with a host family for the first eight days while team-teaching or serving as administrators in British schools. Following this practical experience, participants live at Oriel College, Oxford, and attend a variety of seminars and workshops given by British consultants and guest speakers who are considered to be leaders in their fields. Excursions are taken to nearby points of interest. Group size is limited to 30 participants.

ELIGIBILITY: Participants must be teachers or educational administrators.

LOCATION: Oxfordshire, Oxford, and London, England.

TIME OF YEAR: Summer.

DURATION: Four weeks.

ACCOMMODATIONS: Hotel (one night in London), private homes (eight days in Oxfordshire), and college dormitories (remaining time in Oxford).

COST: In 1992 the program cost approximately $3,500, which included room, board, guest speakers, workshops, field trips, cultural entertainment, coaches, fees, graduate tuition (nine credit hours), and books. Airfare was not included.

AGE OF PARTICIPANTS: The average age is usually about 35, though participants range in age from about 22 to 65.

PERSONS WITH DISABILITIES: The program is open to people with disabilities.

▸⇒▸⇒▸

Western Washington University

Office of Foreign Study
Bellingham, WA 98225
Phone: (206) 676-3298
Fax: (206) 647-6818

INSTITUTION/ORGANIZATION: Founded in 1893, Western Washington University is a state institution with an enrollment of more than 9,000 students. The university is a member of the Council on International Educational Exchange.

PROGRAM: "Greek Odyssey." Focused on the study of art, archaeology, and theater of classical and Hellenic Greece, this study tour combines lectures with on-site visits to places of interest on the Greek mainland. Also included is a sea voyage to the Cycladic Islands. Historians and archaeologists selected by the Hellenic American Union lead the study tour. Group size is limited to 30 participants.

ELIGIBILITY: Interested persons should be older than the traditional college-age student and enthusiasts of art, archaeology, and theater.

LOCATION: Athens, Corinth, Olympia, Epidauros, Delphi, and the Cycladic Islands, Greece.

TIME OF YEAR: Summer.

DURATION: Two weeks.

ACCOMMODATIONS: Participants live in hotels and twin berths on ship.

COST: In 1992 the program cost approximately $3,000, which included round-trip airfare, room, half board on land, double-occupancy board at sea, coach transportation, and a sea voyage.

COMMENTS: Interested students may obtain academic credit for participation.

▸⇉▸⇉▸

Wilderness Southeast

711 Sandtown Road
Savannah, GA 31410
Phone: (912) 897-5108

INSTITUTION/ORGANIZATION: Founded in 1973, Wilderness Southeast is a nonprofit organization specializing in natural history. Small groups camp in diverse wilderness areas for a close-up look at some remarkable ecosystems. The school is committed to earth stewardship and wilderness conservation.

PROGRAMS: Wilderness Southeast offers natural history study tours led by teachers and naturalists with first aid training. The programs for 1993 include the following:

• "Belize/Tikal: Hike and Snorkel." Focused on cultural as well as natural history, this tour includes snorkeling on the Belizean barrier reef and assisting at a working lobster and fishing camp; an excursion to a Black Carib farming and fishing village rooted in West African and Island Carib heritage; a trip to Belize's jaguar preserve in the Cockscomb Basin; and several days in the jungle of Tikal, Guatemala. Participants live in hotels, hostels, and research dormitories. The approximate cost is $1,590 and includes all expenses except international airfare. The program runs for 12 days during the winter. The average age of participants is usually about 50. Group size is limited to 12 people. Applications are accepted from all interested persons.

- "Costa Rica: Lodge/Hike." This study tour takes participants to several tropical habitats, including the rain forest preserve of Rara Avis as well as the dry forests of Palo Verde. A short hike to one of Costa Rica's active volcanoes is also part of the itinerary. Participants live in hotels and research dormitories. The approximate cost is $1,195 and includes all expenses except international airfare. The program runs for 10 days during the winter. The average age of participants is usually about 50. Group size is limited to 14 people. Participants should be in general good health with a desire to actively explore the backcountry of Costa Rica.

- "Costa Rica Jungle Backpack." This program takes participants through Corcovado, part of the Costa Rican national park system. This tropical rain forest is on the Osa Peninsula in southern Costa Rica. In addition to tent camping, participants stay in a ranger/research station during part of the hike. Interested persons should have a strong interest in tropical ecology and be physically fit and accustomed to hiking and exercising. The approximate cost is $960 and includes all expenses except airfare. The program runs for 10 days during the winter. Participants are responsible for bringing sleeping bags; tents are provided, and backpacks are available for rent. The average age of participants is usually about 40. Group size is limited to 14 people.

- "Amazon/Pantanal: Riverboat/Lodge." This study tour takes participants to Brazil on an Amazon riverboat cruise up the Rio Negro for five days, with rain forest hikes along the way. The tour then goes to the Pantanal, one of the world's largest wetland wilderness areas, which is explored by jeep, boat, and on foot. Participants live on a riverboat as well as in hotels and lodges. The approximate cost is $3,000, which includes round-trip airfare from Miami. The program runs for 13 days during the summer. The average age of participants is usually about 50. Group size is limited to 14 people. Applications are accepted from all interested persons.

- "Bahamas/Sea Kayak." This tour includes kayaking across the Gulf Stream, crossing through the Bahamas Banks to the Berry Islands. Participants should be confident swimmers and in excellent health; some paddling experience is recommended. The program takes place for eight days during the summer. Participants live on a boat and should bring snorkel gear, though it is also available for rent. Paddling gear is provided. The approximate cost is $1,200, which includes all expenses from Miami. The average age of participants is about 45. Group size is limited to 10 people.

ELIGIBILITY: Varies according to program. See program descriptions above.

LOCATION: Belize, Guatemala, Costa Rica, Brazil, and the Bahamas.

TIME OF YEAR: Time of year varies. See program descriptions above.

DURATION: Programs vary from eight to 12 days.

PERSONS WITH DISABILITIES: Applicants are considered on an individual basis.

COMMENTS: Financial assistance is available for participation on all excursions; awards are based on need. Contact Wilderness Southeast for more information.

▶═▶═▶

Wildland Adventures/Earth Preservation Fund

3516 NE 155th Street
Seattle, WA 98155
Phone: (206) 365-0686
Fax: (206) 363-6615

INSTITUTION/ORGANIZATION: Founded in 1978, Wildland Adventures is a nonprofit organization that sponsors worldwide nature and culture explorations.

PROGRAMS: The following treks are offered:
- "Inca Trail Preservation Trek." This program takes place in Peru for three weeks during the spring and focuses on archaeology and culture. Guided by a native Peruvian experienced in trekking and building, participants clean and rebuild trails in order to preserve ruins. Lectures are combined with small group discussions. Participants stay in hotels and tents. The approximate cost is $1,295, which includes all land expenses except a few meals and tips. International airfare is additional. The average age of participants is usually between 30 and 60. Group size is limited to 12 people.
- "Himalayan Tree Planting Trek." This trek, which takes place

in Nepal for three weeks during the summer, emphasizes environmental studies and culture. Participants plant trees for reforestation. These outdoor adventures are led by in-country residents with university degrees who have building and trekking experience. Lectures are combined with small group discussions. Participants stay in hotels and tents. The approximate cost is $1,325, which includes all land expenses except a few meals and tips. International airfare is additional. The average age of participants is usually between 30 and 60. Group size is limited to 12 people.

ELIGIBILITY: Applications are accepted from all interested persons.
LOCATION: Peru and Nepal.
TIME OF YEAR: Spring and winter.
DURATION: Both treks run for three weeks.

▶︎⇒▶︎⇒▶︎

Wilson & Lake International

468 "B" Street, Suite #3
Ashland, OR 97520
Phone: (503) 488-3350

INSTITUTION/ORGANIZATION: Founded in 1985, Wilson & Lake is a commercial tour operator that serves as the U.S. representative for a number of small British programs and tour companies.

PROGRAMS: Wilson & Lake represents the following programs:
• "Oxford Heritage Study Programmes." This year-round study program takes place in Oxford and focuses on the history, art, architecture, and literature of England. Participants are taught by Oxford University faculty, who lead seminars, tutorials, and visits to relevant places of interest. Some of the courses offered are "Country Houses, Cathedrals, and Churches," "English Literature: The Oxford Writers," and "Medieval History, Myth and Legend." Participants stay in hotels, private homes, or college dormitories. The program runs for a minimum of one week and takes place throughout the year (except in December). The study visit program, tax, course materials, and entrance fees cost $580 per person per week. Accommodation costs range from about $180 per week for a stay in an English home to $60 per day for a stay in a hotel. Airfare is additional.

• "International Language Centres." This program takes place in Cambridge and focuses on modern English literature and culture. Morning lectures are combined with seminars on literature, art, and aspects of English life. Occasional afternoon visits and Saturday excursions to writer's homes are also included. Classes are taught by Cambridge University senior tutors. Programs run for two to four weeks during the summer, and participants stay in guesthouses and private homes. The cost is about $400 per week, which includes room, breakfast, and tuition. Airfare is not included.

ELIGIBILITY: Applications are accepted from all interested persons ages 18 to 86.

LOCATION: Oxford, the Cotswolds, and Cambridge.

TIME OF YEAR: Time of year varies. See program descriptions above.

DURATION: Programs vary from one week to one year.

COMMENTS: About 25 percent of the participants are usually from the United States.

▸⇒▸⇒▸

University of Wisconsin–Madison

Department of Continuing Education in the Arts
Arts Seminars Abroad
726 Lowell Hall
610 Langdon Street
Madison, WI 53703
Phone: (608) 263-7787
Fax: (608) 265-2475

INSTITUTION/ORGANIZATION: The University of Wisconsin–Madison is a major research institution providing undergraduate and graduate programs, along with comprehensive continuing education and lifelong learning opportunities. The university is a member of the Council on International Educational Exchange.

PROGRAMS: "Arts Seminars Abroad." This program combines educational travel with informal lectures, performances at major centers, and carefully selected complementary events for participants. Offered in 1993 are "Arts Seminars to England, Scotland, Ireland and Wales" and "Arts Seminar to London." Both study tours concentrate on the performing arts and include preperformance lectures. Seminars are limited to about 27 participants.

ELIGIBILITY: Applications are accepted from all interested persons.

LOCATION: Destinations include London, Stratford, Edinburgh (International Festival), Dublin, and various locations in Wales.

TIME OF YEAR: Summer and winter.

DURATION: "Arts Seminars to England, Scotland, Ireland, and Wales": up to three weeks; "Arts Seminar to London": one week (extended time optional).

ACCOMMODATIONS: Hotels and college dormitories.

COST: "Arts Seminars to England, Scotland, Ireland, and Wales": approximately $2,940 plus airfare; "Art Seminar to London": approximately $1,240 plus airfare. Both programs include room and most meals, excellent seats at performances, materials mailed in advance, professional educational leadership, lectures, and transportation to events.

AGE OF PARTICIPANTS: The average age of participants is usually between 40 and 50.

PERSONS WITH DISABILITIES: Anyone interested is invited to participate. Special arrangements are coordinated as needed.

COMMENTS: Minimal funding is available to assist participants. For more information, contact Harv Thompson at the number above.

➤➤➤

University of Wisconsin–Madison

Division of University Outreach/Liberal Studies
610 Langdon Street, Room 624
Madison, WI 53703
Phone: (608) 263-2774
Fax: (608) 265-2479

INSTITUTION/ORGANIZATION: The University of Wisconsin–Madison is a major research institution providing undergraduate and graduate programs, along with comprehensive continuing education and lifelong learning opportunities. The university is a member of the Council on International Educational Exchange.

PROGRAMS: "International Seminars." These seminars combine education and sight-seeing with opportunities to meet local residents. Focused on history, culture, sociology, international relations, religion, dance, and folk music, the seminars are led by university faculty. Lectures are provided en route. Participants attend briefings at U.S. embassies and talks given by journalists, governmental leaders, and other experts. Past seminars have included "The Making of Modern India," "Spain and Morocco," "Israel, Egypt and Jordan," "Eastern Europe Revisited," "A Medieval Pilgrimage to Santiago de Compostela," "Berlin: An Inside View," and "Lands of the Bible," among others. Scheduled for 1993 are "Southeast Asia" and a medieval art history program in France and Belgium. Seminars are limited to 30 to 35 participants.

ELIGIBILITY: Applications are accepted from all interested persons.

LOCATION: Previous destinations have included Israel, Egypt, Jordan, India, Spain, Morocco, Bulgaria, Hungary, and France. Thailand, Indonesia, Malaysia, France, and Belgium are scheduled for 1993.

TIME OF YEAR: Spring, fall, and winter, depending on the program. Some programs are offered every year; some are offered every other year.

DURATION: Approximately three weeks.

ACCOMMODATIONS: Hotels.

COST: Varies with destination; contact the university for an updated list of programs and prices.

AGE OF PARTICIPANTS: The average age of participants is usually about 65.

▶⇒▶⇒▶

Woodswomen

25 West Diamond Lake Road
Minneapolis, MN 55419
Phone: (800) 279-0555

INSTITUTION/ORGANIZATION: Founded in 1977, this nonprofit organization conducts outdoor adventure travel programs for women.

PROGRAMS: Woodswomen offers a number of different programs: wilderness journeys, which include camping, canoeing, and kayaking; cultural odysseys such as trekking in Nepal and Ecuador and hiking in the Swiss Alps; and climbing programs, which include instruction on all levels. Programs emphasize outdoor skills, cultural history, and eco-tourism. Group leaders have language skills and experience traveling in the country. Group sizes vary but generally don't exceed 20 participants.

ELIGIBILITY: Programs are open to women only.

LOCATION: Destinations include Nepal, Switzerland, France, Ireland, Ecuador, Mexico, and New Zealand.

TIME OF YEAR: Spring, fall, and winter.

DURATION: One or two weeks.

ACCOMMODATIONS: Tents and hotels.

COST: Varies. Fees generally include guide services, lodging, and some meals.

AGE OF PARTICIPANTS: The average age of participants is usually about 45.

PERSONS WITH DISABILITIES: Persons with disabilities are encouraged to participate.

COMMENTS: Some funding is available to interested applicants; priority is given to first-time participants.

➤➤➤

World Affairs Council of Philadelphia

206 South Fourth Street
Philadelphia, PA 19106
Phone: (215) 922-2900
Fax: (215) 625-0771

INSTITUTION/ORGANIZATION: The World Affairs Council is a nonprofit, nonpartisan educational organization dedicated to creating a more informed citizenry on matters of national and international significance. The Council serves as a forum for foreign dignitaries, government officials, and journalists who wish an audience with the American public. As a membership organization, the Council sponsors a variety of programs for its constituency, including special lunches, dinners, lectures, and tours.

PROGRAM: "Travel Program." This study travel program includes seven to 10 international trips per year, including briefings at American embassies and meetings with journalists, business leaders, and other professionals. Focused on the discussion of political, economic, cultural, and social issues, an extensive reading list is provided prior to departure. The maximum number of participants permitted on each trip is 35.

ELIGIBILITY: Though the travel study program is marketed chiefly to World Affairs Council members, it is open to all interested persons.
LOCATION: Destinations have included Antarctica, South Africa, China, and Eastern Europe.
TIME OF YEAR: Options are available throughout the year.
DURATION: Each trip runs from one to three weeks.
ACCOMMODATIONS: Hotels.
COST: Costs range from approximately $1,500 to $6,000, which includes airfare, room, some meals, briefings, and sight-seeing.
AGE OF PARTICIPANTS: Most participants are over 55 years old; 65 is the average.
COMMENTS: Membership in the Council is open to all individuals with an interest in world affairs.

➤➤➤

World Learning Inc.
P.O. Box 676
Kipling Road
Brattleboro, VT 05302
Phone: (802) 257-7751

INSTITUTION/ORGANIZATION: Founded in 1932, World Learning, Inc. is a nonprofit organization concerned with providing participants with the knowledge, awareness, attitudes, and skills that enable them to contribute personally to international understanding and global development through citizen exchange. The Experiment is a member of the Council on International Educational Exchange.

PROGRAM: "Elderhostel." Sponsored in cooperation with Elderhostel, an organization that specializes in programs for the 60+ traveler (see description on pages 141–142), this program emphasizes culture, the arts, and development. Homestays are combined with academic work and educational travel. Instructors have advanced degrees and a strong background in the program countries, as well as fluency in the language.
ELIGIBILITY: Participants must be at least 60 years old or accompanying someone who is age-eligible.
LOCATION: Destinations include Ecuador, France, Switzerland, India, Germany, Indonesia, and Mexico.
TIME OF YEAR: Summer.
DURATION: Programs run for six weeks.

ACCOMMODATIONS: Participants stay in hotels, college dormitories, and private homes.

COST: Varies depending on the program; contact World Learning, Inc. for information.

PERSONS WITH DISABILITIES: World Learning, Inc. tries to accommodate persons with disabilities; individuals are considered on a case-by-case basis.

COMMENTS: A three- to four-day orientation is provided, which includes language survival and cultural awareness classes. (Some programs also supply participants with the local dress.)

▶➡▶➡▶

World Neighbors

4127 NW 122 Street
Oklahoma City, OK 73120
Phone: (405) 752-9700
Fax: (405) 752-9393

INSTITUTION/ORGANIZATION: Founded in 1951, World Neighbors is a nonprofit international development organization.

PROGRAM: "Honduras Study Visit." Participants travel to rural Honduran villages with World Neighbor program leaders. These visits are focused on understanding the root causes of global hunger and poverty and learning how these problems can be overcome. Visits begin with an orientation to learn about the appropriate approach to development. Trips end with a period of reflection and evaluation to explore the role of North Americans in helping the poor of the world to help themselves. Groups are limited to 10 people.

ELIGIBILITY: Applications are accepted from all interested persons who are able to climb hills.

LOCATION: Tegucigalpa and various rural locations in Honduras.

TIME OF YEAR: Once a month.

DURATION: Five days (six including travel).

ACCOMMODATIONS: Hostels.

COST: The cost is $800, including round-trip airfare from Houston, room, board, guides, and lunches.

AGE OF PARTICIPANTS: The average age of participants usually ranges from 40 to 65.

PERSONS WITH DISABILITIES: These rural sites are only accessible
by four-wheel drive and walking.

▶⇒▶⇒▶

The 92nd Street YM–YWHA

1395 Lexington Avenue
New York, NY 10128
Phone: (212) 415-5599
Fax: (212) 415-5578

INSTITUTION/ORGANIZATION: Founded in 1874, The 92nd Street
Y is a nonprofit cultural and social services organization.

PROGRAMS: The Y has a continuous program of educational tours
throughout the world that focus on art, history, and architecture. Study
is informal, and small group discussions are combined with guided
tours.
ELIGIBILITY: Applications are accepted from all interested persons,
but an interview is required.
LOCATION: Destinations have included Sweden, Denmark, Norway,
Spain, Italy, Portugal, the Netherlands, China, Hong Kong, Chile,
and Ecuador.
TIME OF YEAR: Options are available throughout the year.
DURATION: One to two weeks.
ACCOMMODATIONS: Hotels.
COST: Varies with the tour. Airfare from New York, accommodations, transportation during tour, specified meals, guides, admission
fees, and porterage are included in price. Contact the Y for more
information.
AGE OF PARTICIPANTS: The average age of participants is usually
between 50 and 60.
PERSONS WITH DISABILITIES: Applicants must be able to keep pace
with the tour and are considered on a case-by-case basis.

▶⇒▶⇒▶

Zoological Society of Philadelphia

34th Street and Girard Avenue
Philadelphia, PA 19104

Phone: (215) 243-1100
Fax: (215) 387-8733

INSTITUTION/ORGANIZATION: Founded in 1859, the Zoological Society of Philadelphia is a nonprofit organization and America's first zoo.

PROGRAMS: "Wildlife Workshops." These educational workshops are designed for educators and zookeepers. Participants meet with respected researchers, scientists, and naturalists in Kenya and Costa Rica. Instructors are zoo staff. Group size is limited to 25 people.
ELIGIBILITY: Applications are accepted from all interested persons, but preference is given to educators and zookeepers.
LOCATION: Kenya and Costa Rica.
TIME OF YEAR: Summer.
DURATION: Workshops run from one to two weeks.
ACCOMMODATIONS: Hotels and lodges.
COST: The workshop in Kenya costs approximately $2,995; Costa Rica costs $1,239. Both include round-trip airfare from Philadelphia, room, board, and transfers.
AGE OF PARTICIPANTS: The average age of participants is usually between 40 and 60.
PERSONS WITH DISABILITIES: Applications are accepted from all interested persons. Individuals are considered on a case-by-case basis.

APPENDIX

MEMBERS OF THE COUNCIL ON INTERNATIONAL EDUCATIONAL EXCHANGE

Adelphi University
Adventist Colleges Abroad
AFS International/Intercultural
  Programs
Albertson College of Idaho
Alma College
American Council on the Teach-
  ing of Foreign Languages
American Graduate School of
  International Management
American Heritage Association
American University
American University in Cairo
American Youth Hostels
Antioch University
Arkansas College
Associated Colleges of the Mid-
  west
Association for International
  Practical Training
Association of Student Councils
  (Canada)
Attila Jozsef University

Augsburg College
Austin Community College
Babson College
Bates College
Beaver College
Beloit College
Boston College
Boston University
Bradford College
Bradley University
Brandeis University
Brethren Colleges Abroad
Brigham Young University
Brown University
Bucknell University
Butler University
California State University
California State University,
  Long Beach
California State University, Sac-
  ramento
Carleton College
Carroll College

Central Michigan University
Central University of Iowa
Central Washington University
Chapman University
College of Charleston
Colorado College
Colorado State University
Cornell University
Curtin University of Technology
Dartmouth College
Davidson College
DePauw University
Drake University
Earlham College
Eastern Michigan University
Eckerd College
Ecole Centrale de Paris (Ecole Centrale des Arts et Manufactures)
Elmira College
Empire State College–SUNY
Flagler College
Florida Atlantic University
Georgetown University
Gonzaga University
Goshen College
Great Lakes Colleges Association
Grinnell College
Guilford College
Gustavus Adolphus College
Hampshire College
Hartwick College
Harvard College
Hebrew University of Jerusalem
Heidelberg College
Hiram College
Hollins College
Hope College
Illinois State University
Indiana University
Institute of International Education

International Christian University
International Christian Youth Exchange
International Student Exchange Program
Iowa State University
James Madison University
Kalamazoo College
Kent State University
Lake Erie College
Lancaster University
LaSalle University
Lehigh University
Lewis & Clark College
The Lisle Fellowship
Longwood College
Louisiana State University
Loyola Marymount University
Macalester College
Marquette University
Mary Baldwin College
Marymount College, Tarrytown
Memphis State University
Miami University
Michigan State University
Middlebury College
Millersville University
Monterey Institute of International Studies
Moorhead State University
Murdoch University
National Association of Secondary School Principals
New York University
North Carolina State University
Northeastern University
Northern Arizona University
Northern Illinois University
Northern Michigan University
Northfield Mount Hermon School
Oberlin College

Ohio University
Ohio State University
Old Dominion University
Open Door Student Exchange
Pace University
Pennsylvania State University
Pepperdine University
Pitzer College
Pomona College
Portland State University
Purdue University
Ramapo College of New Jersey
Reed College
Rochester Institute of Technology
Rollins College
Rosary College
Rutgers, the State University of New Jersey
St. John Fisher College
St. Lawrence University
St. Olaf College
St. Peter's College
Scandinavian Seminar
School Year Abroad
Scripps College
Skidmore College
Southern Illinois University at Carbondale
Southern Methodist University
Southwest Texas State University
Spelman College
Springfield College
Stanford University
State University of New York
Stephens College
Stetson University
Syracuse University
Texas A&M University
Texas Tech University
Trinity College
Tufts University

Tulane University
Universidad Autonama de Guadalajara
Universidad de Belgrano
Université de Bordeaux III
Universidad de Salvador
University College London
University of Alabama
University of Alabama at Birmingham
University of Arkansas at Little Rock
University of British Columbia
University of California
University of Colorado at Boulder
University of Connecticut
University of Copenhagen (DIS Program)
University of Denver
University of Essex
University of Evansville
University of Hartford
University of Illinois
University of Iowa
University of Kansas
University of La Verne
University of Louisville
University of Maine
University of Maryland
University of Massachusetts
University of Michigan
University of Minnesota
University of New Hampshire
University of New Orleans
University of North Carolina at Chapel Hill
University of North Texas
University of Notre Dame
University of Oklahoma
University of Oregon
University of the Pacific
University of Pennsylvania

University of Pittsburgh
University of Rhode Island
University of St. Thomas
University of South Carolina
University of Southern California
University of Sussex
University of Tennessee, Knoxville
University of Texas at Austin
University of Toledo
University of Utah
University of Vermont
University of Virginia
University of Washington
University of Wisconsin at Green Bay
University of Wisconsin at Madison
University of Wisconsin at Milwaukee
University of Wisconsin at Platteville
University of Wisconsin at River Falls
University of Wollongong
University of Wyoming
University System of Georgia
Valparaiso University
Volunteers in Asia
Wake Forest University
Washington State University
Wayne State University
Wesleyan University

Western Michigan University
Western Washington University
Westminster College
Whitman College
Whitworth College
Wichita State University
Wilmington College
Wittenberg University
Wofford College
Worcester Polytechnic Institute
World College West
World Learning, Inc.
YMCA of the USA
Youth for Understanding International Exchange

Associates

American Center for Students and Artists
Association of College Unions—International
Canadian Bureau for International Education
European Association for International Education
Fontainebleau Fine Arts and Music Schools Association
NAFSA: Association of International Educators
National Association for Equal Opportunity in Higher Education
United Negro College Fund

INDEX

GENERAL INDEX (including organizations)